Henry

HENRY

A Life of Henry Ford II

WALTER HAYES

GROVE WEIDENFELD

NEW YORK

Published by Grove Weidenfeld
A division of Wheatland Corporation
841 Broadway
New York, NY 10003-4793

Published in Canada by General Publishing Company, Ltd.

The author wishes especially to thank Mrs. Kathleen Ford
for permission to use her own photographs.

Library of Congress Cataloging-in-Publication Data

Hayes, Walter.
Henry : A Life of Henry Ford II / Walter Hayes. — 1st ed.
p.   cm.
1. Ford, Henry, 1917-1987. 2. Executives—United
States—
Biography.   3. Automobile industry and trade—United
States—
History.   4. Ford Motor Company—History.   I. Title.
HD9710.U52F6638   1990
338.7'6292'092—dc20
[B]   89-70487
                                                 CIP

ISBN 0-8021-1285-4

Manufactured in the United States of America

Printed on acid-free paper

Designed by Brush Horse Books

First Edition 1990

10   9   8   7   6   5   4   3   2

For Elizabeth

Acknowledgments

I am indebted to many people for the opportunities which made this book possible—friends, business colleagues, and the guardians of the Henry Ford Archives in the Edison Institute—but the one man to whom I am most indebted is, of course, Henry Ford II himself. He would have argued perhaps with some of my conclusions—as, indeed, will others. What is beyond argument, however, is my gratitude to Kathy Ford, to Charlotte and Edsel and Anne Ford and many other members of the family. Joe Fowler, John Loudon—who was good enough to read and comment upon some parts of the manuscript—Professor Kenneth Lockridge, and Dr. John Dann of the University of Michigan were generous in helping me to come to my own conclusions. Her Majesty Queen Elizabeth graciously permitted reference to the Windsor Castle Archives for the material on Turville Grange. John Wyer—now, alas, dead—refreshed my own recollections of the GT40 and the campaigns at Le Mans. My wife, Elizabeth, and my children—Jeremy, Richard, and Harriet—not only put up with my preoccupation but also proved occasionally to have more retentive memories than my own. And while it may seem no more than duty to thank one's publisher, I am much indebted to Lord Weidenfeld for his enthusiasm which began as a result of his own friendship with Henry Ford II.

Contents

Preface

It was June 1983 when Henry Ford II arrived one day on my doorstep and said: "I have come to ask you to plan my funeral." He had telephoned the previous evening to make sure I would be at home. "It's no big deal," he said, "just something I want to discuss with you." I had then worked with him and for him over a period of twenty years, and we had fashioned a relationship beyond the normal bounds of business. On and off duty, I had become accustomed to his companionship, often in strange and faraway places, and had coped with other somewhat unusual requests. This, not surprisingly, was the one I found most difficult to respond to.

In the summertime Henry liked iced tea in tall glasses, and we went out into the sunshine to drink it. When we moved from England to Ann Arbor at the beginning of 1980, my wife's first determination was to have a proper English garden. It soon came to provide the only patch of color among the lawns of our less eccentric American neighbors and was much admired. Henry did his duty and said all the right things.

"There's no great rush," he insisted—getting back to the matter at hand—and indeed, there was no reason for anticipating his imminent death. No fewer than five of America's leading heart specialists had been consulted and cross-examined when one of them had diagnosed angina; but that was five years earlier, and they had all been optimistic and unanimous in their verdict: He had a "good few" years to live. He followed their advice, modified his diet, equipped all his homes with exercise bicycles, and pedaled furiously each morning, proving to be a surprisingly obedient patient. He was also able—and how much I envied him—to make do with little sleep, often for days on end, and then refresh himself with twelve or fourteen hours, tucked up in bed in a nightshirt. The reason for the knock on the door was Henry's determination to die as he had lived: in control of the situation.

He was a neat, orderly, tidy man. He never forgot a kindness and was scrupulous with "bread-and-butter" letters even when the debt was trivial; the personal ones were invariably handwritten. He never missed a meeting or an appointment, and he was never late. And he had absolutely no intention of going to heaven unless he had first planned the circumstances of the journey and drawn the map.

It was not until that day in 1983 that I started to think inquisitively about the man who was Henry Ford II and begin a search that has ended—for me, anyway—in this book. I had been invited to join Ford in Britain in 1962, by its chairman, Sir Patrick Hennessy, and fascinated by the vigor of its great Dagenham factory, I gave up a newspaper editorship to become part of this strange new world. Within a few months I was invited to join the board of directors. As years went by, I served on other Ford boards in Switzerland and Germany, became one of the first European vice-presidents of the parent company in the United States—working for some years in Detroit—and then vice-chairman of Ford of Europe. I had every reason for believing I knew Henry well, in public and private—perhaps better than anybody else—but there are many levels of knowing and no certainty that knowledge is truth. Every man inhabits his own island. Some people live together all their lives and are never more than strangers to each other. Moreover, I am suspicious of crystal balls and wary of psychiatric couches and have never demanded of friendship that I should know anybody more comprehensively than he cares to be known. The English writer John Mortimer once told an interviewer: "People should be allowed to be unfathomable."

Nevertheless, I found it impossible to suggest words or music to Henry, or persons or places—all the rigmarole and sentiment of a last farewell—without wondering what Henry thought about himself and what he would wish others to think of him. It was not an easy consideration, for there were many barriers to understanding, not the least of which was Henry himself.

Thrust into the control of what was probably the largest private company in the world when he was a comparative innocent of twenty-seven years of age, he ran it successfully and single-mindedly for thirty-four years, and few others have come anywhere near to matching that achievement. He was a large man in every respect and presented a large target to the world; he was never out of the sights of lesser men, so many of whom were more interested in the boudoir than the boardroom. As a result, he had developed the hide of an armadillo, which stopped the darts from getting in but also inhibited so much from coming out.

He had nothing in common with his grandfather—physically, intellectually, or emotionally—except for his bright blue eyes, which had a vitality and liveliness of a rare kind. People found them penetrating, even dominating. New acquaintances, at their first encounter, would feel them sweep like an impersonal scanner from head to toe, registering, it seemed, their own assessment and tucking it away for future reference. His circle of friends was always small. Company people were rarely included in purely social occasions and even more infrequently in family celebrations. And they always said "Mr. Ford"; until they were unusually invited to do so, very few who worked for him called him Henry, even those who were his near equals in rank.

He was both sensitive and indiscreet. Sometimes he would hold to secrets that might have been better revealed and commit indiscretions that would have benefited from secrecy. He could mislead, occasionally with deliberation to draw others into showing their hands or declaring their opinions, but in one important respect he was like George Washington: He could not tell a lie. The worst thing he could say about anybody was: "He lied to me." It was a sin he rarely forgave.

In the immediate days that followed our Ann Arbor conversation, as I sat down to compose a funeral service, nothing was farther from my mind than this book. The reminiscences of twenty years—the diaries, the letters, the postcards, the photographs—were no more than souvenirs of my own life and the lives of my family. It was not until his death in 1987 that I found it impossible to stop thinking about him and was then persuaded to write this personal memoir. And that is how it began. Of one of the books that was written about him—and the only one he actually read—he said, "I don't recognize myself in these pages," and neither did I. But I certainly came to appreciate the difficulties of the biographer, for who can say with any kind of certainty of any human being, "This is what he was like"? In the long months after his death, as I began to search for him with more purpose—reading his private papers, listening to the spoken memories of his family, his friends, and others who worked with him—it seemed that each, in a sense, looked back on a different man.

A further difficulty, which may be unique to Henry Ford II, is in separating the man from the company—Mr. Ford from Ford—because he never, in sickness or in health, in public or in private, discerned any separation. The company always came first, ahead even of family. What he was was what he did, and it soon became apparent to me that a memoir would have no perspective if it lacked the background against which he lived his life and from which he was inseparable.

I have therefore chosen to portray a man who was more important to my own life than any other, against what I believe to be the most significant circumstances of his own—beginning with his crucial experiences in the ruins of postwar Europe—and I hope the understanding reader will make his or her own discoveries. There were, of course, many events in his life of which I began with little or no knowledge, and some of the days I have covered were "before my time." For the accuracy of these reflections and interpretations, I am indebted to many people, some of whom are acknowledged at the front of the book.

I wish only to add that this is not intended to be a history of the Ford Motor Company; I hope it may still be seen as a contribution toward it.

Chronology

1917
  September 4
    Henry Ford II born in Detroit, the first of four children of Edsel Bryant
    and Eleanor Clay Ford and Henry Ford's first grandson.

1919
  January 1
    Edsel B. Ford succeeds his father, Henry Ford, as president of the Ford
    Motor Company.

1936
  May 15
    The Ford Foundation established by Henry and Edsel Ford.

1938
  December 19
    Henry Ford II elected a director of the Ford Motor Company.

1940
  July 13
    Henry Ford II marries Anne McDonnell.
  August
    Henry Ford II takes his first job with the Ford Motor Company as a me-
    chanic in the dynamometer room.

1941
  April 3
    Charlotte M. Ford born to Anne and Henry Ford II.
  April 10
    Henry Ford II appointed an ensign in the United States Naval Reserve.

1943

January 29
Anne M. Ford born to Anne and Henry Ford II.
May 26
Edsel Ford dies at the age of forty-nine.
June 1
Henry Ford reelected president of the company.
July 26
Henry Ford II released from the navy.
December 15
Henry Ford II elected vice-president.

1945

September 21
Henry Ford II elected president.

1946

July 1
Ernest R. Breech elected executive vice-president.

1947

April 7
Henry Ford dies at his Dearborn home at the age of eighty-three.

1948

February–March
Henry Ford II makes his first official visit to Ford companies in Europe.
December 27
Edsel Bryant Ford II born to Anne and Henry Ford II.

1952–53

Henry Ford II serves as national chairman of the Crusade for Freedom.

1953

July
President Dwight D. Eisenhower nominates Henry Ford II an alternate
United States delegate to the United Nations.

1955

January 25
Ernest R. Breech elected chairman of the board of directors.

1956

January 17
After fifty-three years as a private company, Ford sells its common stock to
the public.

1960

July 13
Ernest R. Breech resigns as chairman of the board of directors. Henry Ford
II elected chairman of the board in addition to being president.

November 9
> Robert S. McNamara elected president of the Ford Motor Company.

December 12
> Robert S. McNamara resigns as Ford president effective January 1, 1961, to become secretary of defense in the administration of President John F. Kennedy.

1961

January 1
> Henry Ford II resumes duties as president.

February
> Henry Ford II appointed by President John F. Kennedy to the Presidential Advisory Committee on Labor-Management Policy.

April 12
> John Dykstra elected president.

1963

May 1
> Arjay Miller elected president.

May
> Henry Ford II appointed cochairman of the Business Committee for Tax Reduction.

1965

February 19
> Henry Ford II marries Maria Cristina Vettore Austin.

1967

July
> Henry Ford II joins the Urban Coalition.

1968

January
> President Lyndon B. Johnson names Henry Ford II to be first chairman of the National Alliance of Businessmen to direct the JOBS program for the hard-core unemployed.

February 6
> Semon E. Knudsen elected president of the Ford Motor Company.

1969

January 18
> President Lyndon B. Johnson awards Henry Ford II the United States Medal of Freedom.

September 11
> Semon E. Knudsen leaves the company. Lee A. Iacocca is appointed president of Ford's North American automotive operations.

1970

April
> Henry Ford II appointed chairman of the National Center for Voluntary Action by President Richard M. Nixon.

December 10
   Lee A. Iacocca elected president of the Ford Motor Company.

1973
   January 4
   Henry Ford II appointed commander of the French Legion of Honor.

1974
   January 7
   Edsel Ford II joins the company as a product analyst.

1976
   October 19
   Eleanor Clay Ford dies at the age of eighty.

1977
   January
   Henry Ford II resigns as trustee of the Ford Foundation.

1978
   October 15
   Lee A. Iacocca leaves the company.
   October 16
   Philip Caldwell elected president of the Ford Motor Company.

1980
   March 13
   Philip Caldwell succeeds Henry Ford II as chairman of the board of directors; Donald E. Petersen elected president.
   June 4
   Henry Ford III born to Cynthia and Edsel Bryant Ford II.
   October 14
   Henry Ford II marries Kathleen Duross.

1982
   January 26
   Henry Ford II appointed honorary knight commander of the Most Excellent Order of the British Empire.
   October 1
   Henry Ford II retires as company officer and employee but remains as a member of the board of directors.

1985
   February 1
   Donald E. Petersen succeeds Philip Caldwell as chairman of the board of directors. Harold A. Poling elected president.

1987
   September 29
   Henry Ford II dies in the Henry Ford Hospital in Detroit at the age of seventy.

Henry

We must begin with the mistake and transform it
into what is true.
That is, we must uncover the source of the error;
otherwise hearing what is true won't help us.
To convince someone of what is true, it is not enough
to state it; we must find the *road* from error to truth.

—Ludwig Wittgenstein,
remarks on Sir James Frazer's *The Golden Bough*

CHAPTER ONE

Appointment in Berlin

The Pan American Airways DC-3 *Yankee Clipper* taxied gingerly to a halt on Tempelhof Airfield, and a ground handler in German military uniform—stripped of its wartime insignia—lodged a flight of steps against the fuselage. A March wind was blowing, clearing the remnants of the morning fog, and the young man shivered as he emerged from the cabin to set his feet on the battleground of Berlin. It was a day, a place, and an experience he would never forget.

In 1948 few civilians were intrepid enough to visit the divided and devastated capital of the Third Reich, for there was little to welcome them. Berlin was still an unhealed war wound, a landscape of walls without roofs and windows without glass. The smell of death lingered in the cellars with the rats. Wreckage extended to the end of the airfield runway. The fine terminal buildings, in which Messerschmitt had built fighter aircraft during the war, were a shell, and the airfield offered no comforts beyond an overcrowded crew rest room and a mobile canteen. Russian occupation forces provided an additional deterrent, for they were obstructively discouraging road and rail traffic from the West in an attempt to dislodge the slender Allied hold on the city.

But the young man was not a tourist. Though scarcely thirty years of age, Henry Ford II bore a name that was known around the world, and he had chartered the *Clipper* for himself, his wife, Anne, and an aide named Graeme Howard, so that he might discover how the Ford Motor Company's European outposts were recovering from the damage inflicted upon them by the Second World War. He had come to Berlin—

as would President John F. Kennedy in the early 1960s—to see for himself, ask his own questions, and make up his own mind.

The surprising thing was that he was there at all. Fewer than five years had gone by since he had been hauled out of the United States Navy— an inexperienced and, some would have said, immature twenty-five-year-old—as heir apparent to the reclusive genius who had put the world on wheels and created the car for the common man. The immediate cause of his demobilization was the death, in May 1943, of his father, Edsel, but July of that year also brought his grandfather's eightieth birthday and further evidence of his senility. The aftermath of two strokes had accentuated Henry Ford's natural quirkiness to the point where it endangered the very existence of the Ford Motor Company and led many insiders, with evident justification, to doubt its survival.

Effective control of the company had long since passed into the hands of Harry Bennett, a shady acolyte who had worked himself into a position of such power and authority that he was able not only to terrorize the management but even to manipulate old Henry himself. His outer office was connected to all Ford service depots in the United States, and the eighteen-hundred-strong factory police force was effectively his private army. He could monitor every step taken by the company's senior executives and maintain contact with them by shortwave radio as they drove along in their cars, although this was as far as modern technology went at Ford; it was otherwise controlled by empirical methods better suited to a small Victorian engineering shop.

By 1945 Henry Ford II had mustered sufficient allies and self-confidence to take charge of the Ford Motor Company although it was still a birthright of doubtful promise. When the Second World War ended, Ford had forty-eight factories in twenty-three countries, a worldwide work force of 150,000 men and women, and cash reserves of $600 million, but it was losing more than $2 million a week because nobody knew how much it cost to build a car or anything else for that matter. Nor was there any department capable of forecasting sales. The value of a pile of invoices was calculated by weighing them. There were only 550 engineers, half the prewar number, and no new cars on the stocks or even on paper.

The problems were to persist for a long time, and Ford was by no means the only company in trouble. Nobody would have been surprised, therefore, had its new president devoted himself to domestic concerns within the United States. Henry Ford II, however—"wet behind the ears," as he freely confessed to friends and acquaintances alike—was not merely content to regenerate the empire his grandfather had founded in Detroit in 1903 and dominated for more than forty years. He wanted to build a world of his own, and in Berlin he began the transformation of the Ford Motor Company and his own extraordinary inheritance.

Henry's parents were young when he was born. Edsel, an only child, was twenty-two and Eleanor was twenty when they married in 1916; Henry arrived ten months later. The family was always close, and its members enjoyed each other's company. Edsel was keen on water sports—he raced yachts and owned an aircraft-engined speedboat—and, until Henry was in his mid-teens, the family went to Seal Harbor in Maine two or three times a year. In the winter there was a private bobsled run, and in summer they all lived on a boat moored to a dock. Guests were accommodated in a beach house, but this was small and Spartan, and everybody was happier afloat. The boys—Henry, Benson, and William—sometimes sailed all day with their father, who often seemed contented when he was freed from any kind of mooring. He was a shy, artistic man with strict moral standards, and he never discussed business with his children. His worries in later life, when he was increasingly in conflict with his father, were shared only with his wife, and the children had no sense of family frictions.

Neither environment nor heredity seems to have given Henry and his son, Edsel, much in common. Even in business they owned to different passions. Edsel was absorbed by design and styling and ever in search of the classic automobile, whereas his father did not really mind how a car looked. Design was the neatest way you could wrap sheet metal around the mechanical parts. Henry Ford was a mechanic.

Edsel's wife, Eleanor—less intellectual but firmer in her views—was a formidable but loving mother. Order, neatness, punctuality, consideration for servants, truthfulness—all these and many more constraining precepts were hammered into the young Henry in such a determined fashion that they became an instinctive aspect of his own personality. He once said in later years, when a swarm of writers were buzzing at his door: "All these people, they are determined to compare me to my grandfather. I am no more like my grandfather than the man in the moon. I am like my mother."

The antagonism between Henry Ford and Edsel might have been

expected to inhibit, at the very least, the relationship with his grand-children, but this was not the case. Young Henry loved his grand-father—and grandmother, Clara—to such an extent that he often had to be dragged away from Fair Lane (their Dearborn house) to his own home, and he and his brother Benson were regularly in trouble for the amount of time they insisted on spending there. Their reaction is not surprising, for Fair Lane was a cavern of delights. Henry Ford had given the boys their own half-acre farm on his property, where they raised their own crops, using equipment specially built to their own scale and size. Their little farmhouse can still be seen at Fair Lane, now part of the Dearborn campus of the University of Michigan, and the Lilliputian farm implements are in the Henry Ford Museum nearby. On the grounds of the house, Henry Ford also built an enchanting Christmas cottage and filled it with toys every December. The boys were encour-aged to use the entire estate as a sort of frontier post, camping out in barns and sleeping in haylofts, often as a reward for their dedication as young farmers. They began raising simple crops but soon had rabbits and geese and chickens and, in a small stable, four Shetland ponies on which they rode this tract of still-virgin Michigan farmland like Daniel Boone—who had once been held hostage by the scalp-hunting "red-skins" of Detroit—or Colonel George Armstrong Custer, who had commanded a regiment of cavalry at Monroe not so many miles away.

It is no wonder that the young Fords came to regard Grandfather's house as a very desirable escape and no surprise that Edsel and Eleanor gave up the battle to keep them at home. They also had another formida-ble attraction to contend with. Clara Ford, denied more than one child of her own, loved playing hostess to her grandchildren and made no effort to apply any kind of discipline. The indoor swimming pool, the powerhouse, the bowling alley—there were no places considered out of bounds. They were also permitted extraordinary liberties with the facili-ties of the Ford Motor Company. They were encouraged to run the railway engines around the River Rouge factory, and when old Henry was working, he would give the boys his chauffeur, who had instructions to take them anywhere they wanted to go and, in effect, to let them run riot. In his old age Henry Ford II could still recall with detailed pleasure the day they went into the cashier's office and dumped the entire payroll on the floor. He remembered, too, that it was his grandfather who taught him to drive a car—showing him how to use the gears—and the never-to-be-forgotten day when he was only twelve years old and Henry Ford sat by his side and made him drive through the streets of downtown Detroit, terror slowly giving way to triumph.

Dynasties, for the most part, secure their survival by passing the trappings or instruments of power to the younger generation in a planned and deliberate fashion. Henry Ford certainly enriched his grandson's experience of childhood by giving young Henry—and his brothers—the opportunity for practical learning. When it came to more formal education, however, and training for responsibility, all was haphazard. Henry was packed off to the Hotchkiss School at Lakeville, Connecticut, and from there he was admitted to Yale University, where he was a member of the class of 1940. I came across a Ford press release—written, I think, since it had no date, in the seventies—which said, "Mr. Ford's entry into a position of responsibility in the company [had been] long planned by his father, Edsel, and his grandfather, Henry," but there is little evidence of planning. He had been appointed a director of the company in 1938, when he was at Yale and Ford was still a private company, but this was no more than a birthday present. Engineering had been chosen for him as his major university course, but he had inherited none of his grandfather's mechanical genius. "I flunked in engineering," Henry said of his Yale years. "The other guys said sociology was a snap course, so I figured that was for me. I flunked it, too." He failed to graduate with the rest of his class, and the only practical talents he demonstrated at this period of his life were as manager of the college rowing crew.

During his senior year at Yale he met, and proposed marriage to, Anne McDonnell—one of fourteen children of a New York stockbroker—and they were married in July 1940. They spent their honeymoon in Honolulu, and within a few weeks of returning home, Henry went to work for the Ford Motor Company, joining Benson, the elder of his two younger brothers, in the engine test room and company garage. It was neither the most elevated nor the most exciting place to be— certainly not for a young man, not yet twenty-three years of age—but he had no discernible ambitions and no qualifications that might have pointed him elsewhere in the company, and had he been shown the press release at that time—with its talk of responsibility—I suspect he might have thought, as I did, that it was fiction.

In any event, he had a better idea. He endured the job through the summer and the beginning of winter and then told Anne and his parents that he had decided to join the navy. He also told Harry Bennett.

The precise role and significance of Harry Bennett in the affairs of the Ford Motor Company have been differently interpreted and occasionally misunderstood for very good reasons. There is no point in being an *éminence grise* if you publish your intentions. Conspirators are not notably extroverts. But Henry's own recollections, together with some letters that were written at the time, leave little doubt—in my mind, at least—that Bennett intended to usurp the throne and believed that command of the Ford Motor Company was not far beyond his fingertips. Had Henry not fought as he did, history might well have told us a different story.

Harry Bennett was a balding, dapper little man, a former prizefighter with a penchant for spotted bow ties and blue shirts, and he had been hired by Henry Ford in the wake of the Lindbergh baby murder to protect his grandchildren from kidnapping. Charles Lindbergh was born in Detroit, and the kidnapping was felt more intensely there than in any other part of the United States. Bennett's recreations were, on the face of it, surprisingly mild. He painted lugubrious oils with bathetic titles such as *The Empty Saddle* and enjoyed accompanying his organist daughter on the clarinet although few people considered him a domesticated animal. His streetwise ways, evident lack of culture, and total obsequiousness appealed to Henry Ford, for they were the kinds of unpretentious qualities he felt Edsel had lost or had never inherited. Of Bennett's closeness to Henry Ford there can be no doubt, just as there can be no question of his power. When Bennett came to write his own autobiography, he said: "During the thirty years I worked for Henry Ford, I became his most intimate companion, closer to him even than his only son." Henry Ford controlled his company in his erratic fashion almost until his death; but in his later years he was rarely seen or heard to give orders, and there were few brave enough to discover whether the voice of command was that of Henry Ford, speaking through Bennett, or Bennett himself. The Ford family was remarkably timid in its dealings with him, and nobody in the management seemed willing to risk his own blood.

Bennett ruled almost unchallenged, and he argued vigorously against Henry's decision to join the navy. Nothing could suit his purpose more than to have the young man innocuously employed in a job where he could keep an eye on him, but immature as he was, Henry was determined not to become a latter-day Prisoner of Zenda. He had not learned very much as an employee of the company, but he had seen and heard enough to give him at least a rough measure of how it was managed, and never doubted the devious nature of "Mr. Bennett." I am sure that his apprehensions were reinforced at that time because nobody else opposed his enlistment; Anne accepted the idea, and Henry thought his parents were enthusiastic. He therefore summoned up the courage to withstand all of Bennett's arguments and blandishments, and on April 10, 1941—eight months before the Japanese attack on Pearl Harbor—he was commissioned an ensign in the United States Naval Reserve.

He did not have to go far to hear his first bugle call. He was posted to the U.S. Naval Training School, which was housed in Dearborn at one end of the Ford Motor Company's River Rouge factory, where he was immediately and pragmatically turned into a schools officer and given charge of some 250 apprentices who were being trained in the plant. The best that can be said about the posting is that it gave him his first experience of command and his first real insight into what makes human beings tick.

There was nothing in Harry Bennett's nature, however, that made it easy to accept defeat. It had not been difficult to frustrate many of Edsel's ambitions; a word in old Henry's ear could usually do the trick. He was sufficiently confident and devious to believe he could retrieve young Henry from the navy, and when the Ford Motor Company pulled up its own civilian sleeves to become an arsenal of war, he had an argument that would stand muster. He began to lobby senior naval officers, Henry Ford, and eventually Henry himself, even to the extent of telling him: "Your grandfather sees the situation as I do." Henry complained to his father, and I know of no moment in Edsel's life when he fought his own father more vigorously or successfully than he did on this occasion. One telephone call convinced him that Henry Ford believed his grandson was already on his way back to the place where Bennett thought he belonged. On March 11, 1942, therefore, Edsel wrote him a letter:

Dear Father:

After talking to you on the telephone tonight we were much disturbed to hear from you that Henry was starting work in the factory tomorrow morning—I telephoned Henry and he said that that was not so and he had no intention of doing so but that he had spent the better part of two days with Bennett and was being high-pressured to do so—Henry is very upset by this situation and does not like it. He is now in the Navy and that decision was made after lots of talk a year ago and mostly with Bennett. Now that he is in the Navy he is trying to do a good job and he can't do it with all the string-pulling and high-pressure from Bennett. Bennett evidently talks to Admiral Downs in Chicago and he talks to Comm. Stoker at Dearborn then Stoker sends Henry to Bennett and the poor boy doesn't know where he is at.

With the country at war, Henry feels that his place is in the Navy and does not want to get into the factory. We, who are after all his parents, have given the whole matter a lot of thought and believe as Henry does and it is his decision to make and he is making it.

You are the only one who can do anything with Bennett and we would appreciate it very much if you would call him off.

It was a careful letter and was first drafted in pencil, and it says a great deal about Edsel's relationship with his father. It was Henry who was upset, Henry who was not going to comply, Henry who wanted to be left alone with his decision, and it proved to be one occasion when Henry Ford remembered his own blood. His grandson kept his uniform.

It is ironical that having fought so hard to keep it, he was not allowed to enjoy it for long. Toward the end of 1942 he applied to go to sea and was posted to the Great Lakes Naval Station, and early in May of the following year he received orders that would have taken him to Africa. On May 26, however, his father died in what should have been the prime of his life, and other hands more powerful than Bennett's began to play their own cards in the game. Henry's uncle Ernest Kanzler, a former director of the War Production Board, warned the United States government that the Ford Motor Company was too important to the war effort to be allowed to flounder in the wake of Edsel's death, with Bennett playing Little Caesar in a war of his own and threatening to become president of the company with Henry Ford's senile approval.

This time Henry was not asked whether or not he wanted to leave the navy; he was told it was his duty to do so, and on July 17 made a formal request to be placed on inactive service. Four days later Navy Secretary Frank Knox sent him a letter. It was not the kind of communication naval lieutenants would expect to find in their mail.

"My Dear Mr. Ford," Knox wrote, "I think the action you are taking is thoroughly justified and understandable and that the services you will render as a private individual will surpass any work you could possibly do in your present position. I wish you all kinds of good luck. Yours Sincerely. . . ."

There was never any doubt that he was going to need it. The best that can be said for his situation at this time is that he at least knew where he was at.

There is no doubt that Henry saw his twenty-seven months in uniform as the beginning of experience. He framed the letter from Frank Knox, and it hung all his life in his bathroom—a private sanctum where only he could see it—and in later life, when he could be induced to reflect upon his apprentice years, he was clear about their formative value. "The navy taught me a lot about how to get along with people," he said.

"It teaches discipline. It teaches you how to read a clock, which a lot of people never learn—and how to take orders and accept them, whether you believe them or not. There has to be a certain amount of that in life, too."

If this was the only knowledge Henry brought to the Ford Motor Company in 1943, it was still a great deal more than the company itself had learned. Henry Ford, though still a commanding figure and a forbidding personality, was neither physically nor mentally vigorous enough to engage in any kind of methodical discussion. The lean Lincoln face had grown puffy with medication, and his eyes were away in their own cloudy reflections. He was taken for a drive every day, stopping now and then to inspect landmarks familiar from his youth, on one occasion making a map of the Dearborn farm where he had been born, marking with a cross a bird's nest he remembered from his childhood, to which, in old age, he was returning.

His young grandson, acutely aware of the responsibility that was all too publicly demonstrated by his return to civilian life, had no alternative—in seeking to "shoulder some of the responsibility"—except to "mosey around" on his own, touring plants, talking to employees, finding out how things happened and, more often, why they did not. The uncrowned prince learned very early in his adult life to keep his own counsel, hide his disappointments, reveal no emotion, and answer the more direct interrogations with a handy anodyne: "I am green and searching for answers." Within the massive frustration that was then the Ford Motor Company, he discovered quickly that questions were in greater supply.

At one of their meetings he screwed up enough courage to tell his grandfather that "something should be done" to clean up the mess. Clara was there at the time and added her support, saying to her husband, "I think young Henry should take over," but there was no response, and the drift continued.

Week after week Henry went back to Fair Lane, ever hopeful that the period of indecision would come to an end. Among the many legends surrounding the Ford Motor Company is the one about Clara's recognizing that the affairs of the business were getting dangerously out of hand and threatening to sell her stock in the company and force some kind of insurrection unless her grandson were allowed to ascend gracefully to the throne. But Henry Ford II was always scornful of this melodramatic exaggeration of the painful enough reality. All he remembered of the circumstances that finally brought him his inheritance was his going to his grandfather sometime later with stronger arguments, which were again supported by Clara. "I have got to get some things done," he said, "and I have to have the freedom to do them myself." But he could not muster the courage to ascribe all, or even some, of the problems to Harry Bennett because Henry Ford was incapable of seeing anything but virtue in his underling. This encounter therefore ended as inconclusively as all the others. "He had been a wonderful guy," Henry recalled later in life, "but I just couldn't make contact anymore."

Faced therefore with the inescapable fact that the man who, more than any other, had created the automobile was no longer capable of drive or direction, Henry Ford II decided to fill the vacuum. He would still report back, for his affection never wavered, but he would grasp the power that was so nearly his anyway. Fortunately he knew what he wanted, and in 1944 he began seriously to search for a mentor, a man who could understand the organization charts that other companies had (and business schools talked about), somebody who could bring order, stability, and common sense to his disorganized individuals. Like so many of the Fords, he was left-handed, and in his large, round writing he made lists of jobs and titles. He drew management charts like family trees. He had no doubt that what Ford needed was professional management, and he was wise enough to recognize the limits of his own experience.

In January 1946 he began to court Ernest R. Breech, president of the General Motors subsidiary Bendix Aviation. Breech had risen through the GM ranks to become a vice-president in 1939. He was a renowned management troubleshooter and a strong contender for the top job at GM. By April, after several meetings with Henry Ford II, Breech, who was beginning to feel almost a personal obligation to him, finally accepted the offer and became executive vice-president of the Ford Motor Company. He was forty-nine years old. His job, said Henry, was to remake Ford along the lines of General Motors—which was evidently the outstanding automobile management—and though relative fortunes varied and this would not always be the accepted view, Henry kept a General Motors organization chart on his office wall every day of his working life and even into retirement.

The new team went quickly to work. As late as the first half of 1946 Ford would still find itself losing $55 million, but thereafter Breech's surgery was to pay rapid results. The management that Henry had wanted was taking shape, its bible, the recently published *Concept of the Corporation*, an evaluation of the General Motors organization by Peter F. Drucker. A "staff and line" structure—a concept originating with the Prussian Army—was introduced into the uncharted Ford world by a new director (soon to be a vice-president), appropriately called Crusoe, and ten remarkable and recently demobilized air force officers, who had applied to Ford for jobs en masse, were taken on as a group, and were given responsibility for analysis and planning.

Once a week Henry continued to make progress reports to his grand-father at Fair Lane. He discussed his new appointments and talked about the first all-new postwar car. One weekend, when he knew nobody would be in the styling department, he bundled the old man into a back seat and took him to see it. It may well have been this action—although the suggestion is purely conjecture—that persuaded Henry Ford to come to terms with the inevitable, for in the early-autumn days of 1945 he told his grandson that the time had come. Henry Ford I would hand over his authority and his power. Henry Ford II said the first thing he would do would be to fire Harry Bennett. There was no objection. On September 20, 1945, Henry Ford surrendered unconditional control of the Ford Motor Company, and a board of directors' meeting was convened to ratify Henry Ford II's appointment as president. Bennett was gone within a week.

What had been the worst of times soon became the best of times. A mass of hungry people was wanting and waiting to buy automobiles of any kind and quality. The new management, aided by the eagerness in the market, soon began to show results. By the end of 1946, on gross sales of $1.2 billion, Ford had scraped a profit of $2 million. The following year sales revenue increased to $1.6 billion, profits were $64.8 million, and Henry Ford II, by then chairman of the board, was pleased to secure unanimous approval to pay a $2 dividend.

The dividend came too late for old Henry Ford. He died from a cerebral hemorrhage on April 7, 1947, leaving his heirs a fortune that was estimated to be somewhere between $500 million and $700 million. His influence on the company he had created was, at the end, negligible. Freed from his cracker-barrel philosophy of doing things, the shambles that had been the Ford Motor Company was beginning once again to look determined and in some kind of order. Ernie Breech had worked wonders and was taking good care of things, and so, with the ghosts of the past finally exorcised and a good housekeeper who could be trusted,

Henry Ford II felt the time had come for him to explore the rest of his world. For it was, without a doubt, all his now.

By the end of 1947, when Pan American Airways was asked if it could provide an aircraft and crew for a private tour of Ford operations in Europe, Henry Ford II had already learned a great deal. He was wiser in the ways of business, more pragmatic, and perhaps less trusting. He had become something of a public figure, and his occasional speeches were increasingly imaginative and human, suggesting to many that it was now indeed a different Ford Motor Company and commanded by a very different Henry Ford. Everything he did was observed, and he was no stranger to gossip columns; but among his peers in America at large and with the influential in Washington, he was getting a good press. Henry always had what he called seat-of-the-pants judgment about people, and this became more obvious as he sought to enlarge his experience and find other mentors who could teach him the "thing or two" in which his knowledge and understanding were still lacking. Ernie Breech, of course, knew everything, but Henry was not sure he was the right man to advise him about Ford overseas. In particular, where Europe was concerned, he was sure he needed somebody who really knew his way around.

Once again, General Motors supplied the need in Graeme Howard, a recently resigned GM vice-president. For all its aptitude in the science and application of management, GM sometimes, it seemed, found it difficult to accommodate or use the odd man out. And Howard was odd. A tall, gaunt, humorless Californian with a clipped military mustache, he had joined GM in 1920, graduated from Harvard Business School in 1921, and climbed through the ranks of the Export Division to a vice-presidency in 1939. He was appointed colonel and deputy chief of the U.S. Army Motor Transport Division in 1942 and eventually joined Dwight Eisenhower's staff in Europe. He was responsible for economic planning at the U.S. Control Council for Germany and recruited many of the staff, but he left the army in 1945 to rejoin GM, where he still did not quite fit in. In June 1947, at Henry Ford II's request, he became a consultant to the newly formed International Division of the Ford Motor Company and proved an ideal amanuensis for Henry on his European journey. Howard at least knew the people who controlled the destiny of the part of Germany that remained in the West.

It is dangerous for anybody to indulge his hindsight and confer some kind of symbolic stature upon past events. Significance is always easy to assign in retrospect. Yet it is still appropriate to see Henry's trip to Europe in 1948 as a remarkable example of the young man's prescience.

The company Henry had inherited was American only in birth; its affairs were worldwide. Nevertheless, there were few industrialists of any age thinking seriously beyond the United States in 1948. For one thing, there was too much to be done at home as America's almighty economy turned from war into avenues of pacific endeavor. The slow tap-tap-tap of trowel on mortar, the most characteristic sound in Berlin as the German *Trümmerfrauen* (women of the rubble) recovered bricks from the wreckage for the task of rebuilding, was in a different key from the sounds of optimism that postwar America was hearing on its radios. All opportunity seemed to reside there. Some few politicians talked of the need to rebuild the shattered economies of Europe, even drawing blueprints of a United States of Europe with the combined resources to defend its bitterly won freedom. But the United States was where the action was.

One incentive Henry Ford II recognized as a motive for the trip to Europe was curiosity because he had been there before. He had first seen the overseas domain old Henry Ford had created as a round-faced eleven-year-old in knickerbockers and Buster Brown cap, fidgeting among a crowd of civic dignitaries, while his father performed the ground-breaking ceremony for the new British factory at Dagenham in May 1929. (In 1924 Ford had bought 310 acres of desolate Thames-side marshland—the location of Pip's meeting with the convict Magwitch in Dickens's *Great Expectations*—as the site for a new Detroit of Europe.) More to young Henry's taste was a visit to the Ford France plant, Asnières, in Paris. The assistant works manager, Gabriel Panier, drove the family around, showed them the Bois de Boulogne, and took the boys to a fun fair. Afterward they toured the châteaux of the Loire, and young Henry kept a diary and drew maps of the entire journey, transferring them all into a leather-bound album when he returned to Detroit, captions neatly written under pictures of each château. The album was in his study when he died. But nostalgia was only peripheral to the European journey in 1948. Henry could be persuaded to reminisce when the mood and the moment came together, but his reverence was always for the future. When he poured his tea and my coffee in Ford's World Headquarters in the seventies and eighties at the start of so many working days, he would invariably ask: "Well, what are we going to do today?"

Edmund Burke once observed that a great empire and little minds go ill together, but empires are often assembled in a haphazard fashion, with chauvinism as their most distinctive feature. In its earliest days Ford had a factory in Copenhagen, Denmark, for the same reason it had one in Cork, Ireland: sentiment. Henry Ford built a tractor plant in southern Ireland in 1917 because his father had come to the United States from County Cork, and Copenhagen was chosen as a location in 1919 because William Knudsen had been born there; coincidentally, both plants produced their first vehicles on the same day, July 3, 1919. Knudsen and his compatriot Charles Sorensen were the most prominent of old Henry's manufacturing men, and just as Cork was to prove vital to Ford of Britain by providing its most dynamic postwar leader, Patrick Hennessy, so Copenhagen was to prove essential to the Ford interests in Germany by recruiting an ambitious young Danish clerk named Erhard Vitger in 1920.

The subsidiaries simply grew up one by one, each fitting into Henry Ford's prejudices and their own national culture as best they could. The new German subsidiary was a case in point. In 1925, when a Ford company was incorporated in Germany and began operations in a rented canal-side warehouse, Vitger, who read but did not speak German, was sent to Berlin by train from Copenhagen to take up a new post as chief clerk. He was firmly in the ascendant by the end of the twenties, when Ford was looking for a bigger site on which to build a new factory and when the staunchly anti-Nazi *Oberbürgermeister* of Cologne, Konrad Adenauer, offered the most favorable package of inducements— including six years of reduced taxes—to persuade Ford to buy fifty-two acres on the Rhine in the Cologne suburb of Niehl. The factory opened in 1931, but its location was not to the liking of Adolf Hitler, who was elected chancellor in 1933. The following year Wilhelm Keppler, Hitler's minister for economic affairs, wrote to Prince Louis-Ferdinand of Prussia (the kaiser's nephew and a closet Nazi, who was working in Dearborn as a Ford production trainee):

Hamburg circles are informing me that the Ford Motor Company is contemplating at the moment the expansion of its German Ford works. Knowing that you are interested in the question, I take the liberty of calling your attention to the point that it would not agree with the wishes of the Führer if the Cologne works should be enlarged. Almost the whole German motor industry is located along the western and southeastern frontier of our country and, therefore, the government is forced to give greatest attention to the fact that when new investments are being made, the new constructions are erected in locations more convenient for Germany. I, therefore, would be very thankful to Your Royal Highness if you could call Mr. Ford's attention to this point during your conversations with him. The Führer decidedly favors the foundation of new motor car factories in order to create the Volksauto, and he always stresses the point that he does not wish any discrimination whatsoever of foreign capital among the German industries. Our country is, as far as motorization is concerned, utterly backward.

Henry Ford's attitude to the Germans had been one of naive admiration. In the confessional of the barber's chair at the Dearborn Inn (built to serve the Ford airport in 1931), he told his barber, Joseph Zaroski, that his favorite nationality was German. "He once said," Zaroski recalled, "that he liked the Germans because they were industrious, productive, hardworking people. They invented things, built things, and kept things beautiful." His admiration did not extend to Keppler's letter. Cologne had been built, as had all Ford plants throughout the world, on the water—on the great highway of the Rhine—and that was where it was going to stay. Adenauer proved equally inflexible, and eventually Hitler must have decided to forgive because Henry Ford was offered and accepted the Grand Cross of the Supreme Order of the German Eagle on his seventy-fifth birthday in July 1938.

The forgiveness was nevertheless partial; Ford-Germany was regarded as an alien company in a way that General Motors' subsidiary, Opel, was not. "Indeed," recalled Vitger, who joined the Cologne board of directors in 1937, "it was not permitted to park a Ford car in a public place or in the parking areas of authorities and official bodies. Only German cars were allowed. And later, when we began to supply Ford in America with parts so that we could obtain foreign currency to buy raw materials, we found that a quarter of the overseas earnings had to be handed to the government." Cologne did its best to Germanicize its products in an attempt to achieve Aryan purity, endowing them with patriotic names such as Taunus, Eifel, and Rheinland, but the changes were purely cosmetic since Cologne was only an assembly plant for American cars and had no independent engineering facilities.

The modern Ford manager, familiar with all the offspring of microchip technology, for whom no place on earth is more than a push button away, has to make a considerable mental effort to comprehend the way things were in the good old unsophisticated days of his company. The relationship of Ford to its overseas subsidiaries at that time often seems like something from the silent movies when you could see the action but fail to catch the words.

Initially, in the decade that followed the First World War, Ford's European subsidiaries had been little more than unruly puppies. A visit to headquarters in the United States demanded that the general manager of each outpost take a train to the nearest transatlantic port, then a ship to New York, and finally another train to Detroit. The fastest return journey took six weeks. Reporting to Dearborn was entirely individualistic, conforming to no pattern, and the English in which reports were written was often more picturesque than descriptive.

In 1928 Henry Ford—no devotee of sophisticated management—was nevertheless able to see that something had to be done to control and direct the evidently prosperous future that was there for the making. The result was the "1928 Plan," which was duly explained to Percival Perry, the founding father of Ford of Britain, and this xenophobic Englishman was then charged with the task of bringing some sense of common purpose into a complex set of European managements and markets.

In 1919 Perry had resigned in a bitter quarrel and retired to his small Channel Island of Herm. Nine years later Henry Ford enticed him back, confident that Perry—who had been knighted for his government work during the First World War—was the right man to run Europe. Resolutely unwilling to learn any language but English, Perry hired Maurice Buckmaster, who spoke some German and Spanish and was bilingual in French, and set out to explain the plan to an assortment of resolute individualists who were equally reluctant to learn. Perry took his wife, sister, valet, and Buckmaster to London's Victoria Railway Station to board the Golden Arrow, and they crossed the Channel to France to visit the plant at Asnières and on to Hoboken (Antwerp), Rotterdam, and Cologne and then farther still into Scandinavia, stopping at Copenhagen and Stockholm. There was another trip to Finland, where they were stranded in Helsinki waiting for the St. Petersburg express to Warsaw, since one other item on the agenda was the prospect of building a plant in Poland.

The "1928 Plan," which was really little more than an idea and not a plan at all, had no chance of succeeding from the outset. For one thing, there were too many iconoclasts at the head of the individual and individualistic companies. Perry sacked Alexander Lie, the Norwegian-born manager of Ford France, and four successors in rapid succession. In 1930, when Maurice Dollfus—a former director of Hispano-Suiza and a French rugby player with money of his own—was appointed general manager, he paid no attention to Perry at all and developed his own relationship with Henry Ford, who seemed perfectly content with this rebel. In 1938 Ford gave him $1 million, which he doubled with a loan from Ford Belgium, to build a new factory at Poissy on a site from which there had once started a crusade to the Holy Land.

The plan had other, larger issues to contend with. The Spanish Civil War broke out on July 18, 1936, and Ford Spain's assembly plant in Barcelona was an early victim. Progovernment Loyalists occupied the factory within a fortnight of the outbreak of hostilities and forced it to operate under their chaotic control. Most of the company's managers and directors were made to flee the country. Ford Italy had been founded in 1923 and poured out Model Ts to thirty-four countries across the world; but five years after Mussolini's Fascist legions marched on Rome, mounting Italian nationalism forced the closure of the Trieste factory, and Ford Italy was no more. It did not worry Perry. He had always believed that the safest place for Ford in Europe was England.

The present-day Ford executive traveling to Europe or anywhere else in the world has at his immediate disposal every fact he needs to discipline his judgment, often enough to fill an encyclopedia. If he has an appetite for more, the information system installed outside London in England can provide facts, figures, or pictures in minutes. When Henry Ford II set out for Europe in 1948, he had a very rudimentary Baedeker of the eight countries on his schedule, a sheaf of papers in a three-ring binder consisting principally of biographies of senior management. That is what he had asked for and all he had asked for. Graeme Howard had had six months to bring some of the disciplines of the Harvard Business School to bear on the matters ahead, and he reached his own conclusion: ". . . there is embarrassing evidence that the principal weakness in the Ford International scheme of things rests in ourselves—our own top management." It is not the sort of sentiment that comparatively junior executives would commit to paper today—even if they believed it—but nobody within the Ford Motor Company was looking for alibis in 1948. Their new young leader had absolved them from the sins of the past, and none of them felt they bore any responsibility save for the future. Henry

Ford himself did not need to travel to Europe with a file of statistical information. All he needed was a clean sheet of paper.

Henry set out for Europe, as he had many years before, by ship: on the *Queen Mary*. It was a rough crossing. Tugboats nudged the great liner into its Southampton berth at 11:15 A.M. on Tuesday, February 10, and Henry was relieved to arrive precisely on time. For two days the ship had rolled in heavy weather; but his spirits were high, and he waved cheerily to crowds gathered on the quayside. Glamorous visitors were hot news in austere Britain, and the newspapermen waiting at the foot of the gangway were as keen to speak to Henry Ford II and his wife as they were to photograph film star Merle Oberon, another of the *Queen Mary's* passengers. Anne Ford and Miss Oberon were arm in arm as they stepped ashore. A new Ford V8 Pilot was waiting for the Fords on the quay, its enamel gleaming raven black. The Ford of Britain directors sent this flagship of their fleet to meet the Fords with a certain amount of trepidation. It was a prewar design, reintroduced six months before and, in a sense, already antique. On the ride to London the car impressed Henry no more than the competitive models he saw on the roads. Three weeks later he was to make a speech in front of these same directors in which he said: "In respect of English cars, I would say that I myself do not like them."

The problem was that the car market in England was not encouraging to the development of new models. Restrictions imposed upon industry and the private motorist by the socialist government of Clement Attlee made the future look anything but expansive. Compelled to export most of its production or forgo an ungenerous allocation of steel, the industry was told in a government white paper that the home market had been assessed at fifty thousand cars a year "for essential users." Would-be customers had been informed at the end of 1947 by the ascetic chancellor of the exchequeur, Sir Stafford Cripps, that the basic gas ration was being withdrawn to save dollars, which made big cars like the Pilot, with its 3.6-liter engine, unsalable. Other public pronouncements were equally chilling. The member of Parliament for Dagenham, many of whose constituents depended upon Ford for a living, condemned car ownership altogether as an "advantage of wealth."

Against such a background it might have been thought impossible for Henry Ford II to be optimistic, yet at his first press conference in Europe—held at the Savoy Hotel on his first evening—he was cheerful and open. Conforming in full measure to the newspaper reporters' idea of the young American executive—in an easy-fitting light gray suit, white silk shirt, and silk tie, emblazoned with pictures of military heroes in full regalia—Henry was flanked by Graeme Howard and Ford of Britain's triumvirate of recently knighted (for war service) directors: Sir Rowland Smith, Sir Stanford Cooper, and Sir Patrick Hennessy. The fact that none of his companions was under fifty years of age made him seem all the younger. After telling the journalists that over the next six months Dagenham planned to export some 6,000 cars worth £125,000 to the United States, he pointed out that 1947 had been Ford's best production year in Britain, despite all the restrictions, with 114,872 vehicles produced, beating the previous record of 1937 by more than 100. He dealt with persistent questions and was stumped by only one. "Can you tell us the cash value of the concerns that you control?" asked one reporter.

"No," said Henry, "I haven't the slightest idea."

There were formal luncheons and meetings and black-tie dinners in England, and then it was time to board the Pan American *Yankee Clipper* for the trip to France. A dinner at the Hôtel Plaza d'Athénée was his formal introduction, and he crossed the first divide by talking fluently in French, an ability he owed to his Parisienne childhood nanny. *"C'est pour moi un grand plaisir de me retrouver de nouveau à Paris . . ."* he began, although when it later came to fielding questions from journalists, Dollfus acted as interpreter.

Henry's own wartime horizons had not extended beyond the Great Lakes and its training station, but he soon came face-to-face in Europe with the reality of war and began to appreciate the often bizarre consequences of trying to run a company with subsidiaries that had been forced to fight on different sides. The outbreak of war in Europe set Ford of Britain and Ford of Germany in opposite camps although until America entered the war, both were still free to communicate with each other via the mother company in Dearborn. There was also at least one meeting on neutral ground. In 1940 Thornhill Cooper, an Englishman, met Erhard Vitger from Cologne, and Arthur Beck and Otto Brondum from Stockholm on the neutral soil of Sweden. The meeting was relaxed, and when Vitger suggested a souvenir photograph with his three colleagues, they jokingly raised their arms in a "Heil Hitler" salute. After the war the American authorities saw the picture; they did not appreciate the joke, and Vitger had some questions to answer.

Nobody is likely to fight over the issue, but I have sometimes wondered if the Allies could have won the war without Ford, and the question is not as fanciful as it might sound. The Japanese attack on Pearl Harbor broke the spell that had been binding old Henry Ford, and he emerged from his home in the stone recesses of Fair Lane to play once again—until the first of his damaging strokes—an active role in the running of the company. Ford factories in North America joined those in the empire that still belonged to Britain and poured forth everything from mobile canteens to four-wheel-drive trucks, airfield wind socks to grenades and bombs. Ford engines powered landing craft, high-speed patrol boats, balloon winches, and every one of the ubiquitous Bren gun carriers, the go-anywhere light-tracked armored vehicles designed by Sir John Carden. Ford Britain built nearly 14,000 of them, Ford United States another 14,000, and Ford Canada almost 44,000. Ford United States was the prime mover in the development of the immortal jeep and built 277,896, a substantial portion of the more than a million fighting vehicles supplied to the Allies by Ford operations in the United States, Canada, Britain, India, South Africa, and New Zealand. Ford played an equally constructive role in the air.

To the west of Dearborn, Henry Ford ordered a huge assembly plant to be built at Willow Run on the site of one of his combined farms and boys' camps to produce four-engine B-24 Liberator bombers on a mile-long production line. The first concrete was poured in April 1941, the first steel structure went up three weeks later, the first machinery was installed the following September, and the first bomber rolled out in May 1942. By the spring of 1944 Willow Run, which had encountered many problems, had triumphantly confounded the critics who called it Willit Run? and was producing several hundred aircraft a month. It had become the largest supplier of B-24s to the army air forces and, at the beginning of May, achieved old Henry's ambition of a bomber an hour. By the end of the war Ford had built 86,865 complete aircraft, plus 57,851 aero engines, 24,000 jet bomb engines, many thousands of engine superchargers and generators, and 4,291 invasion gliders.

The British company's contribution to the war effort was no less emphatic. Patrick Hennessy was seconded from Dagenham to help Lord Beaverbrook at the Ministry of Aircraft Production, where his unique talents—determination spiced with blarney—were directed to coordinating materials requirements and working out a production plan for the entire aircraft industry to cope with the extraordinary demands of the Battle of Britain. Rowland Smith, who lived to celebrate his one hundredth birthday in 1988, was asked in November 1939 if Ford could mass-produce Rolls-Royce Merlin engines for Spitfires and Hurricanes at the rate of four hundred a month. He said it could, and a new factory was erected at Urmston, not far from Ford's first British factory at Trafford Park, Manchester. Key Ford workers were trained for the venture at the Rolls-Royce works at nearby Derby, and Rolls-Royce blueprints were redrawn to Ford standards of accuracy at Dagenham. Precision jig boring machines obtainable only from neutral Switzerland were nevertheless delivered safely in 1943 after traveling unhindered through German-occupied France and Spain. The Swiss, uncompromising but staunchly commercial in their neutrality, insisted on their right to trade with all belligerents, and since the Germans were also dependent upon Swiss machine tools, they were forced to agree to export shipments to their enemies. It was, as Hennessy later recalled, a very funny war. The new Merlin factory was already manufacturing Merlin crankshafts and spare parts before its roof was in place. The first engine was produced in June 1941, and from then until the war's end, Ford built more than thirty thousand of these complex supercharged V12s—more than Rolls-Royce built at Derby—and they were later installed in Mosquito and Lancaster bombers.

The Third Reich, on the other hand, benefited little from the activities of the Cologne factory. In the wake of the Munich crisis of 1938, Robert Schmidt, a German working in Dearborn, was sent to Cologne and appointed general manager. When France, Belgium, Holland, and Denmark all fell under Nazi control, he was made *Verwalter* (administrator) of all these national Ford companies and was commanded to produce trucks for the German armies. In 1942, however, it was decreed that only Germans could manage industrial companies during the war, and Schmidt was made chairman of the Management Board. Though he was joint manager, Vitger, the Dane, was not permitted to enter the factory and had to restrict his activities to the offices. Under effective but industrially inexperienced military control, Cologne now had to enter more fully into war production and turned out a considerable number of trucks. It continued working until late October 1944, when production became virtually impossible, and then it ceased altogether because of constant air raids.

Before the air raids the Ford plant at Cologne was working flat-out, though output was less than half that of the late 1930s. Wilhelm Inden, who started at Ford-Werke as an apprentice in 1944, recalls two shifts a day of twelve hours each and a special form of air-raid protection.

"When there was no wind, artificial fog was blown across the factory." The facility was better protected by the fact that it was surrounded by fields and located some miles from the city, which was destroyed by air attack. Most damage to the Ford factory was done by German artillery as the German Army fell back across the Rhine and Cologne was occupied by American troops. George Orwell, who was working as a war reporter for the British Sunday newspaper the *Observer*, provided a definitive, if dispassionate, account of the city at this time. In a dispatch datelined Cologne, March 24, 1945, he wrote: "There are still a hundred thousand Germans living among the ruins of Cologne. The whole central part of the city, once famous for its romanesque churches and its museums, is simply a chaos of jagged walls, overturned trams, shattered statues and enormous piles of rubble out of which girders thrust themselves like sticks of rhubarb." He approved of the military government— in this area a purely American concern—which was tackling the job of reorganization with "praiseworthy energy" and had appointed as chief of police a Jew who had held the same post in 1933, when the Nazis evicted him. And "energy" seems almost a restrained word to use in the circumstances. Before the war was officially over, a call was made to the Supreme Headquarters of the Allied Expeditionary Force, and SHAEF asked for immediate help from Dagenham to start things going again in the Ford plant. A three-man team, headed by Ford Britain's sales manager, Charles Thacker, was there within days of the request's being made, and the first postwar truck, assembled from components on hand, left the plant on V-E Day, May 8, watched by Thacker, his two assistants, Jack Horlock and Tom McCarthy, and American army officers. But the real heroes of this dramatic rebirth were the German employees of Ford-Werke. At the end of the war the German authorities had given instructions for the production machinery to be relocated in dispersal factories and then, later, to be blown up to prevent its falling into Allied hands, but the Ford men had disobeyed orders. All that remained was to get the machinery back into Cologne, where its mounts and power sources were waiting.

It was in those bleak days that Vitger was the saving of the company. He had been in an unenviable position during the war but now emerged to wheel and deal and horse-trade and get the operation into continuous production. The American authorities appointed him custodian of Ford interests not only in Germany but also in Budapest, Hungary (though the company was moribund), and in Salzburg, Austria, where the machinery from Budapest had been taken to keep it out of the hands of the Russians. Vitger managed to borrow transport from an American colonel by somewhat devious means to bring back eighteen hundred machines that had been moved across the Rhine to escape the bombs. They were delivered and installed before the last shots were fired. He was inventive also in dispatching borrowed trucks to the south and east of Germany, where there were potatoes to be had, and he bartered them for cigarettes and bicycles. Out of the new production, he gave two trucks to a cycle factory in return for one hundred more bicycles, which were given to employees so that they could come to work, for no trams were running. He made another deal with the French zone of occupation that got him three tons of potatoes. Barter was his only recourse since the reichsmark was worthless. Vitger, who in his late eighties was still Danish consul in Lugano, Switzerland, remembered every kind of opportunism. "A farmer used to graze cattle in a paddock near the factory. One day a heifer trod on a land mine, and our people were there quickly. That day we had potatoes and stew. Another day I saw a horse pulling a float which collapsed and died on the spot. When I passed the same way in the evening, all that was left was the skeleton." Some indication of the spirit that was being rekindled on the bank of the Rhine can be gathered from the reaction to the order that was given in Dearborn in 1947 when Henry Ford died: All Ford plants throughout the world were to close for a day out of respect for their founding father. Cologne ignored the order and kept working. Ford and Germany had to be rebuilt. To do this, old enemies were going to have to work together.

All his life Henry Ford II loved going around his factories. An overseas visit that did not take him through the places where things were made or put together was out of the question. And there was always a guard or a foreman or a janitor who could "remember when." None of them was running for office, and there was no reason not to talk openly and naturally to the boss. I always suspected that it was this tide of goodwill that manifested itself everywhere on the many miles and kilometers of Ford shop floors that directed Henry's first public thoughts to the power of people. His apprentice speeches on public platforms were about "human engineering." He was no populist and never had to canvass for votes, but he was, I often thought, instinctively aware that people who bring their minds as well as their muscles to work do both a better and a more rewarding job. The belief that nobody can live by bread alone is a lot older than manufacturing industry. In Europe Henry discovered that no one can live without it.

He also began to have some personal and immediate awareness of just how hungry Europe had been during the years of war. Sometimes the discovery was a little abrupt. The British minister of supply, George Strauss, who had dined with him at Claridges, had observed: "I hope our distinguished visitor is not so unwise as to judge the food our people are able to eat here today by the repasts he can get in this hotel." The empty stomachs of France made the same point, although in rather more gracious fashion.

From Paris Henry traveled to Antwerp and Amsterdam to visit the Ford plants, but it was Cologne that he wanted to see and Cologne that wanted to see him. The *Yankee Clipper* had been unable to leave Amsterdam because of fog, and the journey had to be made in a big American Lincoln limousine. He was late, but at least he was there. Journalists had been waiting at the Ford plant, and it was not until the afternoon that the car drove through the gates. There was no sign of the fog that had grounded the *Yankee Clipper*; a warm spring sun shone out of a clear blue sky. The journalists swarmed as he stepped out of the car, and Anne Ford, alarmed, returned to the safety of the back seat. But Henry happily answered as many questions as he could, although, as the *Kölnische Rundschau* complained, "his replies were typically American, friendly but noncommittal, giving hope without promising too much. . . ." The day's schedule, however, already dented by the morning's delays, was by now irretrievably damaged.

In the plant the employees who had been waiting for him to drive the ten thousandth postwar truck off the assembly line shrugged their shoulders, gave up, and went home. The Ford party was lodged just outside the city of Cologne at Röttgen Castle, a big stud farm that had escaped the general destruction and had become the residential head-quarters of the British military governor and senior members of his staff. When the bags were unpacked, it was more than obvious that the American visitors had little idea of the total loss suffered at all levels of German society. Forty years later, when Vitger was in retirement and living in distant comfort, his wife remembered the occasion in the way that a woman would. "We were invited to meet the Fords and the other members of their party at dinner that evening," she said. "The ladies had brought long evening dresses, but of course, we had nothing of the sort. They all looked very smart indeed. My husband saw Mr. Ford in the office, of course, but we could not invite him to our house because it was still in ruins and we simply had nowhere to entertain." "Entertain" was a hollow concept in the country of *der Grosse Hunger*, where a third of all deaths were caused by malnutrition and exhaustion, though Vitger was at least fortunate that the new British management team in Cologne shared its rations with its German colleagues. But it was in Berlin that Henry faced, as he had known he would, all the consequences of war in the starkest form yet.

He was wiser about many things by the time he got to Berlin, and both surprised and delighted to discover that the American commander of defeated Germany was also looking beyond the rubble of the city where he had his headquarters. Graeme Howard had known General Lucius D. Clay, commander of the U.S. Control Council for Germany, and served briefly under him during his own army service. Howard had always considered Clay a tense and dour, if combative, officer, and like Henry was pleased to find him relaxed and in good spirits. Clay was the reason Berlin had been planned as the last stop on the German tour. All his life Henry had been accustomed to dealing with the men whose pants were on the seats of power, as he put it. For one thing, it tended to save time. And the chain-smoking Clay, in his immaculately pressed military pants, was a man with power and knowledge. If the future of Germany and, indeed, of a reconstructed Europe hinged on any one man, that man was Lucius D. Clay.

Born in Georgia, son of a U.S. senator, and great-grandnephew of statesman Henry Clay, he was one of the army's top engineers, and had made his name by damming the Red River in Texas before the war. Clay was endowed with a phenomenal memory and able, it was said, to read six times faster than any other officer in the army. It was reported of him that "he could run anything—General Motors or General Eisenhower's army." He had been called to Europe by Eisenhower to break the supply bottleneck after the Normandy landings. Now Washington had given him the impossible task of reaching agreement with the intransigent Russians over the reform of Germany's worthless currency, though he confessed to Henry Ford II that the prospect of the $1 billion he had been promised to finance raw material imports together with a surprisingly good harvest had brought him a new sense of optimism about the future.

He might have been more optimistic about currency reform, for the Federal Republic's own D day was not far distant. In June 1948 the worthless reichsmark was replaced by the deutsche mark. Everybody in the country was given twenty-five deutsche marks for each reichsmark he or she held. In June 1988, when I attended a meeting with Helmut Kohl in the Chancellery in Bonn, he talked at some length about the fortieth anniversary of that event, which was then only a few days away. It is a moment burned into the German soul, and it also taught Henry a lesson about the value of money. When the deutsche mark was issued and he was back in the United States, he sent Lucius Clay a telegram of congratulations.

In 1948, however, Clay had more fearful apprehensions at the back of his mind. As the Ford party arrived in Berlin, he was putting the finishing touches to a confidential document telling Washington that his dealings with the Soviet authorities had given him the "gut feeling" that its erstwhile allies were planning some new action in Germany and he no longer felt war with Russia was impossible, a report that led to a speedup in American defense preparations. Accused of being alarmist, Clay retorted: "I did not want Pearl Harbor in Berlin." Sixteen short weeks later Clay, who had previously doubted that the Russians would try to drive Westerners out by blockading Berlin, was compelled to call General Curtis LeMay, the U.S. air force commander in Europe, to set in action Operation Vittles, the U.S. airlift that shuttled thousands of tons of supplies into Tempelhof to supply the beleaguered U.S. garrison and prevent the cold war from turning hot. "The events which accompanied the imposition of the blockade could have created war if they had been permitted to do so," he said later. Clay's determination to call the Soviet bluff and rebuild the German economy was the message Henry had come all that way to hear. It confirmed his own growing optimism and his sense of responsibility.

When Henry Ford II came to sum up the things he had seen and the people he had met on this venture into another world, there was little doubt of the acuteness of his perception or the urgency of his response. It was clear, too, that it was not the condition of the business but rather that of the people that had made the most cutting impression upon him. His reactions can be accurately assessed from an instruction dated April 5, 1948, presented to the Ford Policy Committee—the controlling operating group—and signed jointly with Graeme Howard. "Both at Dagenham and Poissy," it read, "we were acutely aware of the difficult food situation faced by the working force as a result of slim rations and inability to fulfill the ration. In Germany, an entire *weekly* ration consisted of three very small bowls of cereal, a coffee cup of brown sugar, another coffee cup of synthetic coffee, and two small loaves of black hard bread. Even this ration was not actually available. No meats or fats had been distributed since early December." Therefore, "a food package for the specific diet requirements and ration, costing approximately four to five dollars each, will be forwarded to every member of the Dagenham and Poissy organizations. For Antwerp, Amsterdam, Copenhagen, Stockholm, and Helsingfors [Helsinki] assembly plants, a carton of cigarettes will be supplied each worker." Every one was to contain the personal card of Henry Ford II. For Ford-Werke in Germany, $50,000 had been authorized on the spot to provide "a supplemental supply to give a minimum diet to each worker for the balance of the year."

The instructions were precise. Roy Larson, "an expert in food sources, packaging, transportation, insurance, and dietetical requirements," had been told to make it all happen and present a sample package to Dollfus and Patrick Hennessy "to be sure that the contents are acceptable. . . . Actual delivery will be made to each worker when he receives his weekly pay check."

This same report, which Henry Ford II kept in his office until the very end of his life—among the small collection of private documents he considered too personal to destroy—revealed some other aspects of his character. When it came to Ford's European executives, there was little criticism. "The British organization needs assistance and encouragement, an appreciation of their difficulties, and a recognition of the job done under conditions of extraordinary obstacles. Carping, unconstructive criticism"—in one of Henry Ford's typical expressions—"will butter no parsnips. Encouragement and help is [sic] what is required." Comments were nevertheless succinct: "Maurice Dollfus is a fine asset, one of our ablest executives in Europe, who has made great accomplishments under most difficult circumstances. With no help from, on the contrary despite Lord Perry, it is to the great credit of Mr. Dollfus that he has kept the Ford flag flying in France."

With the praise there was evidence of personal concern. Charles Thacker was an Englishman who had helped Ford of Germany back on its feet almost as the last post had sounded, and he was then sent to Belgium as managing director. Henry was "very favorably impressed" with him, although he was not a natural for the post "as he is not familiar with the language, customs, tradition, and history of the country," but even that was not the principal concern. "We were shocked at the salary paid the managing director," the report continued. "He receives a monthly salary which is equivalent to $12,280 per annum. At present, Mr. and Mrs. Thacker are not only forced to live on their own capital, but under circumstances detrimental to the Company's interests."

Things were as bad in Amsterdam:

The general manager, Stenger, seems a good sound man, supported by a fine wife (mentioned since the wife of any general manager of one of our overseas operations can and should play a very important role). Although 54 years of age with 23 years of service, Mr. Stenger receives a salary which approximates $12,000 per annum. As a result, he is not able to live up to his position; although managing director of the principal automotive company in Holland, he ironically is unable to afford either the initial investment or operating expense of the least expensive Ford passenger car.

Where the business was concerned, and for all his inexperience, Henry Ford II had no difficulty asking the right questions of the many executives he saw on the journey or observing the weakness in existing or projected cars and trucks. He was surprised to discover that Dagenham had no chief engineer, no body or styling engineers, and no engineering building; he demanded such a facility as a pressing need. He had not known that Ford Britain had its car bodies manufactured by another company. The styling of the products had to be modernized and costs reduced, and nobody should forget that one-third of the British production was tractors and farming implements. In France he asked to see the Peugeot operations and was given a special tour. Like Ford, he noted, Peugeot had been a family business since its inception, and he was surprised to find "order, system, modern methods, modern equipment." He sat down to talk with Jean-Pierre Peugeot and discussed the possibility of the two companies working together.

In Spain Miguel Mateu, who served as an intermediary between the Spanish king in exile and General Francisco Franco, said he thought he could talk the government into a joint venture—49 percent Ford; 51 percent government—which would make Ford the only supplier of commercial vehicles in the country. Henry said he was against any program that smacked of monopoly. Competitive individual enterprise was in the best interests of Spain and the consumer. He avoided a meeting with Franco, and it was another thirty-five years before he and the generalissimo talked together.

It was Germany where he felt most involved, though not, as was the case with his grandfather, out of any special sense of identity with the Germans. It was England to which Henry Ford was most strongly drawn.

He felt at home there and in the latter years of his life made it his real home, even at times claiming to be English in all but nationality. What made Germany in 1948 so significant to him was its desolation and sense of hopelessness. Cologne, apart from its great gaunt Gothic cathedral, was a rat-infested ruin. As ever, though, he was practical. And again, management—the recurring theme of his life—was foremost among his business concerns. He noted of Erhard Vitger in the jottings he kept at the time: "He is a man of more than average ability. Unprepossessing in appearance, shrewd in finance and law, . . . personally ambitious . . . Still a man of some ability. Smooth and bright . . . But not the man to head the Company."

It was, perhaps, the only unfair judgment, for it was Vitger's ability to wheel and deal that had enabled Ford-Werke to resume production after the war, when one could get things done only by breaking the rules. "You have no idea what it was like in those days," I was once told by the daughter of a German industrialist. "Only the foxes survived. . . ." And Vitger was certainly a fox.

If Vitger was not the man, who was? Was there perhaps a German Ernie Breech who could tackle the German shambles as Ernie had tackled Dearborn? Graeme Howard suggested a meeting with Heinz Nordhoff, who had been the outstanding head of Opel, the GM subsidiary, before and during the war and was now general manager of Volkswagen. When they met Nordhoff, he accepted the job as head of Ford-Werke and suggested that Ford should take over Volkswagen altogether. He offered to produce a study that would show how Ford might at least obtain a controlling interest. There were others in favor of this move. Volkswagen Werke AG, which had been constructed and owned by the German government, went into production just after the outbreak of war. It was located in what became, after the war, the British zone of Germany and had been taken over by Allied Property Control, which, under the Potsdam Agreement, had its disposition in its power.

Henry Ford II was considerably more perceptive about Volkswagen than most of the people who greeted the arrival of its products in the American market some years later with amusement. In the paper he presented to the Policy Committee at the end of the European tour he noted: "The product—known as the Volkswagon [sic]—has a definite appeal. There is ample room for improvement in its design and particularly in the quality of its materials and fabrication. These weaknesses are, however, correctable and do not prevent an amazing future for this little car." There was, as it turned out, too much politics involved in

Volkswagen's future at that time. Allied Property Control was not over-joyed at the prospect of an American company taking over any European enterprise, and when Nordhoff discovered that VW might retain its own independence as some kind of nationalized or partly nationalized enterprise, he also changed direction and withdrew his acceptance of the Ford job. Henry had decided anyway, pragmatic as ever, that a VW takeover was at best a slight possibility and that the Ford Motor Company should first learn how to run its own affairs before assuming other people's burdens. The more immediate need, he urged, was for better management in Europe—particularly in engineering and manu-facturing—and he insisted that these appointments should be given priority.

With the Continental part of their tour over, Henry and Anne took a brief holiday in Switzerland in the remaining days of March and then went back to England for some last farewells before their return to the United States by sea from Southampton. On the way back, he began to sort out his principal conclusions and reflect in more leisure upon the things he had heard and seen and upon the coincidence of thoughts that was to shape the future of his entire company and even, in the eighties, prove to be its salvation.

On March 20, 1948, George Marshall, the United States secretary of state, had made a speech in Los Angeles that had a decisive influence on the passage by Congress of his recently formulated European Recovery Program, later to be known and all too soon forgotten as the Marshall Plan. It was a resounding declaration and deserves to be remembered for it says so much about postwar America and the dream that was then so vigorously alive:

Our position of pre-eminence demands on our part a full realization of the degree to which future events depend upon what we say and upon what we do. We can no longer count on others to carry the initial burden of safeguarding our civilization. They will share our burdens, but the primary responsibility is now clearly ours. The fact is, the decisive factor for good in the present circum-stances of Europe will be the action of the United States. By the power of our decision we can strengthen the free nations of Europe in the defense of their freedom.

Henry Ford II, a little less loftily, had already come to the same conclusion, and Marshall's words, which rang like an echo in his mind, left no doubt about the rightness of his own vision. What was most likely to save European civilization, he considered, was an industrial renais-sance and an improvement in industrial leadership. Western Europe, he decided, was "in the beginning stages of industrial convalescence." Britain was a "job-shop nation" that needed conversion to mass production and a philosophy of competitive individual enterprise. But "those traits in the British people that have made England great still exist," and "there can be little doubt that five to ten years hence the country will resume an important role in the international economic scheme of things." France, with the aid of the European Recovery Program, "appears to have a better economic outlook than it has in any of the years before the wars." Germany was "an unbelievably sick country," and "the extent of her physical and spiritual misery has to be seen to be appreciated. Germany has a long, hard road ahead but the extraordinary capacity of the people for hard work, their technical genius and managerial ability—if given the opportunity for expression—can combine to produce results that might astonish even the most optimistic."

In its conclusion the paper that Henry tidied up to his liking on the transatlantic voyage home was unequivocal:

I believe that the policy of the Ford Motor Company should be to invest dollars in Europe where such an investment is obviously in the interests of the countries and the people involved. I further believe that in the years ahead, the success of the large American manufacturer will be measured equally on the national and international scales. The material rewards can, of course, be great; but of equal importance is the satisfaction of knowing that the Ford organization will be making a real and significant contribution to the general welfare. These two considerations are inseparable.

There was one other immediate consequence of this trip. The senior managers of all the Ford subsidiaries throughout the world were called to the first-ever international management meeting. It was held in Dearborn from June 23 to July 1, 1948. Henry Ford II took his notes with him to the meeting and then put them into his files, where they remained until he came across them again, housecleaning after his retirement. He brought them to my office the next day and dropped them on the desk. "I don't suppose anybody cares about these anymore," he said, "but I think you'll find them interesting."

CHAPTER TWO

Detroit's Crown Prince

Men who leave their mark on the world—even those who build their own—still cannot escape the influence of their environment. The Ford family in America had, in a sense, grown up with the city of Detroit. Henry Ford II was born and brought up there, in a black and white cosmopolis, and all his life he felt a special responsibility for the place and the people. As with all relationships, it was a mixture of love and fury, hope and despair.

The Ford family was originally English and Anglican and made its first emigration from England to County Cork in Ireland before joining the Irish exodus across the Atlantic. When Henry Ford's father, William, arrived in 1847, to settle on a forty-acre farm—ten miles or so from the center of Detroit—it was still a predominantly French, Catholic, and French-speaking community of only ten thousand people. Robert Beverley, the first native Virginian to write a history of that colony, had declared in 1705, " 'Tis not likely that any man of a plentiful estate should voluntarily abandon a happy certainty to roam after imaginary advantages in a new world," but the hundreds of thousands of people for whom America had become a dream had no estates and no certainty, and the advantages of emigration were far from imaginary. America was "where it was happening," and Detroit, in the middle of the nineteenth century, was a good place in which to begin.

Americans, new and old, lived on the land and off the land, but foundries and steel mills, electricity, and the telegraph (which arrived sensationally in 1844) quickly became the symbols and catalysts of change, and when Henry Ford was born on the farm on July 30, 1863, the American Industrial Revolution was outpacing the ambition of pioneers and newcomers alike. Necessity is truly the mother of invention, and necessity was not long in producing the automobile. Waterways and railroads could build cities; they could not build a country—and the overwhelming need for farming, for industry, and, above all, for an essentially restless people was transport.

The adventurous genes that made Henry Ford an inspired mechanic never managed to disturb the roots that always held him to the soil, and indeed, much of his early ingenuity was directed toward easing the hard work of farming. In 1885, when he was twenty-two years of age, he met at a dance a farmer's daughter who proved—as he put it in one of his letters to her—"loving and kind and true," and on April 11, 1888, he married her and settled down on his own forty acres, which he bought from his father. When they met, Clara Jane Bryant, the eldest of ten children and then approaching her nineteenth birthday, was a great deal more than loving and kind and true. She was a practical and economical young woman. Being the eldest in farming families of this size inevitably brought with it a set of subparental responsibilities, but what was more to the point was that she seemed as fascinated by machinery as Henry and spent long hours during their courtship listening to his strange mechanical ideas, wondering at the new watch he had made, and riding the newfangled farm engine he built.

The age of the automobile is generally considered to have begun ten years before Henry's wedding day at the Paris Exposition of 1878, when William Otto exhibited his four-cycle engine, and the first car is most often credited to Karl Benz in 1885. The speed with which these inventions were adapted to the needs of America is staggering even by today's standards. The Otto engine was being developed under license in America by 1882, and Henry Ford drove his first car through the streets of Detroit in 1896. By then Detroit was a metropolis of some two hundred thousand people. The Olds Motor Works was established in 1899; Ford, Cadillac, and Packard were founded in 1902 and 1903; and by 1904 there were eighteen auto manufacturers in Detroit.

There was certainly no conviction at that time that Detroit would become the automobile capital of the world, for it had many rivals. Before 1905, 445 different makes of cars were being produced in 175 separate locations from New York to California. Both Indianapolis and Cleveland had hopes of becoming the principal auto cities. New York, Chicago, and Boston were not far behind. Yet by 1914 three-quarters of all vehicle production in America was based in Detroit, and Ford accounted for more than half: nearly 300,000. The hunger to possess a car of one's own was exceeded only by the compulsion of its makers to produce them. Henry Ford's Highland Park factory, opened on January 1, 1910, had enabled assembly time to be reduced to fourteen hours a car. When the moving line was introduced there in 1913, assembly time tumbled astonishingly to ninety-three minutes. The Model T, which was born on October 1, 1908, had been priced at $850. With the moving line a proved success, Henry Ford cut the price to $600. Demand for cars was as insatiable as it was for people. The company had 14,000 employees but had to hire 53,000 a year for a period to maintain a stable labor force. Henry Ford dealt with this problem in the same pragmatic way he faced all challenges: On January 15, 1914, he invented the $5 day, after which he had to turn job seekers away from his doors. By 1916 the price of the Model T was down to $360 and 577,036 of them were sold. The following year there were 135,000 people employed in the Detroit industry and production exceeded 1 million for the first time.

The year 1917 was notable for two other reasons: The Ford family—at least the American Ford family—entered its third generation, and work began on a new factory unlike any other in the universe. A son was born to Edsel Bryant and Eleanor Clay Ford on September 4 at 6:00 P.M. in their home at 439 Iroquois Avenue (now 2171) in what is still called Indian Village. He was named Henry Ford II. Edsel was twenty-three. Eleanor, who gave her occupation merely as "wife," was twenty-one. Eleanor Lowthian Clay had married Edsel the previous November, and the wedding had clearly surprised the local newspapers, one of which reported that it was singularly lacking in the ostentation, show, glitter, and display of wealth usually associated with the union of scions of great and wealthy families. Eleanor's mother was a sister of J. L. Hudson, who had established Detroit's largest department store and, with Roy Chapin and Howard Coffin, had founded the Hudson Motor Car Company, and she brought, as the newspapers observed, a heritage of her own to the marriage.

The factory was born on the banks of the River Rouge and was designed to be the world's largest industrial complex. It was a self-contained auto city with twenty-seven miles of conveyors and ninety-three miles of railroad, and Henry Ford took his first grandson as a child in arms to see it. Its twenty-three main and seventy subsidiary buildings covered a floor space of 160 acres. A fleet of Great Lakes steamboats was built to bring ore to the blast furnaces. Henry Ford spent $360 million between 1919 and 1925 to perfect this enterprise, and everything needed for production was at the tips of his inventive fingers. He was a mechanic who made himself into an engineer, and in the process he also made Detroit.

Many Americans, and people in other countries, carry in their minds an unconsidered representation of Detroit as an inferno of smokestacks and furnaces, but it is a distorted picture of then and now. I recall hearing the reminiscences of a grand old lady who had visited Detroit once in 1914, when she was still in her teens, and what she most remembered—and this was after sixty years—was that it was the cleanest and neatest place she had ever seen. Everything was brand-new. The city had all the money it wanted for parks, curbs, streetlights, and the outdoor embellishments of downtown life. Well over half the houses were ten years old or less, and they were well built. It was a good city in which to grow up.

When Henry Ford II was three years old (and his brother Benson was two), the family moved to 7930 Jefferson Avenue, a limestone mansion with twenty-five rooms originally built for Albert Stephens, who had made a fortune from lumber. It overlooked the Detroit River, and the garden ran down to its edge, which was a big part of its attraction for Edsel, who lived and loved boats and passed on this passion to his son. His only daughter, Josephine, was born at the Jefferson Avenue house in 1923, and his youngest son, William Clay, in 1925. Their perambulators were safe in its landscaped grounds. Young Henry learned to swim in the pool and sat for hours watching his grandfather's ore boats go by. There was one for which he kept a special watch; it had been given his name. His school was ten blocks away, and he was permitted to cycle there unaccompanied.

But no industrial city is an island, and none is safe from intrusion and the rising tide of outside events. Detroit has been no exception. It has created its own problems, and it has had the sins of others visited upon it. Perhaps the principal problem of its own making was the inevitable human growth that accompanied the industrial gold rush. It went from being a city of a hundred thousand people in the nineties to well over a million by the First World War. Until the mid-twenties nine Detroiters out of every ten had grown up elsewhere, and although the city offered money and jobs, it was never home. It was a shifting, wide-open, multieverything society, which made it unusually vulnerable to three other uniquely American influences: prohibition, the Depression, and race.

Nobody knows why one nation drinks more than another any more than why one man drinks more than another. Sophisticated and apparently secure societies have felt impelled to prohibit alcohol. What persuaded U.S. politicians to attempt to stem the Niagara of booze they felt was about to engulf them is a complex question and defies easy explanation. Try they did, nevertheless. The Eighteenth Amendment to the American Constitution, which came into effect on January 16, 1920, prohibited the production or consumption of any drink containing more than 0.5 percent alcohol. The state of Michigan had anticipated this federal prohibition and had enacted its own law effective on May 1, 1918. Detroit at that time had more than fifteen hundred licensed saloons. The major breweries, such as Stroh's—which still sells its beer in Detroit—were too visible for defiance and turned swiftly to the production of innocuous mineral waters, ginger ale, and ice cream. Others who felt less exposed elected for free and private enterprise. In no time at all the number of drinking places had multiplied twenty times over. The licensed bar put up its shutters and along came speakeasies, gin palaces, and blind pigs—the perhaps deliberately unromantic name given to unlawful and often lawless bars. Private garages, which were springing up all over town to enclose the growing number of private cars, began to have a secondary importance as more and more of them were converted into private stills.

Prohibition did not deter the forces of the law in Detroit from following their own off-duty inclinations. They went to their favorite speakeasies along with everybody else. On duty it was a different matter. The neighboring state of Ohio remained doggedly wet after Michigan had gone dry—until federal Prohibition brought everybody into line—and early summer 1918 began to see armed bootleggers, occasionally in armored cars, machine-gunning their way from Ohio past police barriers and inspections. The police were outmanned from the beginning. On January 1, 1920, when Canada dropped its own prohibition law, introduced during the war, Detroit lawmen found themselves fighting a battle on land and water and losing it.

Indeed, the D day landings may well have involved fewer people than those who joined what Detroit newspapers called the "Prohibition Navy." Certainly, some of the "sea battles" on the Detroit River—no wider than the Thames in London, the Rhine in Cologne, or the Seine in Paris—were bitter and bloody. Prohibition was not repealed until 1933, and by then it had had an ineradicable impact. In the middle of the twenties Detroit had 1.5 million people. It also had the Mafia.

Gangs with names straight out of dime novels exceeded any fictional imaginings. The newspapers did not have the space to dwell upon every one of the five murders that took place on average every week or the kidnappings, extortions, and gangland executions.

The colors of the rainbow, mixed together, produce something that looks like mud, and societies, no matter how vigorous their separate communities, are often perceived at the lowest common denominator. In the twenties in Detroit everything happened—everything imaginable and many things that were not—yet it was a livelier city than its literature suggests. Detroit *was* baseball. Ty Cobb, who played for and managed the Detroit Tigers, was the nation's greatest baseball hero and possibly the finest player ever. Local son Charles Lindbergh made history with his solo flight to Paris. Skyscrapers went up almost (or so it seemed) overnight. Jazz had walked to Detroit in the hearts of its southern blacks, and the jazz craze was at its height. And Detroit had Bix. Bix Beiderbecke, who had difficulty reading and no formal training, was the aficionados' trumpeter, the greatest horn player of the Jazz Age and a symbolic figure in his own short lifetime. Before he died in his late twenties (of drink), he had played in Detroit with the Goldkette Orchestra and recorded at the Detroit Athletic Club. When Bix blew his horn, people said, it was like a girl saying yes, and the Detroit boosters added his reputation to that of their other heroes and swore that it was the biggest and the best and the richest and the liveliest damned place in the whole damned country. In the twenties people still went dancing, and the dance halls were always packed. In 1927, when John Philip Sousa was seventy-two, Detroiters gave him a weeklong birthday party, and Sousa, who liked the city, wrote "Pride of the Wolverines" and dedicated it to Detroit, which immediately adopted the work as its official march. The theaters were crowded, too. Magician Harry Houdini, who had once jumped into the Detroit River with handcuffs on his wrists, refused to disappoint an audience at the Garrick Theater despite the fact that he had appendicitis and collapsed to die as the curtain fell.

It seemed in 1929 as if the gangland wars and the Jazz Age and the Charleston and the days when everybody was young and gay would last forever, but on October 29, Wall Street crashed into crisis and the country discovered other things on its mind. The consequences of the crash were felt immediately by Detroit's auto companies. Production dropped quickly to half its prewar level. Nearly half the city—perhaps two-fifths of its working population—was unemployed, and the escalator up to a consumer heaven (which Detroit had seemed to be for all of the twentieth century so far) stuttered to a stop. The Great Depression was worse in Detroit than in most other industrial cities because even those who were not employed in the automobile industry were economically dependent upon it. Thousands of jobs in the supply and service industries existed only to serve those who were themselves the servants of car production. By the end of 1930, 125,000 families in Detroit had no money and no other means of support, and this accounted for one family in three. Job creation schemes flickered and died, for the city itself was bankrupt, and inevitably it was upon the blacks that the reversal of the nation's fortunes fell most heavily. People with skills were prepared to trade down to less skilled jobs; those without skills had nowhere to go. A return to the South was no solution to their distress because black unemployment there was 80 percent. Crime in the city shot up.

It was not to be expected—then any more than now—that visiting intellectuals would judge Detroit and its noisy, labor-hungry factories except in the light of their own experiences. They certainly did so, both before and—with extra enthusiasm—after the Depression. In 1925 the curmudgeonly H. L. Mencken told readers of the *American Mercury*:

Michigan is the seat of Henry Ford, the billionaire automobile manufacturer. Its chief city, Detroit, is mainly devoted to making automobiles and is immensely rich. Canada is separated from Detroit by a narrow river; thus the city is tremendously wet. The rest of Michigan is negligible—farms and forests, inhabited by a half-civilized peasantry. At Ann Arbor, there is a State university with 10,000 students. In 1924, the British poet Laureate lived there for a few months and was politely gaped at. The Detroit intelligentsia begin to show a considerable literary activity.

Aldous Huxley and Charlie Chaplin, in their different ways, came to the same conclusion about the machine age. In Huxley's *Brave New World*, "Our Ford" was the icon of an anesthetic and impersonal universe. Huxley had no firsthand experience of the real world that provoked his satire, but Charlie Chaplin was given a personal tour of the Rouge by Henry Ford in October 1923, emerging deafened and unforgettably mesmerized, as he was to show when he produced and starred in *Modern Times* thirteen years later and committed to all our memories his own mockery of the factory system.

It is not, of course, difficult to understand the effect of Detroit upon writers looking for subject matter and perhaps an anvil upon which to grind their own axes. The consequences of the Depression; the demanding discipline of the assembly line; the discovery that there could also be unemployment in Shangri-La; the struggle for recognition by organized labor—all these things drove deep rifts into a social fabric as kaleidoscopic as Joseph's coat and provided raw, and often bloody, material for any lurking typewriter or fountain pen. But the concerns and the conditions they described were by no means confined to this one city, and it is never easy—and sometimes is a dangerous distortion—to be simplistic about any part of the United States, for it defies classification. Nothing in America is typical of America. It was Edmund Wilson who said, "The United States is not a nation in the sense that England or France is. It is a society, a political system, which is still in a somewhat experimental state. Hence our panics of various kinds."

Panic may be too strong a word to apply to Detroit at this time, but no one can doubt its volatility. In the same way that everything had been built in the city about the same time, it all started to fall apart at the same time, and Detroiters who did not have multigenerational roots—and for many the city was not much more than a transit camp, a place on the road to somewhere else—did not care enough or were not conditioned to keep the city healthy and repair it in the face of continuing immigration. It was easier just to move out. The white and black middle class had every incentive to head for suburban safety.

The rich prefaced the exodus to residential pastures on the shores of Lake St. Clair and among the woods that fanned around the city. Edsel Ford, who had been happy with Eleanor and his four children in the house by the river on Jefferson Avenue, acquired nearly ninety acres of land from his father fifteen miles northeast of downtown Detroit. The land was known as Gaukler's Point, and he built a large house there on what was originally a Chippewa and Huron campsite, taking up residence in the autumn of 1929. It was not where Henry Ford would have chosen to live. The site, which was part of the larger area known as Grosse Pointe, was becoming a baronial enclave, and Henry thought its new residents were "damn stiff-necked sons of bitches," but Gaukler's Point provided three thousand feet of lakeside frontage and offered the prospect of pleasure on bigger boats than could comfortably be kept on the Detroit River. Edsel and particularly Eleanor were keen to create a major residence and traveled to England for architectural inspiration. In common with other automobile magnates, they fell in love with the stone houses of England's Cotswold country and commissioned Albert Kahn, a prolific architect, to design a sixty-room mansion built of rough sandstone in the Cotswold style. They imported from England roofing stones, paneling, fireplaces, and a great oak staircase dating from 1600 for the hall. The walls were hung with paintings by Titian, Joshua Reynolds, Jean Renoir, and Paul Cézanne and with some glorious tapestries. Among the library's sixteen hundred books were first editions of John Milton's *Paradise Lost* and *Paradise Regained*. The house cost $3 million, but money was scarcely a consideration. Apart from everything else, Henry had given his son $1 million in gold on his twenty-first birthday. And paradise of a sort it was. The children were safe from kidnappers, and the family was able to make its own life there. *

The exodus from the dangerous city was given new impetus by World War II. After the Japanese attack on Pearl Harbor and America's declaration of war, there began a period during which the patina of gold could again be seen on Detroit's sidewalks. One-third of a million people arrived in the city, cramming themselves into any kind of available housing and sending rents sky-high. But the war also offered new temptations to those who could afford to escape, for new roads turned open country into suburbia. The Willow Run Expressway opened in 1943 to expedite movement to the enormous Ford aircraft plant in this distant suburb.

Detroit became a largely black city and one hot summer night in 1967, a timid and ineffective raid by Detroit police on a blind pig boiled into a riot. It was not the first; there had been others and at least one had been significant. But this took everybody including the U.S. Army— 17,000 people in all—to quell it, and by the time it was over there were 48 dead, 657 injured, 7,231 arrests and 682 fires, and 1,700 stores had been looted. It need never have happened, for the ingredients were by no means unique. By 1967 Detroit was regarded as a model of comparative racial harmony, and there is ample evidence that Detroiters of every color and racial origin were appalled at this new and spontaneous combustion of inflammable emotions.

To Henry Ford II—three years old when the twenties came strutting in, twelve when Wall Street crashed, twenty-four when America entered the war—the sidewalks of Detroit were as familiar as they were to those who had to walk them. He was strictly and tidily brought up, and his lessons in charity began at home. His parents and grandparents were

---

* When Edsel died, Eleanor hesitantly put the house on the market but, on second thoughts, withdrew from this instinctive intention, and when she died on October 19, 1976, at eighty years of age, she left the house and a $15 million endowment fund as "an historical property and cultural center." It was the last of the great houses of Grosse Pointe and remains so today.

benefactors to Detroit and either built or endowed concert halls, li-
braries, art galleries, and museums. His mother bossed and fussed at the
guardians of the Henry Ford Hospital, which was much more than a
hospital; in its care for the sick it had to develop a conscience. Nor was
there any doubt about his grandfather's concern for social welfare, although it sometimes took strange directions.

It was not until 1943, when he was demobilized from one battlefront
and recruited for another, that Henry began to see that his inheritance
included the care and even the feeding of the city beyond his own factory
gates. It also meant coming to terms with a society of which he was only
imperfectly aware. The statistics of race were never of more consequence
to him than those of gender, but nobody can live in Detroit without
knowing it lives by and for the motorcar; nobody who manufactures
automobiles can afford to forget that it is still human beings who make
them. As he surveyed his new dominions in 1943—beginning with that
dependency he could see in the distance outside his office windows—
Henry knew that Detroit and its people were also part of the job. He also
thought he knew of an instrument that could afford a social conscience.
It was called the Ford Foundation.

Henry took over the presidency of the Ford Foundation upon his
father's death in 1943—when it was seven years old and he was twenty-
five—and began a postgraduate course in philanthropy that had a
crucial impact on his thinking and his life.

His grandfather had created the foundation in 1936 to "receive and
administer funds for scientific, educational, and cultural purposes." It
was established and chartered in Michigan, and Edsel was appointed
president. It was the direct consequence of an inheritance tax, passed
into law the previous year by the federal government, providing authority
for the appropriation of one-half of all estates over $4 million and 70
percent of all fortunes over $50 million. America at that time was three
years into Franklin Roosevelt's New Deal, and this tax on wealth was in
tune with the times. Henry Ford had no difficulty coming to the conclusion that one or two deaths in the family—his own, in particular—
would mightily enrich the U.S. government but substantially impov-
erish the Fords. The fate of the family fortune, however, was not his
immediate concern. Nothing Henry Ford did was ever dictated by
money; he had an inveterate disrespect for the stuff except as a means to
an end. Money was the Ford Motor Company's basic material and the
seed corn of its future, and the important thing, in his eyes, was to be
able to fund the development of the business and control its destiny.

Having established the foundation, he made it a founding gift of $25,000, and nineteen days later signed a codicil to his will guaranteeing a great deal more. The Ford family at that time owned 172,645 shares in the Ford Motor Company, and a scheme was devised to split these into foundation stock and family stock. The shares were multiplied by twenty and converted into 3,452,000 units, of which 95 percent was nominated Class A, or nonvoting stock, and 5 percent Class B, or voting stock. Henry Ford's will formally bequeathed all his A stock to the foundation and all his B stock, in five equal parts, to his son and grandchildren. Edsel enacted a similar codicil, again giving the foundation the A stock and leaving the B stock to his wife and children. It was neat, it was intelligent, and there was a surprising lack of argument about the maneuver and no suggestion of any consequence about tax dodging.

The foundation began, as the family intended, by confining its grants almost entirely to activities and institutions in which the family had a special interest. The principal beneficiaries were Detroit's Henry Ford Hospital and the Edison Institute—the extraordinary enclosed and open-air museum in Dearborn that housed the artifacts of Henry Ford's own history and of other makers of America. In 1937 Henry and Edsel made the first substantial transfer by giving the foundation 125,000 A shares apiece. At this time its trustees—principally members of the family—could only guess at the eventual value of future holdings. Ford stock, being privately held, was not publicly quoted, and there was no hint of the illness that would bring about Edsel's early death.

In 1943, however, when Edsel died at the age of forty-nine, the stock had to be valued for death duties, and the government came up with its own assessment of $190 a share. Edsel's widow replied that in her opinion, $58 was a more realistic figure. It was finally agreed to establish the valuation at more or less the difference between the two points of view, and Ford stock was declared to be worth $135 a share.

Henry Ford died in 1947, and his widow, Clara, lived for another three years; but when she died and the three blocks of A stock went to the foundation, it was sitting on a nest egg of $500 million—a large sum today by any standards, but in the fifties a treasure of truly immense proportions.

Henry Ford II set about his foundation responsibilities in 1943 with only one sense of foreboding. Harry Bennett was still at large, and his powers of voodoo were sufficiently strong to convince Henry that he had his eyes not only on the Ford Motor Company but on its charitable golden goose as well. When he became president of the Ford Motor

Company itself in 1945 and got rid of Bennett, he decided it was now sensible to achieve a proper separation of goods and deeds and moved the foundation to a separate location, in the Buhl Building in downtown Detroit, with a small staff effectively controlled by a young man from the company's finance department.

Henry knew the foundation had to be a national instrument for good and felt he could not give it all the time it required even though its offices were on his own doorstep. For one thing, the Ford Motor Company was an insisting and demanding monster; he was also sufficiently realistic to believe he was "wet behind the ears." He lacked the experience to run the foundation himself and could think of nobody within the company who might tackle the job—at least no one who could be spared—so he decided to look outside. He selected, and made himself chairman of, a board of trustees, and in 1948 it appointed a San Francisco lawyer, Rowan Gaither, to develop a specific order of priorities for the organization.

Henry also found a president. Paul G. Hoffman, a former head of Studebaker (then the world's fourth- or fifth-largest automobile company), had gone on to become the first director of the Marshall Plan. His business credentials seemed more than adequate, and Henry himself was one of the staunchest supporters of the European Recovery Program.

The mistake Henry made at this time—at least in his subsequent opinion, although he went into it with open eyes—was to agree to amendment of the articles of the foundation, formally separating it from family control. There was no legal obligation upon him to do so, and the only arguments in its favor came from the nonfamily trustees and officials; but there is no reason to ascribe self-interest or bad faith to them. Idealism has all the arguments in its favor. Henry's brother Benson, who was a trustee, and some of his friends argued against the move, insisting that Rockefeller and Carnegie and other lesser foundations that had been formed out of family fortunes had stayed in family control. Henry would have none of it. There was plenty of money. Income from the endowments was more than adequate to help his pet Michigan charities, and the Ford Motor Company itself had aspirations beyond the insular boundaries of Detroit.

The first benefactions caused no alarm. The Henry Ford Hospital promptly received a 1950 grant of $13.6 million to build a diagnostic clinic, and the first overseas development program went to help the obviously needy in Southeast Asia and the Middle East. So far, so good.

But soon things began to go wrong, and what caused them to go wrong was the enlargement of the board and the arrival of what Henry called "the liberals." The word *liberal* in American parlance has a very different implication from its meaning in other parts of the world, and one must be careful not to attach the wrong definition to Henry's use of the word. He was a very liberal man himself, generous, concerned for people, often surprisingly and instinctively sensitive to the tenderness of others, and he was, to a large extent, color-blind, as he showed beyond doubt in the aftermath of both Detroit riots and through his lifelong interest in the welfare of minorities and black education. His closest relationship with an American president was with Lyndon Johnson, and he regularly voted Democrat in U.S. elections. "Liberals" in his definition were those who pursued sectarian, impractical, or emotive causes that had no relevance to the "real world." Henry was all for changing the circumstances of life, but people were what God made them. It was all right to help them improve themselves and their circumstances—indeed, one had a duty to do what was possible in that regard—but they should be allowed to keep their psyches intact.

Lacking the power to control and the experience to shape Hoffman's new appointments, he began to have his first experience of what happens to perfectly normal, even distinguished people when they are provided with the power to give away money they have done nothing to earn. The rot, as Henry saw it, set in with the move to Pasadena. Hoffman insisted that a foundation as important as Ford could not do its job if it were cloistered in provincial Detroit, and so off it went to California where its liberals had more freedom to plan the transformation of American society. On February 9, 1950, Senator Joseph R. McCarthy made his name notorious with a speech at Wheeling, West Virgina, waving a list of 205 names of people he said were known members of the Communist Party in the State Department. He then flew around the country in a converted bomber, cheered on by Walter Winchell and other strident voices in the press. He brought terror to Hollywood, California, but not to Pasadena. Blithely convinced of their own virtuous designs for social reform—and with no evident awareness of the way the McCarthy winds were blowing—the architects of change in the foundation pushed ahead with black and Hispanic "freedom" programs, legal aid for the poor, and cultural and social exchanges with Eastern Europe.

It has to be said that other liberally minded American foundations—notably Carnegie—were on the same track, and in these days (when there are no surprises in anybody's closet) it might be thought a matter of pride to be so socially avant garde. But America didn't think so then, and increasing public concern provoked the House of Representatives to set up a committee to investigate alleged subversive or Communist-influenced activities among all U.S. foundations. By the end of 1952 Henry had had enough, and although family control had been surrendered, he carried with him enough of the trustees to arrange an expensive but effective departure for Hoffman. Aided by Donald K. David, dean of Harvard Business School—who had joined Ford Motor Company's board of directors in 1950—Henry then devised a $568 million benefaction which increased salaries in 630 private universities and colleges and provided large sums of money for nonprofit hospitals, medical schools, and college scholarships. Henry was delighted to achieve the approval of the foundation's trustees, almost as delighted as were the recipients. Benevolence on this scale removed a lot of money from the vaults and helped to crystallize the concern of some of the trustees and many of the foundation's administrators about its continuing dependence upon Ford Motor Company. More than 98 percent of its annual income was derived from Ford dividends. I know of at least one trustee who also felt its activities would become less controversial if it were Ford Foundation in name only.

The restlessness of the foundation in its desire for financial, as well as operational, independence thereupon brought about one of the decisive actions in the history of American capitalism. In 1955 Ford decided to end its long years as a private company, and the stock was reclassified to permit a public issue. The foundation agreed to sell 10.2 million units of stock at $63.00 a share to 722 underwriters across America and Canada. It was offered to the public at $64.50, and on January 17, 1956, when trading began, it closed at $69.50. The foundation pocketed $640,725,445.00, and the Ford Motor Company had three hundred thousand owners. A leading figure on the New York Stock Exchange called it "a landmark in the history of public ownership," and David Halberstam declared it "a historic shift in American capitalism," and both comments were true, for it can fairly be regarded as the beginning of popular capitalism. Millions of Americans who had previously locked up their savings in the banks began to buy stocks and shares. Financial journalism became a growth industry; analysts on Wall Street began to talk of a new era. Rowan Gaither, who confessed that the pain of decision making had made him ill, saw the issue through and then resigned the presidency to Henry T. Heald, who was considered a businesslike educator and who came to the foundation from the top position at New York University. Henry Ford II resigned the chairman-ship of the trustees, and Gaither took over this less taxing role for two years while a search was undertaken for a more permanent chairman.

The following years, however, did nothing to increase the popularity of the Ford Foundation except among the recipients of its bounty, and although Henry was a party to its decisions, he began more and more to feel outnumbered. The foundation was on the agenda of every Ford Dealer Council meeting in Dearborn. The protests never stopped com-ing, and Henry found himself in the less than diverting position of trying to charm customers into his company's products, continue the building of a worldwide enterprise, and, at the same time, defend an enterprise that also had his name over its doors and was apparently doing its best to enrage potential purchasers.

In 1958 John J. McCloy, chairman of the board of the Chase Man-hattan Bank, succeeded Gaither as chairman of the foundation, and with Heald securely in the president's chair, a somewhat calmer period ensued. It would be wrong to typify the life of the foundation as one of continuing discord, and there were many outstanding trustees—John Cowles and Mark Ethridge; Don David; Larry Gould; Vivian Hender-son; Jim Ellis; John Loudon—and their traditional Wednesday night dinner before the board meeting was always convivial, outspoken, and relaxed, and before women were admitted to the board, occasionally very frank indeed.

Benefactions were substantial and eclectic. The Institute for Strategic Studies was established with foundation money. The United Nations received $6.2 million to build a new library; $11 million went toward improving the teaching of engineering in universities; overseas develop-ment assistance was extended to the Caribbean and South America; a family-planning program was introduced into India; the Kennedy Cen-ter got $5 million; $30 million was spent on experiments in classroom television; $8 million went to ballet training and "performing resources." No charitable organization ever opened its arms so wide or permitted so many diverse causes to dip their hands in the cornucopia.

For Henry Ford II, alas, the bad old days returned in 1965, when Henry Heald resigned, John McCloy retired, and (in 1966) Julius A. Stratton, president of MIT, became chairman, with McGeorge Bundy as president. Henry had first met Bundy when they were both at Yale, although the acquaintance was no more than that. Bundy, a former dean at Harvard, had been ushered into the limelight when John F. Kennedy was elected president in November 1960. Bundy, a Bostonian, became one of the white knights of the new Camelot and served in the Kennedy administration as national security adviser. The assassination of John Kennedy in November 1963 required him to look for a new stage on which to parade his zeal.

Bundy was proposed as president of the foundation by Charles Wyzanski, a federal judge from Boston. Henry wanted Franklin Murphy, a distinguished medical doctor and university administrator, who, as a member of the board of directors of the Ford Motor Company, became his closest friend and ally at that institution. Bundy was nevertheless elected and was quick to fly his colors. He made it clear that he saw the foundation as an instrument of social change and an antidote to urban conflict; and in 1967, when race riots erupted in one hundred American cities—and the foundation moved to a glamorous new headquarters on New York's East Forty-third Street—he began to take up controversial positions on such house-burning public issues as equal rights for minorities. The foundation substantially increased its support of civil rights— thrusting itself more prominently into the political arena—with major grants to the National Association for the Advancement of Colored People, the National Urban League, and the Southern Christian Leadership Conference. It established a Legal Defense and Educational Fund for Mexican-Americans. It was accused of making grants even to street gangs, and critics said that its activism on social and racial issues was actually contributing to violence.

By 1967 Henry Ford II had become, through example and achievement rather than heredity, the acknowledged first citizen of Detroit. With his support, things tended to happen; without it, the hills were steeper. An enormous effort had been made to build social and cultural institutions in the city in the well-off years, and its medical, charitable, and educational institutions were as good as those anywhere in the country; but the pressures upon them were growing by leaps and bounds.

In June 1967 Henry was in Europe. His horizons were always broad and distant, and he had become a man of the world, but his attention was more immediately focused on his own backyard when he got back to Detroit.

The great riot of 1967 erupted on July 23 on Twelfth Street. Within a week an organization called the New Detroit Committee was formed by the mayor and the governor of Michigan, and Henry was immediately invited to join its deliberations. Levi Jackson, who had come to work for Ford after making history as the first black football player to play for Yale University, told him that what Detroit needed was jobs for people who had no skills or, at best, the most elementary ones. He had written his thoughts on paper and tucked the memorandum into Henry's pocket. "You have got to find jobs," he said to Henry, "for the blacks in the inner city." Henry had no jobs to offer at that time because the United Automobile Workers was engaged in a strike against the company, but when this came to an end, Ford announced sixty-five hundred job vacancies, adding that five thousand would be hired from the ghettos. Written job tests were dispensed with, and special buses were put into service to ferry the new labor force to the plants.

In two years New Detroit raised and spent $10 million on black social problems, the encouragement of black businesses, and even cultural activities. Max Fisher, who had made a fortune in the Marathon Oil Company, began to develop his close personal relationship with Henry Ford II, and they sat together in their offices and over dinner, wondering what more could be done. Both were impatient with the pace of New Detroit. Henry wanted, as ever, to paint the future on a bigger canvas. The White House was the place where national initiatives began—or, at least, received their blessing—and although the man in the White House was preoccupied with the problems of Vietnam, Henry went to see Lyndon Johnson with the suggestion that Ford's inner-city hiring program could become a model for the country. On March 1, 1968, the president took the hint and formed the National Alliance of Businessmen to operate the JOBS program—an acronym for Job Opportunities in the Business Sector. Its objective was to find employment for one hundred thousand long-term unemployed, and Henry was glad to be offered the chairmanship of this body. Leo Beebe, who had been one of Henry's instructors during his period of training in the United States Navy and had subsequently held a variety of senior jobs in the Ford Motor Company, was hauled out of his Dearborn office and dispatched to Washington as JOBS executive director. The hundred thousand target was quickly met, and on January 31, 1969, Lyndon Johnson sent Henry a letter of thanks. "Without your vision and commitment," he wrote, "I seriously doubt if the National Alliance of Businessmen would have succeeded as it has. And there are so many other programs and hopes that owe as much to your leadership. I will remember them all for long years to come."

Henry's frustration with the Ford Foundation at this time is more easily understood in the context of Detroit and what the riot had revealed of its needs. Henry had no doubt that a major commitment to black education in Detroit and vocational training would have been more significant and productive than "long papers on educational theory." He understood the foundation men when they argued that Detroit was no more than a symptom of a deeper national malaise, but it seemed to him that if America was to be saved, that was a federal responsibility. Detroit was his. Events, however, convinced the foundation of its mission to act out its destiny on a bigger stage than Detroit could provide.

For in 1968 the Tet, or New Year, offensive was launched in Vietnam, and guerrillas attacked one hundred cities from the Mekong Delta to Saigon, where the American Embassy came under siege. In April Martin Luther King, Jr., was shot, and riots swept more American cities. Students occupied American universities. In June Robert Kennedy was shot and killed, and Dr. Benjamin Spock, the patron saint of the American nursery, was found guilty of conspiring to counsel draft evasion. In August Soviet tanks invaded Prague in Czechoslovakia, and a turbulent election in November put Richard Nixon into the White House. On Christmas Eve three Apollo astronauts reached the moon and three days later returned to earth after ten orbits. If they were looking for a new world, they appeared to have gone to the wrong place.

Henry nevertheless continued to back civic ventures in Detroit. New Detroit and Detroit Renaissance Incorporated brought together the leaders of business and local government, and the many honors conferred upon him in his later years testified to the real and symbolic nature of his concern and practical assistance. When Coleman Young won election as Detroit's first black mayor in 1974, he found in Henry Ford II a convinced ally and a friend whose telephone was always answered when he called. It delighted Coleman Young to call Henry Hank the Deuce, and it amused Henry. They were never close friends; but the relationship was initially more important than that, for they were allies, and when I arrived in Dearborn in January 1980 to begin four working years there, Henry told me politely that he had volunteered two evenings of my private time each month to meet with Coleman in his residence and consider what more could be done for the city, its people, and its children. More than 85 percent of all pupils in Detroit's public schools were black.

By then Detroit had other things to worry about. Perhaps it is more accurate to say that it had the same things to worry about in a different fashion. The first U.S. soldier was killed in Vietnam just before Christmas 1961, and the war did not end until January 1973, by which time 47,321 Americans had died in battle. On March 21, 1918—one day—Britain, in an earlier war, lost 150,000 young men, but Vietnam did more harm to the United States than all its previous wars, for it destroyed America's self-confidence, opened the doors to a new drug culture, and handed over the government of the country to television. Tons of drugs came into America, showing the greatest malevolence toward black families. Dope dealers recruited underage runners, parents were separated, and children no longer knew the grandparents who had long provided the stabilizing force in black society.

A foundation that had dedicated itself to the strengthening of the economy, education, and human relations could have settled without controversy upon any number of practical initiatives to help a society in such turmoil; but it chose to remain controversial, and Henry was not the only critic of the monster his family had brought into being. Angry voices were raised in Congress, and the Ford Foundation was called "the most politically active foundation in the country." The press joined the chorus of disapproval, and *The New York Times* of February 12, 1969, reported with evident amazement that the foundation had made eight grants to prominent members of President Kennedy's staff to assist them in their transition back to private life, despite the fact that some of them went straight into well-paid jobs.

The trustees were themselves appalled by Bundy, and private meetings were held to discuss ways of getting rid of him. It says something for their good nature that they were surprisingly gentle in their response. It was argued he was not particularly bright and would have difficulty making his own transition into another job. "He'd have had to go on welfare," Henry said with forgivable exaggeration, "and so everybody got compassionate." Not Henry.

The wrath of Ford dealers in the United States continued to mount. An enraged dealer deputation went to New York to tell Bundy face-to-face that his policies were ruining their businesses by alienating thousands of Americans whose only practical form of revenge against foundation radicalism was an individual boycott of Ford products. The public was not sophisticated enough to know that the company and the foundation were not the same thing. The dealers hotfooted back to Dearborn and told the management of the company that Bundy not only had delivered a lecture to them on what was good for America but had told them how to run their own businesses. Henry Ford II was never more tempted to call it a day and walk out of the elegant ambience of the foundation. He stayed because he saw himself as a buffer to some, at least, of Bundy's wilder whims.

By 1970 it was obvious to the trustees that Henry was sufficiently isolated and so out of tune with the foundation that he could no longer see any virtue in anything it did. Any who doubted his rising anger must have been convinced when a request for support from the Henry Ford Hospital was rejected out of hand. Henry lobbied the trustees individually, and John Loudon privately, and at meetings argued the case for the hospital, pointing out that Detroit and the Ford family were where the money had come from in the first place and that by any standard of judgment, it was as deserving of support as any other medical establishment. The trustees eventually came together and agreed to the donation, although Bundy fought to the bitter end, resisting every blandishment. In the end the Henry Ford Hospital got the money but only at the expense of some severely wounded spirits.

The ties that might have bound the foundation to Detroit had long been severed, and by 1974 not even a strand remained. In that year it disposed of its remaining Ford stock and depended upon income from other diversified sources. Henry was surprised the Ford stock had lasted so long. Upon taking over, Bundy had concluded that there was not enough money—even in the richest foundation in the world—to meet his ambitions, and he had vigorously promoted and undertaken an aggressive investment policy. The collapse of the New York securities market in the first years of the seventies quickly showed how wrong he had been. When Bundy arrived at the foundation, its portfolio of investments was worth $3.7 billion. By 1970 nearly $1 billion had been knocked off its value, and it continued to fall to $1.7 billion in 1974. In eight years its resources had been halved. The management of its assets seemed to bear no relationship to its true resources. Between 1967 and 1974 it overspent its income by an average of more than $100 million a year, and it took a further five years to break even. In 1970 the foundation had a staff of fifteen hundred people; by the time Bundy left in 1979, it was down to seven hundred.

Waldemar A. Nielsen, a former Rhodes scholar who became America's most knowledgeable commentator on the vagaries of U.S. foundations—and was an adviser to John D. Rockefeller, Jr., J. Paul Getty, and Robert O. Anderson—said of this rake's progress (in his book

The Golden Donors): "No disaster of comparable magnitude has ever been recorded."

On December 11, 1976, I flew to New York from London to meet Henry Ford II and John Loudon at the foundation. John had already offered his resignation, and Henry said: "I don't think I can stand this much longer. This place is a madhouse."

Nor did he. Three months later he sat down in his home at Grosse Pointe on the shore of Lake St. Clair and began to compose his resignation. He poured it all on paper, edited it with care, and on December 11, 1976, had it delivered to Alexander Heard, chancellor of Vanderbilt University, who had become the foundation's chairman in 1971.

After the break I never heard Henry mention the foundation again except on two occasions when I brought him back to it—one of them in 1979 when Bundy left. He still had no doubt that it was "the worst mistake of my life." He said, "I didn't have the guts or experience to scream or yell and tell them; 'Over my dead body.' That's what I should have done but I didn't know enough and I wasn't tough enough and it was kind of hard to go to older people for advice and learning and say, 'Thanks for the lesson, but now I know better!' " Had he kept the foundation in Detroit under family control and at his own elbow, and had it grown up and existed in the same environment as the Ford Motor Company, it might have come to be the instrument he wanted it to be. It certainly could have proved that charity is best when it begins at home, and above everything else, Detroit and its needy people could have kept the lion's share of old Henry's golden cornucopia—and kept it in the place where the gold was mined in the first place. There would have been more than enough money to fund national causes and initiatives, but Detroit would have been first in line. I could not help reflecting that this would also have avoided the necessity for its crown prince to go cap in hand to the guardians of the treasury that he and his family had created. I wondered if the enormous funds that the foundation had distributed over the years would not have been too much for Detroit's institutions alone to handle. "They couldn't have done a worse job than the one that has been done," was Henry's answer, "no matter what they did."

I believe, however, that the significance of the Ford Foundation in Henry's life extends far beyond the problems it caused. It taught him— and he began to learn the lesson quite early in his business career—that he must never, under any circumstances, allow the family to lose control of the Ford Motor Company as it had lost control of the foundation. It shaped—I think to a very large extent—the manner in which he ran the company, his relationships with Lee Iacocca and others who worked for it, the planning of his retirement, the writing of his will, and even family attitudes. He was by nature imbued with a sense of mission and occasionally trampled over the sensibilities of his sister, brothers, wives, and children because he thought he had been permitted a larger revelation. The foundation added steel to his dedication and cast iron to his single-mindedness.

CHAPTER THREE

The Making of a Management

In an interview published in the *Chicago Tribune* in 1916, Henry Ford gave birth to his best known and most quoted declaration, although its meaning has been generally misunderstood over the following years. "History," he said, "is more or less bunk. It's tradition. We don't want tradition. We want to live in the present, and the only history that is worth a tinker's damn is the history we make today." More and more of our present business leaders would beg to differ.

Alfred Chandler, Straus professor of business history at the Harvard Business School, has devoted the past thirty years of his life to the development of an historical theory of big business. "The historian," Chandler has written, "by the very nature of his task, must be concerned with change. Why did it come when it did? What in the American past has given businessmen the opportunity or created the need for them to change what they were doing or the way they were doing it?" Chandler's analysis of response to change in large American corporations has directed the attention of boardrooms and business schools to issues deeper than the bottom line and broader than the last ten-day sales report. Great companies, particularly those making what are now known in the impersonal jargon of modern business as consumer products and certainly those that survive in the long run, are conditioned by change, and so are the people who run them. This may seem a fairly unremarkable observation today, but it is surprising how many people forget it.

It is evident that the forces that made the Ford Motor Company and the manner in which they were confronted determined both the deeds and the personality of Henry Ford II. The company itself would not be what it is today had it been less personally controlled and had he been less aware of his family heritage. Business is a science or business is an art; at Ford, within the ambience Henry created, it was both. In a speech delivered at Vanderbilt University in March 1969—its title was "The Individual and the Establishment"—he said:

Power is never monopolized by a few people at the top. Important changes almost always occur in little steps as a result of the complex interaction of many people at many levels all pulling in somewhat different directions. Nothing ever changes very much because someone with a big title issues an order. Orders always have to be carried out by stubborn and unpredictable people. Unless these people agree with the order, either nothing much happens or something happens that is quite different from the intent of the order. It's true that events are hard to control and reform is difficult to achieve. But the basic reason why reform comes slowly . . . is that nobody has enough power to set things straight in a hurry.

When he made these remarks—which might be considered something of a maxim for our times—he had a quarter of a century of experience behind him, and he had won himself time for reflection. In 1945, when he began the making of a management, and when he was essentially creating an entirely new Ford Motor Company, he had no alternative but to do things in a hurry.

Henry was the captain of his ship and, for most of his life, the admiral of his own fleet. He was only once seriously challenged from within the company, but like the enterprise he ran, he was as much at the mercy of the tides and turbulences as all the other mariners who sail the seas of big business. Knowing this, he gathered a remarkable crew, and the officers' mess was never without some extraordinary—sometimes flamboyant— talents. General Motors might serve as his wistful model of the corporate ideal, but to many others it often seemed more like a branch of the civil service, where succession was invariably unremarkable and conflict either unknown or hidden from public observation. Ford was never like this. At its worst it managed to give the impression that power was synonymous with struggle and even intrigue, and there was a sense in which this was true. Chandler once observed that "business activities are often still treated as shallow morality plays of great men and scoundrels, depending upon the narrator's inclination." Few onlookers see enough of the game or get close enough to the coach to give them a deeper perspective.

Somebody once said to me that only Henry Ford II worked for "Ford";

everybody else worked for a person, somebody who was his or her immediate boss. What was meant was that Henry was alone in being obsessed with the idea of family, heritage, and continuity, and it was this idea—perhaps ideal—above all others that drove the company forward. All his life was dominated by the need to find and develop a management that could manage change so that his Ford Motor Company could survive. In the beginning he never had the opportunity to fulfill his needs by promotion from within, for the talent was not available. Moreover, he had little reason for trusting its existing management. He had to build an entire new one, top to bottom, bringing together people who might well have no previous experience of each other. He came early to understand that management implied organization and system, but he did not rate experience higher than character, insisting that a team was only as good as its players and its players, together, every bit as important as the captain.

The football analogy is not inappropriate and can be carried further, for such was his own sense of mission that he could never quite see why aging players could not be persuaded to stay on the team in a secondary position—or even put in the reserves—if a new star was available for selection or transfer. Most of the men concerned, at least those in the larger offices, understandably took a different view, feeling that their demotion was not an improvement and seeing it, naturally enough, as a discouraging lack of confidence in their ability. There was a certain ingenuousness in Henry where these things were concerned, and he never successfully communicated his point of view because businessmen, on the whole, do not offer themselves as sacrifices to the larger good. They have their own egos to address.

In the beginning Henry Ford II was lucky to discover within the Ford Motor Company one tough, loyal, and resourceful ally. John Bugas had been the principal FBI agent in Detroit when he was hired by Harry Bennett as an assistant. It has been suggested that Bennett wanted access to his knowledge of the Detroit underworld and saw the new recruit as an important reinforcement for his own intelligence network. Bugas was a tall, lean, rangy man with the heart of a cowboy. He later owned an enormous ranch in Wyoming and shed his business cares riding the range. Bugas, however, was a good enough agent to perceive very quickly that he had been hired as a gunslinger by an evident badman, and he saw the arrival of the young Henry as not unlike a scene from Dodge City; a new marshal had ridden into town. There was a moment when John Bugas thought he might be faced with a real shoot-out with

Bennett; but the bad guys backed down, and Bugas and Henry, between them, secured Bennett's departure. In April 1945 Henry appointed Bugas vice-president for industrial relations, giving him far-ranging powers over all personnel and appointments. It was Henry's first key appointment.

Henry's second piece of good fortune that year—after Bennett's departure—was the engagement of a group of ten remarkably brilliant U.S. Army Air Forces officers who had provided General Henry ("Hap") Arnold, commander in chief of America's air legions, with the most scintillating planning group any military commander can ever have enjoyed. Most of them had been graduated as the brightest stars of America's top universities, and if genius is the infinite capacity for dealing with numbers, they were geniuses without a doubt. I think they also had a genius for friendship. Their story has been told before but too often in isolation. They may have provided the shiniest threads in the tapestry that Henry was weaving; they were by no means the whole of it.

When the United States entered the war, it was evident that planning and control would present as big a challenge as the battlefields themselves. The U.S. Army Air Corps (later the U.S. Army Air Forces), lacking any kind of statistical system, did not even know how many aircraft it had. The deficiency was quickly remedied when Donald David, dean of the Harvard Business School—its classes increasingly depleted by military enlistment—sent two of his professors to Washington to discover how the university might help the war effort. Arrangements were quickly made to run special courses for the air force, which itself established an office of Statistical Control. When Charles Bates ("Tex") Thornton was put in charge of this staff operation—becoming in the process one of the youngest colonels in the U.S. Army—he applied himself to the task with scientific care. The wise men from Harvard were dispatched to officers' training schools, where the brightest recruits were given written and oral tests; those who distinguished themselves most in the examination were then sent to the Statistical School at Harvard for a six-week course. From there they were posted to specific assignments in Thornton's group. It was not unlike a controller's office of a kind that is now commonplace in private business or industry. Its job was to accumulate and analyze all the information available about air force resources and operations and provide factual reports and special studies for the high command rather than for top management.

When the war ended in Europe, the young men working for Thornton in General Arnold's headquarters became preoccupied with targets in the Far East and preparations for a concentrated Pacific campaign; but two bombs on Japan wrote an end to all their planning, and they began to think earnestly about finding jobs in business or returning to the ivory towers they had vacated for the business of war.

They all might be remembered now as venerable academics or individual businessmen were it not for Thornton's determination to sell his most able officers as a group to a private corporation or even set up a company of their own. There were nearly fifty officers in the Statistical Control section, and Thornton picked nine names from the roster, obtaining agreement from each one to start canvassing likely employers. A brochure was prepared to demonstrate the diversity of their talents, and this was dispatched to Eastman Kodak, U.S. Steel, the Allegheny Corporation, and other big businesses. Allegheny said it would be happy to hire an even larger group, and that might have been their destiny were it not for a cover story about Henry Ford II in the *Life* magazine issue of October 1, 1945, leaving little doubt in the minds of its readers about the problems Henry was facing and therefore the opportunities the Ford Motor Company offered. Lieutenant Arjay Miller showed the magazine to Colonel Thornton, who submitted it to Lieutenant Colonel James O. Wright, who, at thirty-four years of age, was the oldest of the group and a member of a rich Detroit family. Enthusiasm for Ford when the others were consulted was far from universal; but all agreed to an approach, and Thornton sent a telegram to Henry Ford II suggesting a meeting.

The ten men were immediately invited to Dearborn, and eight of them, still in uniform, traveled there by train late in 1945 and were taken to dinner at Cliff Bell's restaurant by John Bugas. Wright's father had produced guest passes for the Detroit Athletic Club, and later that night they sat on its sofas and considered their prospects. Bugas liked them immediately; he was impressed by their directness and their talents, but he was nevertheless cautious in his recommendation to Henry Ford II. He composed a careful memorandum urging that "we should not slide into it without a little more consideration." He also observed that they were asking for too much money.

It has often been assumed that the Whiz Kids, as they quickly came to be known, were always a close-knit group of friends, but initially they were only brothers-in-arms. Lieutenant Miller, who had just achieved his captain's stars before demobilization and whose magazine reading had inspired the approach to Ford, was the youngest of eight children born to Rawley John and Gertrude Miller in Shelby, Nebraska, and had grown up among the farms and cattle of Nebraska's treeless plains. The person who filled out his birth certificate had not been provided with christian names, so the entry read "Rawley John Miller Jr.," but R.J. preferred his initials and turned them, early in life, into a distinctive christian name. It was a determined thing to do, but not perhaps out of character, for Arjay always knew who and what he wanted to be. He had graduated with the highest honors from the University of California, worked on a Ph.D., done some teaching, and then graduated first in his class from the Harvard Statistical School. He had married a fellow student in 1940. He was tall, self-contained, infinitely curious, and a gentle man.

J. Edward Lundy, who was born in Clarion, Iowa, had joined the economics faculty at Princeton when he was twenty-five as a specialist in international trade and accounting and had been voted the best teacher there by the students, many of whom remained friends for life and were still sending him Christmas cards and presents forty years later. His eyesight was less than perfect, but he was drafted into the army as a private and sent to Miami for basic training with a bewildering assortment of other recruits, including a number of men of Italian and Greek descent from New Jersey. Transferred to an officers' training school, he was quickly confronted by two of Thornton's visiting professors and scored 100 percent in their tests. From Harvard's Statistical School, he went to Washington with no specific assignment and looked around for what was not being done. His first significant task was to give a presentation to General Arnold, and he went from private to major in eighteen months. Before long he was arguing the air force point of view before congressional committees. Lundy and Miller were friends and have remained so. Lundy, a lifelong bachelor and an extraordinary philanthropist who never forgot a favor, became over time a virtual member of the Miller family. But in 1945 he was by no means overwhelmed at the prospect of working for Ford since his ties with Princeton remained strong and, in planning his own future, he had thought of nothing more than returning to its familiar environment. He took a day or two to make up his mind and then said he would join the group if Miller went along.

Robert McNamara had graduated from the University of California and from the Harvard Business School, where a professorship was awaiting him upon demobilization. Lundy had met McNamara at the Pentagon and had been impressed by a presentation he had given to General Marshall. McNamara could read numbers the way ordinary mortals read words, but he was only reluctantly recruited by Thornton. He was nevertheless persuaded because he knew that the gap between academic and business salaries was as large then as it is now and McNamara had a family to think of. His wife also had recently contracted polio, and he had to face substantial medical bills.

The other six members of the group—Francis Reith, Wilbur Andreson, James Wright, Charles Bosworth, Ben Mills, and George Moore—brought other and perhaps more varied experience with them, and it is no wonder that John Bugas was impressed.

When Henry Ford II met them the day after their arrival, he took little time to make up his mind, and they, individually and together, were "bowled over" by him. All his life Henry made an immediate impression on people of every rank, shape, and color, partly because of who he was but, more important, because of what he was. Ben Mills, who eventually became a vice-president at Ford, retained sharp memories of the meeting long after he retired. "Mr. Ford was a very self-assured young man," he said, "who intended to turn his company around and wasn't afraid to take chances. He was completely and utterly self-confident. He had a quality of perception that seemed a little inordinate to me because I didn't know where he got it. To this day he seems to have an ability to cut through the garbage and get right down to the nut cutting."

The question of salaries was easily resolved. Tex Thornton was asked to write down what he thought each should be paid and produced a list, strictly in order of rank, with the highest salary at $12,000 and the lowest at $8,000. Arjay Miller got $8,000. He had only just made captain.

The group was due to report for work on February 1, 1946, but arrived enthusiastically a day early and began with a four-month period of orientation during which it was designated in company records as "Mr. Ford's office—Special." "The only thing we knew was how to ask questions, and we asked them by the thousands," Mills recalled. "Word got around, and we were dubbed the Quiz Kids. It just got turned around later to Whiz Kids."

The arrival of the Whiz Kids is now part of Ford mythology, but they never liked the appellation and did nothing to encourage it, partly because of their own aversion to its comic strip allusions but also because of their own reticence: They made few speeches and gave even fewer interviews. As time went by, the individuality of their own achievements and the force of their characters reinforced their status as singular geniuses in their own right. In 1946, however, there was no reason to view these fresh young talents as anything other than supporting actors in the drama that was being written. At the time of their interview in Dearborn, Henry was stalking bigger game; he was looking for an accomplished leader with all the talents to lead Ford from the top.

Once again Uncle Ernie came up with a good idea. Ernest Kanzler's attitude to his nephew was both close and curiously distant. His wife and Henry's mother were sisters, and he had shared in the frustrations Edsel had been forced to endure. He had listened as a brother-in-law to Edsel's hopes and fears for the Ford Motor Company—when good and sympathetic listeners were hard to find—and his service on the War Production Board in Washington until June 1943 gave him the entrée that secured Henry's release from the navy. Within days of Edsel's death he accompanied Henry on several foraging expeditions to the Ford vault to excavate Edsel's will and otherwise unregarded papers setting out Edsel's own hopes for the company.

He was there as a listener, too, when Henry—still uncomfortable out of uniform—took the blame for things he could not remedy. "I haven't any power here; I'm just walking around," Henry told his uncle. When Henry did come into power, he continued to talk to Ernest Kanzler, but he did not ask him to join the company. In later life Kanzler thought it would not have been right for two people from the same family to share the top rungs of the same ladder, but he also came to believe that Henry regarded him as somebody from another generation. "He never consulted me from day to day on the whole thing," he recalled. "From the very first he had his own ideas. He had figured them out by himself. He never consulted his younger brothers either. He took the bull by the horns and set out to do it himself. He knew it was his job."

But Henry also knew that Uncle Ernie was a shrewd judge of business ability, and when Kanzler suggested that another Ernie, in his opinion, was the right man for the top of the pyramid Henry was building, his nephew was quick to act. Ernie Breech—nobody ever called him Ernest—was an accountant who had been twenty-three years with General Motors and was then president of Bendix Aviation. Kanzler was a member of the Bendix board, and had watched Breech in action. Henry, who had met Breech three times—twice at business functions and once when he had come to Dearborn as a supplier in an attempt to sell components to Ford—called Breech at his office on Friday, April 5, 1946, making an appointment to see him the following Monday. He felt he had a chance. Breech's long career with GM and his success at Bendix made him a candidate for the presidency of General Motors, but rumor in Detroit—which is usually accurate where such things are concerned—had it that Breech would be passed over and might therefore nurse some resentment.

Henry spent most of Monday morning in Breech's office, offering to make him executive vice-president and operational head of Ford, but Breech was hesitant. He liked Bendix. Ford was at best a risk, and those who looked down from the topmost towers of GM had no reason to admire its supposed competitor, which had already been relegated below Chrysler into third position among America's automotive hierarchy. Henry felt he was losing the argument and said finally: "Well, will you at least give me some advice? Look things over. Tell me what you think. You've nothing to lose." In later years Henry confessed: "I knew he was sympathetic and wanted to help. I could feel it. I thought if I could hang in for a bit, he might be persuaded." On April 12 Breech went to Ford's Dearborn test track and drove prototypes of the revamped Ford car that was being developed for production. He asked how many Ford could build in a year, but nobody could do more than guess. He asked to see the balance sheet, but all it told him was that losses were in the region of $10 million a month. Breech was not a risk taker, but he began to be captivated by the young man who was a little more than half his age. He went back to his office and called a handful of GM colleagues to see if they would accompany him should he decide to join Ford. Two engineers, Harold Youngren and Delmar ("Del") Harder (the man who coined the word *automation*); William Gossett, Bendix's top lawyer; and Lewis Crusoe all said yes. Crusoe had worked for GM's Fisher body-building division for thirty-two years. With his own team of mature whiz kids duly signed up for the adventure, Breech felt relaxed enough to call Henry and accept the job. He signed a contract on May 11, 1946. "If I was ever asked to name the best month of my life," Henry told me, "that would be it."

A week or two before Breech joined the Ford Motor Company, Tex Thornton made his own bid for the top job, taking Henry Ford II a memorandum (approval of which would have given him veto power) recommending the creation of a planning and control group effectively to run the company. Henry called Breech, who said: "Why don't you wait until I get there?" It was wise counsel. Thornton was still learning his new trade; Breech had already forgotten more about cars than Thornton would ever know, and when Breech joined Ford, he had the Whiz Kids report to Crusoe, who promptly fired Thornton and split up the rest of the group. McNamara, Miller, and Lundy remained in finance, and when Crusoe was given the task of heading up a new Ford Division—the first major move toward decentralization and the creation of profit centers—they gained another and equally important mentor. Henry was determined to find himself a full-time economist, certainly a prime necessity since the company—astonishing though it may seem— had never made a profit forecast in its life and had no way of anticipating either the sale of its products or the external factors that conditioned its markets. Once again Ernest Kanzler had a name up his sleeve and suggested Henry might look at Theodore Yntema, who had taught economics at the University of Chicago from 1923 and was now a consultant. Henry flew to Chicago, and Yntema agreed to surrender his wide-ranging freedom and become vice-president for finance.

The finance staff, to which Robert McNamara, Ed Lundy, and Arjay Miller were assigned in 1946 after their four-month familiarization, was no more than a fledgling; but progress was rapid, and by 1949 McNamara was controller of the company, Lundy was assistant controller, and Miller, assistant treasurer. No greater concentration of brainpower has ever been brought to bear on financial control and analysis, but the three of them contributed much more than that. Henry had insisted from the beginning that the acquisition of top people from the outside was obviously sensible when talent was not available within the company but was nevertheless a sign of weakness. If you could grow your own talent in your own backyard, you could grow loyalty. Finding and developing talent, however, had to become a universal preoccupation. Recruitment was not a function of a personnel department; it was everybody's business. The sign of a good manager, Ford was soon to insist, was how well he developed his successors (in the plural), and it was a lesson Henry did not need to hammer home to the Whiz Men— no longer kids—who commanded the high ground in corporate finance.

With their own air force experience and distinguished academic backgrounds, it was inevitable that they would maintain their links with the best business schools, and within months the news was getting around: if you were bright and ambitious, Ford was the place to be. The deans and professors at Stanford, Harvard, California, Carnegie, and UCLA almost became part of the recruiting process by urging their best students to think about Ford. The top three graduates from Carnegie regularly went to Ford year after year. By 1969 the company's remarkable hiring offensive had recruited twelve hundred executives with M.B.A. degrees and twenty-two hundred with undergraduate degrees in business administration. Half of the M.B.A.'s had engineering degrees as well. Most of them were in finance—either on the staff or in the operations— and it was commonplace in the company to talk of "members of the finance staff." Nobody thought the words strange because they were, in every important respect, members of a club. They had good jobs. The M.B.A., particularly if it was one of the "right" ones, got you a starting salary about a quarter above those who were not members of the order. More important, it got you visibility. Lundy took enormous professional and even paternal pride in showing off his young lions to top management and letting them out of their cages. If they worked on special studies or papers of some kind, they were permitted to make the presentations themselves. They were even coached in the art of financial lucidity.

When I sat among the gods on the twelfth floor of Ford's World Headquarters in Dearborn, I once sent for a manager who worked in the basement. He was oddly diffident throughout our discussion and would not touch the coffee I offered. When he left, I asked my secretary what was the matter with him. "Well, he naturally feels strange," she said. "He has worked here for fifteen years, and this is the first time he has been on this floor." It was never that way with Miller or Lundy. Nobody joined finance unless Lundy approved of his academic record, and if he found that satisfactory, the candidate was invited for an interview. Lundy conducted every one himself no matter the proposed ranking of the appointment. He watched the newcomers like a schoolteacher, and he talked to others among his working family to see how they got along with other people. There were jobs for talented introverts who feared the heat of the sun. Ed accepted that it took all sorts and that not everybody was at ease in company, in conversation, or in the sanctified arena represented by the horseshoe table in the boardroom. The introverts were not overlooked when suitable promotion was available, but his ideal men had presence and made it felt.

Many people on other staffs and operations were daunted by the "members" of the financial community who looked so much alike and thought alike and dressed similarly, but their inferiority complexes were their own fault. McNamara, Miller, and Lundy wanted the best young men they could find, the best that America contained, because their own personal and academic confidence was of such a dimension that they could not imagine the possibility of hiring somebody better than they were. And to give them credit, I think they would have enjoyed the intellectual challenge had they found somebody who just perhaps one day might be better. Neither Manufacturing nor Engineering placed the same emphasis on the caliber of its recruits, and this also was understandable, for it is in the nature of men who make and design things to believe that there are practical virtues that outweigh the academic. Nevertheless, it was not surprising that they were so often outdebated in their own specialty by finance men.

Finance was an extraordinary inner world. Rising stars were permitted to leave and not discouraged if the outside offer was better. They were also welcomed back if they came to believe that the outside grass was not as green as they had imagined. They sent each other birthday cards and were never heard to utter a word of criticism of other members of the clan.

One mature and experienced journalist who wrote a long book about Ford came to the conclusion that this financial aristocracy was what was wrong with Ford. What it needed, he wrote—and he was told—were more "car men." This conclusion seemed to satisfy him because Ford at the time was a company with serious problems, and its principal trouble was that it was not selling enough cars and trucks. A likelier explanation was that other areas of the company were not as good as finance; their deficiency, not finance power, was the root of the problem.

In the adolescent years of the American automobile industry up to World War II, there were two distinct and different approaches to the business—Fordism and Sloanism. Fordism was essentially the science of mass-producing cars with the widest appeal and application, sometimes cars that were quite technically advanced but also—as they have often been characterized—"simple, homely, and cheap." Sloanism—derived from the surname of the General Motors chairman Alfred Sloan—implied annual model changes (next year's models invariably appeared the previous autumn), "styling," proliferation of gadgets, and, to an extent, promotion of the car as fashion or a status symbol. Sloanism had evidently paid off. Old Henry Ford had resisted change for the sake of change with all his might. If it was a good idea, it was forever. If recessions came along or the market turned down, you could cut prices or spend more on advertising. The problem was not the cars themselves but the lack of customers with the will or money to buy them. But more and more customers came to believe Sloan or, at least, submit to his influence, and in the decade after the war General Motors maintained a position of such dominance that in some years it had more than half the U.S. market. It takes great courage in any business or industry to defy the market leader, particularly one with apparently inexhaustible reserves of money. It always seems safer to follow the pathfinder, especially when its principal asset appears to be infallibility.

When Charles E. Wilson, president of General Motors, appeared before the U.S. Senate in 1955 at hearings conducted to confirm his nomination as Dwight Eisenhower's secretary of defense, he was asked if he would make a decision in his cabinet post that was not in the interests of GM shareholders. He said in reply that he could not imagine that any such conflict could happen. "I cannot conceive of one because for years I thought what was good for the country was good for General Motors and vice versa. The difference did not exist." The press reported his remarks in abbreviated form, and he was chastised for corporate arrogance; but he was not attacked or misunderstood in Detroit, where his remarks seemed no more than a statement of the obvious. If GM prospered, so did America. And, as "Engine Charlie" had put it, "vice versa." It was not surprising that the Ford Motor Company should separately come to the conclusion that what was good for GM was also good for Ford.

When the war ended, there were nine motor manufacturers in the United States: the Big Three (GM, Chrysler, and Ford), plus Hudson, Crosley, Kaiser, Nash, Studebaker, and Packard. The smaller six had only 15 percent of the market among them. By 1954 only two remained, for in that year Hudson and Nash came together to form American Motors and Studebaker merged with Packard.

Under Sloan, General Motors served its mass public with Chevrolet; the middle class with Buick, Oldsmobile, and Pontiac; and the rich with Cadillac. It was called market coverage, and this approach was highly profitable, for one basic design could be adapted to serve many publics and much variation in taste through styling-influenced changes in sheet metal, different levels of appointment, and distinctive radiator grilles and badges of marque. The technique is alive and well today and is sometimes called badge engineering.

Ford followed suit and created three other product divisions— Lincoln, Mercury, and Continental—each of which marketed contenders for the more lucrative segments of an apparently insatiable market. Jack Reith, one of the Whiz Kids, was appointed vice-president and general manager of the Mercury Division, having returned from two years with Ford France, where he had won a reputation as a good manager. He was full of ideas but not all of them were successful, as events were quickly to demonstrate. On April 15, 1955, Jack Reith came up with a plan for a new division that was promptly opposed by some senior members of management. Robert McNamara, who had been appointed vice-president and general manager of Ford Division, and Henry's brother Bill, who held the same position as overlord of the Continental Division, both thought that there was no need for a fifth franchise with its own distinctive products, distribution system, and dealers, but the plan was blessed by Ernie Breech and Henry Ford II. One evident attraction was that this proposed initiative would give Ford five product divisions, just like General Motors, and although the revived Ford Motor Company was decidedly immature at this time, it was still chin-high in confidence. Profits for the year proved to be $437 million, almost double those of the previous year and by far the highest in the company's history, and that was encouraging. Public attitudes toward Ford were also good, and *Time* magazine was to select Henry Ford II as its "marketing man of the year."

The venture, however, testifies to nothing so much as the continuing inexperience of Ford management. In 1945 it had had no sophisticated management at all; ten years later the development of management into "line," or operations, and "staff," or analysis, was still proceeding slowly, and the new Special Products Division seems not to have been submitted to any kind of staff analysis. Yet the engineers were put to work and committed to the new franchise. Enormous investments went into manufacturing plants and even more effort into finding a name for the division and its future cars. The right name was probably Euphoria. Candles were burned late into the night by intelligent men seeking one. It was a search for a touchstone as much as a derivation.

One of my most thumbed bedside books the years over has been a slim, limited (550 copies) edition published by New York's Pierpont Morgan Library and produced, with wood engravings, by America's most respected fine printer, which contains an exchange of letters between Ford's marketing research department and the renowned poet Marianne Moore. The letters, written (on Ford's behalf) by a young man called David Wallace, are enough to make one regret that the dream did not come true, for they show that romance and wit and a sense of style were alive and well, if a little ponderous, and one likes to believe that these virtues lingered long after the fiasco.

The first letter to Miss Moore, dated October 19, 1955, and sent to her in Brooklyn, New York, declared:

This is a morning we find ourselves with a problem which, strangely enough, is more in the field of words and the fragile meaning of words than in car-making. And we just wonder whether you might be intrigued with it sufficiently to lend us a hand.

Our dilemma is a name for a rather important new series of cars.

We should like the name to be more than a label. Specifically, we should like it to have a compelling quality in itself and by itself. To convey, through association or other conjuration, some visceral feeling of elegance, fleetness, advanced features, and design. . . .

Over the past few weeks, this office has confected a list of three-hundred-odd candidates which, it pains me to relate, are characterized by an embarrassing pedestrianism. We are miles short of our ambition. And so we are seeking the help of one who knows more about this sort of magic than we.

Miss Moore replied charmingly two days later. She was, she said, "complimented to be recruited in this high matter. I have seen and admired 'Thunderbird' as a Ford designation. It would be hard to match, but let me, the coming week, talk with my brother who would bring ardor and imagination to bear on the quest."

The correspondence continued over three months, during which Miss Moore evidently gave the matter much thought. Mr. Wallace sent her a philodendron, which she paused to water as she paced around her room, seeking inspiration. And she was resourceful. Ever since I came across the letters, I have longed to have such a poet on my own staff. She suggested: The Resilient Bullet, Arcenciel (from *arc-en-ciel*, or rainbow), Aeroterre, and *andante con moto*—"description of a good motor?" —tongue, one hopes, in cheek. In one brief note she asked: "May I submit UTOPIAN TURTLETOP? Do not trouble to answer unless you like it." The response from Ford was gentlemanly; it sent her a Christmas card and a floral tribute containing two dozen American Beauty roses. The card said: "To our favorite Turtletopper."

The final letter in the correspondence came on Armistice Day 1956, when peace had descended on their labors. Miss Moore was acknowledging a communication of November 8 that said: "We have chosen a name of the more than six-thousand-odd candidates that we gathered. It has a certain ring to it. An air of gaiety and zest. At least, that's what we keep saying. Our name, dear Miss Moore, is—Edsel. I know you will share your sympathies with us."

There are some Edsel alumni—nowadays, a diminishing band—who will tell you that this literate exchange was no more than a publicity exercise to acquaint American car buyers with the coming of something importantly new, but it all seems to have been taken seriously by those who were engaged in the exercise. *The New Yorker* published the letters with a straight face. One person, who seems never to have attended to the name hunt, was never concerned by the process of christening. He had much earlier come to the conclusion that naming the new division and its cars after his father would delicately flatter Henry Ford II but neither Henry nor his mother thought much of the choice. He nevertheless let Breech have his way and Edsel it was.

The first of the cars was launched in 1957 with much noise but produced a deafening silence. The U.S. economy was in poor shape, a little poorer, it turned out, than the car itself. There was insufficient resolution or, more likely, singleness of mind among the management of the company so that the Edsel Division, its cars, and its dealers lived for another two years before disappearing as completely as a tribe of nomads. The intended gaiety and the zest were no more than whispers in the night. Only the dust of failure and the wounds inflicted by the loss of some $250 million involved in the venture remained. The Continental Division was brought to an untimely end soon after. Lincoln and Mercury were combined into one.

The Edsel became a legend in its time. Books were written about it, and they remain on the shelves of business schools as a case history of how not to do things. The true circumstances have always been misunderstood, and the lessons mistaught, but they were not lost on Henry Ford II, for they showed him that men of talent could still come to the wrong conclusions. Ernie Breech, who had been chairman of the board of directors since January 1955, had—despite all his experience—let it happen. Henry was shocked, but he was not frightened by the Edsel experience, for the tide was rising. World automobile production in 1955 exceeded ten million for the first time. In 1956 the federal government decided to build (and finance 90 percent of) a new interstate highway system that would create forty-four thousand miles of expressways. At the same time McNamara was quick to take advantage of the investments in plant and equipment that the Edsel had brought about, and in 1959 he used them to create the Falcon, the first Ford compact, which five years later would father the all-conquering Mustang. Without the Edsel, there would have been no Falcon.

Robert McNamara is not remembered as a "car man." His reputation, even within Ford, lingers as the quintessential bean counter, never happier than among numbers, a connoisseur of brainpower rather than horsepower. Chroniclers of automania still categorize the industry's executives and fall easily in love with the glittering few who drive home with straight arms and driving gloves and turbos under their heavy right feet. Yet the red ink in which much of the motor industry's history has been written has been freely expended in cautionary tales of companies whose designers were allowed to ignore the financial disciplines of their business. McNamara was not a "car man," but he could read signs and symbols as well as he could read figures.

After becoming assistant general manager of the Ford Division in August 1953, he rose steadily in the product side of the business until 1960, by which time—as group vice-president for cars and trucks—he was responsible for everything Ford put on the American roads. He was also more than smart enough to see that there were intruders on those highways, which many regarded as the preserve of big, chrome-laden, gas-guzzling dinosaurs. By 1957 Volkswagen had 350 dealerships in the United States selling the Beetle—the car that Hitler had inspired—for as little as $1,500, and by 1958 European imports accounted for more than 8 percent of the entire United States market.

The Falcon was only one exercise in thinking small and countering this challenge. McNamara knew that if he were forced to rely upon off-the-shelf components—even if he could give them a new exterior appearance—he would not really address the growing number of Americans for whom the Beetle was becoming a cult. Something new and different was required. The Beetle came from Volkswagen in Germany; Ford had a substantial resource in Germany, so why not go there to provide the missing link? With the active encouragement of Henry Ford II, he initiated a cooperative program with his own engineers and the German company for a small front-wheel-drive car to be manufactured in both Germany and the United States and be introduced in 1962 and thereby tackle the imports with a homegrown invader of his own. The program was given a code name, as all the projects were, and called the Cardinal after an American bird he could sometimes see in his own back garden in Ann Arbor. The plan never came to fruition because Lee Iacocca, who was a chrome-and-power man, killed it. It nevertheless proved itself of inestimable value to Ford. Sir Patrick Hennessy on a trip to Dearborn saw the prototypes and was impressed and returned to England determined not to be outdone. He immediately initiated a program of his own and gave it the code name Archbishop—one up, he thought, on a Cardinal, not knowing that the American code name was not derived from a Roman Catholic dignitary—and his product was right, and so was its timing.

The Archbishop had all the dedication of Ford of Britain behind it, and the bureaucracy, such as it was, took only a couple of weeks to choose a name for the car. It came to market in 1962 as the Consul Cortina—"the small car with a big difference"—and it laid the foundation for the future unchallenged strength of Ford in the British market. Among the activities I had under my control at the time was motor sport, and I took some of the early models to Cortina d'Ampezzo in Italy, where, with the lively connivance of the mayor, the entire city council, and a handful of racing drivers, we drove them down the bobsled run just to have a good time. The irreplaceable Jim Clark, who three years later won the Indianapolis 500 for Ford, said he didn't believe it could be done, but it was the sort of thing we made happen in those days.

On both sides of the Atlantic the planets seemed to be in their right conjunction. More than 1.2 million children had been born in the United States in 1945, the first bumper crop from the postwar baby boom, and there were more every year. The peak was reached in 1957, when 1,837,000 new Americans came confidently into the world and every one was a future car owner. In 1960 the United States had almost as many students as Britain had people, and you did not need a degree in demographics to know the automobile industry could anticipate years of abundant markets. In 1945 there were twenty-five million cars on American roads; by 1960 there were sixty million. Any car that had panache or power—and preferably both—was certain of success. The Edsel debacle was certainly an enormous setback for the Ford Motor Company; the financial losses were substantial, and so was the loss of face. But whereas in 1957—the year the Edsel was introduced—Ford profits were $283 million and the following year, as a consequence, they tumbled to $96 million, by 1959 they were sharply up to $451 million, and another $428 million was reported for 1960. It was a time to be confident and do bold things. Automania had become epidemic.

Henry Ford II therefore entered the Swinging Sixties, as we all did, with a growing sense of self-fulfillment and certainty, and he had every reason for his contentment. With growing resources in the bank and an international management that had learned some hard lessons and was beginning to prove its competence, he was coming to the conclusion that he had served his apprenticeship. For fifteen years he had understudied Ernie Breech, and he was increasingly restless. Ernie had turned the company around and taught it all he could about management and was himself sensible enough to see that Henry was fidgeting and frustrated.

In March 1960 Ernest Kanzler had given a dinner at Maxim's in Paris, and it was there that Henry met a provocatively vivacious divorcée, Cristina Austin, who had been married to a Canadian naval officer. He invited her to the United States, and by the time he returned home, he had come to conclusions about both the lady and Ernie Breech. Henry was convinced that Ernie would see that the time had come for Henry to take over the chairmanship, and there would be no problem in selecting a candidate for his own president's chair. McNamara, the architect of discipline and financial responsibility, had all the virtues and qualifications anybody could desire. He would become the first president of the Ford Motor Company whose surname was not Ford. Henry's dream of a professional, assured, sophisticated management—operating under his control—seemed to him on the point of achievement. And there was Cristina. Perhaps she was an omen. After seventeen years of single-minded devotion to his demanding inheritance, the time might even be approaching when he could take things easier, relax a little, buy pictures, spend more time overseas. The scene was set, and the words were written; but the play never got much farther than the opening curtain.

It has been said that Breech was cruelly ousted and that his departure was at best a sign of ingratitude, but there is no evidence to suggest this is either fair or true. Ernie had enjoyed his fifteen-year task of civilizing a monster, and he was proud of this new Ford Motor Company of which he had become godfather. He was sixty-three years of age, and the two men both had too much respect for each other to regard the moment as anything but inevitable. Breech said to Henry, "I guess you've graduated," and they had an amicable parting. The friendship endured, and Henry kept in touch with Ernie's widow long after he was dead. In the early eighties he dedicated the Ernest and Thelma Breech Pavilion, an extension to the Henry Ford Hospital, and seized upon the occasion to remark publicly upon his debt to a remarkable mentor. He never wanted Ernie to leave Ford, and in July 1960 created the Finance Committee and made him chairman, believing that this—with his continuing seat on the board of directors—would secure his continuing loyalty. But the arrangement lasted no more than six months, for Ernie was a proud man, too, and had become accustomed to being at the top of every ladder he climbed. There was a number one job available at Trans World Airways that could rekindle his old love for the aviation business, and he took it.

Bob McNamara accepted his promotion without demur, and at his suggestion, a young man of thirty-six named Lido Anthony Iacocca was appointed vice-president and general manager of the Ford Division. The year 1960 promised to be a vintage one. It was good to be alive and in love. Japan built a mere 165,000 cars, a drop in a distant ocean.

Bob McNamara's elevation to the presidency was unanimously approved by the board of directors and formally announced on November 9, 1960. Nothing could have seemed more timely. The previous day the American people had gone into the polling booths across the nation, and by the slenderest of margins—only 120,000 votes—John Fitzgerald Kennedy had beaten Richard Nixon and won the presidency of the United States. Within hours of his triumph, the young (he was forty-three) and impatient victor had begun to draw an organization chart for his administration, and one of the first calls he made was to McNamara, whose achievements at Ford had been approvingly observed by the world at large and the powers that be in Washington. McNamara was invited to become secretary of the treasury but declined the post. Kennedy did not give up and came back later to suggest another cabinet position and more or less gave McNamara a free choice. McNamara said he would accept the Defense Department, and his resignation from the Ford Motor Company was made public on January 3, 1961. He had been president of the company for fifty-one days, and Henry was back to the drawing board.

Many different motives have been put forward to explain McNamara's defection, and some people have used words like *betrayal*. D. H. Lawrence once wrote, "The only principle I can see in this life is that one *must* forfeit the lesser for the greater," and I suspect that no other explanation is needed. McNamara's close friends say that he was always fascinated by the corridors of power and even more so by the aura of the Kennedys, a not uncommon feeling at the time.

Henry was, as ever, pragmatic. The loss of a leader around whom so much was to be built, and for whom Henry had such high hopes, was a devastating blow, the kind of reverse that can force many a good general to flee the battlefield. But all his life Henry had an extraordinary respect for the integrity of other people's motives and their right to deal with their own lives in their chosen fashion. To step from the world of business to government was not unusual; Charlie Wilson had left GM when

Eisenhower called. McNamara said that the prospect of being warlord of Camelot was irresistible and rode off like Sir Lancelot to a destiny more challenging than he knew, and he would always bear the scars of Vietnam. Henry wished him luck.

Unfortunately the process of change or development in the management of any substantial company is rarely as easy as it seems when the choice is made and the newspapers have had their say. There are never enough qualified candidates for any position of responsibility. Change at the top can be even more complex, for it leads inevitably to a kind of musical chairs, and all the other consequential repositionings have to be taken into account. The departure of Breech and the appointment of McNamara took Henry Ford II a long time to plan and resolve, and when McNamara departed, there was no evident replacement. After much consideration and conversations with Ernie, who was still on the board and still proud enough of his own handiwork to be concerned, Henry turned in April 1961 to a man who was in some respects not unlike his grandfather.

John Dykstra had left General Motors and was living in virtual retirement in California, where he bumped into Ernie Breech. An introduction to Henry Ford II followed, and he joined Ford in October 1947 as assistant to the vice-president and director of manufacturing. Dykstra knew how to make things. He was first taught tool- and diemaking at Cass Technical High School in Detroit and started in manufacturing at the age of sixteen. He had taken part-time courses in foremanship and factory management at La Salle University and had gone on to become a plant manager at Hudson and Oldsmobile. During the Korean War Ford set up a plant in Chicago to make Pratt & Whitney aircraft engines, and John Dykstra showed a craftsman's ability to innovate and get things done. He also built one thousand tanks.

Dykstra might well have flourished in the old Ford Motor Company, but he was out of place and out of tune with the new company and the times. He lasted seventeen months and was replaced, almost inevitably, by Arjay Miller. The second Whiz Kid had made it to the top.

CHAPTER FOUR

Total Performance

Lido Anthony Iacocca, who had shortened his christian name to Lee, always intended to be a Ford vice-president by his thirty-fifth birthday, but he missed it by one year and twenty-five days. He had benefited from Henry Ford II's early determination to reinforce the company's meager engineering resources with bright young men from the universities and was hired on August 27, 1946, as a college graduate trainee. He had an engineering degree, and rheumatic fever had exempted him from being drafted for the Second World War. After seven months with Ford, at his own request, he had been sent to Chester, Pennsylvania—not far from his birthplace in Allentown—as a sales trainee, and his entire career had consisted of selling American cars and trucks to Americans in America. He married Mary McCleary, a receptionist at the Ford assembly plant in Chester, in 1956 and that same year was called back to Dearborn as the Ford Division's truck—and later car—marketing manager. It was a comparatively modest job, but he was streetwise and inventive; he made rapid progress, and McNamara recommended his appointment as vice-president and general manager of the Ford Division on November 9, 1960.

Henry Ford II asked to meet the young man he had not previously encountered, and the gods were surely on Iacocca's side. Within two months McNamara had left to join the government in Washington. John Dykstra, who had been appointed president in his place, obviously lacked the flair and apparently the power to stand in the way of Iacocca's next ambitions. Nature abhors a vacuum as much as a hostess dislikes an empty chair, and while Iacocca felt himself some distance still from the presidency of the Ford Motor Company, he was prepared to seize every opportunity to advance the boundaries of his own estate and his place in it.

The range of Ford cars for which Lee Iacocca was given responsibility was functional but lacking in excitement and presence. The two divisions—Ford and Lincoln-Mercury—had 26.6 percent of the U.S. market, which was respectable but a long way below General Motors. McNamara, in his time, had at least one major success to his credit. He had fathered the Falcon in 1959 at a time when other manufacturers were also responding to the trend. Chevrolet introduced the Corvair, and Chrysler the Plymouth Valiant, but McNamara won the battle. The Falcon sold 417,174 in various versions in its first year on the market, creating an industry record in its initial twelve months. Lee Iacocca might have been expected to capitalize on the evident strength of the market for smaller cars and the move away from the age of fins and chrome and dinosaurs; but he was young, and he suspected there was a bigger market for more glamorous and what were beginning to be called image cars. One in every two cars sold in America in the sixties would find a buyer between the ages of eighteen and thirty-four, and Iacocca wanted to respond to their youthfulness. Ford, he argued, had a "rather stodgy, non-youth image," which was true enough. Its only previous venture into the business of making "dream cars" had been the prestigiously successful Thunderbird; but McNamara doubted its enduring value, for Ford was in the mass market, and dreams, it seemed to him, were something only the minority could afford.

The Ford Thunderbird, a pretty little two-seater, had been introduced on September 9, 1954, following a trip to the Paris Motor Show by Lewis Crusoe, who was then vice-president in charge of the Ford Division, and his chief stylist, George Walker. The fact that we call them designers now rather than stylists is itself an indication of the American view of the automobile at this period. Crusoe and Walker were less interested in the new European products on display in the Paris exhibition than in GM's new Chevrolet Corvette. Here, they concluded, in all its splendor was another home run for General Motors, although Walker wryly remarked that it could have been a Ford; he had something even more exciting in his styling studios. Crusoe promptly phoned Dearborn and told the stylists to get going, and Henry Ford II quickly approved the program when Crusoe brought it to him; Henry was himself only thirty-seven and not too old to be young at heart.

Annual sales of the Thunderbird were originally projected at 10,000, but it sold 16,155 in its first year. A much improved model was introduced the following year—with thirteen two-color paint combinations and seven solid colors—at a factory price of only $3,408, and the car was not just a styling success. The top overhead-valve V8 engine delivered 225 horsepower, and its designers had concentrated on safety so that they could proudly offer a new concave steering wheel, safety door latches, seat belts, a padded dashboard, and visors. None of these things was freely available or much in demand, and Ford was way ahead of its time. The "Bird" at introduction sold substantially more than all the other American sports cars together and reached a sales figure of 21,380 in 1957. Unfortunately these were still modest figures for a mass producer, and Crusoe turned later Thunderbirds into cars with four seats, which doubled sales but destroyed their unique character.

In all his years at Ford, McNamara made no secret of his aversion to performance and power and architectural excesses in design, and he was not alone. In 1957 the Automobile Manufacturers Association (AMA) had adopted a safety resolution that ostensibly outlawed all participation by its members in motor-racing events. Iacocca in 1960, however, searching for a fast sales track, set his team of young bloods to write a new prospectus for the Iacocca Ford Division, and with a little help from the advertising and public relations men, they came up with the two words *Total Performance*. They were open to all and any ideas, and when Carroll Shelby, one of America's best racing drivers, walked into Ford the following year and suggested marrying a big lightweight American engine to a European sports car chassis, he could scarcely have found a more willing group of listeners. A tall, rangy Texan with a mop of hair and a beguiling grin—persuasive, as are all top racing drivers who have to talk their way onto teams and into contracts—Shelby wanted to put American engines into the British AC roadster. General Motors had turned him down when he approached it, but he had no difficulty selling the idea to Ford.

On January 30, 1962—one month after I had joined Ford in Britain—the first Shelby Cobra prototype was tested on the perimeter track of a wartime airfield at Silverstone in England that had become a motor-racing circuit. AC Cars was a modest operation in the center of an English village called Thames Ditton; it was three or four miles away from the house where I was living at the time, and I wandered around there, cloaked in my new authority, running into Shelby and glad to have done so. The Atlantic was wider in those days, communication was intermittent and casual, and although I had no knowledge of the plans for "Total Performance" in America, I was determined to put Ford of Britain on the map with its own motor-racing program. I had one ally in Colin Chapman, a persuasive genius who had founded Lotus Cars; but I needed more, and I knew that Shelby had forgotten more about cars than I had ever learned.

Shelby had no idea where to find AC Cars when he first came over to sell it the idea, and he called on an English motoring journalist, John Blunsden, to drive him there; but when I encountered him in Thames Ditton, he certainly knew where he was going. "I was going to drive for that bastard Ferrari," Shelby said—in 1959 he had won the Twenty-Four-Hour Race at Le Mans and just about everything that could be won in the United States—"but they tried to screw me. I told them I'd blow their asses off someday. And with this, I sure as hell will."

Coincidence continued to play its cards the way Lee Iacocca wanted, and Shelby's preoccupation with beating, or at least administering some kind of lesson to, Enzo Ferrari was taken a step farther the following year, when the German consul in Milan told Robert Layton, one of the senior executives in Ford Germany, that Ferrari was for sale. The "old man," he reported, was growing tired of the legendary "stable" he had built so carefully since his early, glorious days as Alfa Romeo's racing manager, and he thought that Ford would be the right company to take over. When Layton contacted Dearborn, its first reaction was "We're not interested," but Don Frey, one of Iacocca's top and most imaginative executives, went to Modena, and although he discovered Ferrari's price—$18 million—was about twice as large as expected, he insisted the deal still looked good. Ferrari said that he would sell the entire enterprise to Ford, which would take over the car production business in its entirety, but that he would retain absolute control of Scuderia Ferrari, the racing operation.

Ferrari, who remained an imperious and mercurial figure until his death in 1988 at the age of ninety, found the business of making road cars a burden. He broke away from Alfa Romeo in 1938 and built his first cars in 1940; but he could not contractually use his own name until after the war, and the first Ferraris were assembled in December 1946. But the cars were not right, and the customers were a nuisance. We once had a halting conversation in Italian and English, and it was clear to me that Ferrari had always found road cars a diversion from the real business of racing and he had always found it difficult to raise enough money to do both.

Iacocca's knowledge of Ferrari went no farther than the papers Don

Frey provided, but he was aware of the mystique enshrined in the name and, ever inventive, could also see the possibility of using Ferrari's body-building experience—which was, in fact, nonexistent since he relied on *carozzerie*, such as Ghia and Pininfarina—by putting "Body by Ferrari" on his American luxury cars. He therefore had an additional reason for pressing ahead, and another Ford team was sent to Modena to audit the Ferrari facility and see just what Ford would be getting for its money. Ferrari asked what the Ford men were doing about the place since he had not yet made any deal. He was told they were making an inventory. "What's that?" he asked, and again they told him. Like a latter-day Henry Ford, he said: "What would anybody want to know that for?" It was an amusing story, but it was not this that brought the exciting prospect to an end. Ferrari very simply wanted to be rid of the cares and woes of a car manufacturer—even if he was making only one or two a week—but he was determined to continue as the reclusive, erratic, and absolute monarch of what amounted to a small racing principality, and he could see that these men from Ford were not likely to be sleeping partners. A joint Ford-Ferrari announcement of the takeover had been drafted when he canceled all discussion and went onward in his own idiosyncratic way until financial problems forced him into the arms of Fiat in 1969. Giovanni Agnelli, a good and close friend of Henry Ford II, agreed to take over Automobili Ferrari, or road car production, leaving the *commendatore* alone to crack the whip in his own stable. Agnelli also agreed to keep Ferrari's illegitimate son, Piero Lardi, on the payroll, an agreement that Ford had refused to contemplate, and I was convinced at the time that this more than anything else may have aborted the deal.

But failure to buy Ferrari was merely a hiccup and by no means a setback toward the imminent achievement of "Total Performance." In June 1962 Henry Ford II joined the battle. He was more than willing to back Iacocca—as he would always support new men in new jobs—and he was becoming increasingly irritated by the back-door racing activities of Chevrolet and Pontiac, which were openly flouting the safety resolution of the AMA. Henry was president of the association, but this was not likely to stop him from expressing his own beliefs any more than his position with the Ford Foundation inhibited his criticism of that body. He issued a public statement that left nobody in doubt:

The so-called safety resolution adopted by the Automobile Manufacturers Association in 1957 has come in for considerable discussion in the last couple of years. I have a statement to make on this subject.

I want to make it plain that I am speaking in this instance only for Ford

Motor Company. I am not speaking for the AMA, of which I am currently president, or for the other manufacturers.

Following the adoption of the AMA resolution, we at Ford inaugurated a policy of adhering to the spirit and letter of the recommendations contained in the resolution. We tried very hard to live with this policy. We discontinued activities that we felt might be considered contrary to the principles embodied in the resolution and also modified our advertising and promotion programs appropriately.

For a while, other companies did the same. As time passed, however, some car divisions, including our own, interpreted the resolution more and more freely, with the result that increasing emphasis was placed on speed, horse-power, and racing. As a result, Ford Motor Company feels that the resolution has come to have neither purpose nor effect. Accordingly, we have notified the board of directors of the Automobile Manufacturers Association that we feel we can better establish our own standards of conduct with respect to the manner in which the performance of our vehicles is to be promoted and advertised.

This action in no way represents a change in our attitude towards highway safety. Indeed, I think everyone is aware that Ford has been a pioneer in the promotion of automobile safety. We will continue with unabated vigor our efforts to design, engineer, and build safety into our products and promote their safe use. We will also support every legitimate program—both inside and outside the automobile industry—which we believe contributes materially to safer vehicles and safer driving.

This declaration of independence with its unmistakable tone of voice brought immediate jubilation to Iacocca's young men and also provided another insight into Henry's character. He could not abide cheating in any form or under any conditions, and was particularly unforgiving when he detected subterfuge within his own company. It was a pronouncement that carried great weight inside and outside the headquarters of the Ford Motor Company, and it unlocked the door to days of triumph at Indianapolis, Monte Carlo, Le Mans, and other places with names engraved on silver trophies. It also led the way to the Mustang.

Success produces many heroes, and there is no shortage of fathers willing to claim parenthood; only failures become orphans. Yet the Mustang began with a kind of orphan. The door had scarcely closed on McNamara when Iacocca was off to Germany, his first visit to Europe, to kill the Cardinal—the small front-wheel-drive car that had been planned as a joint German-U.S. venture, an antidote to Beetlemania. If Germany wanted to go it alone, Iacocca insisted, that was O.K., but there would be no Cardinal in America. He did not like the way it looked, and it was too small. The German management, under the redoubtable John Andrews, was left to complete the engineering on its own, but did fortunately persevere and introduced the car as the Taunus 12/15M. Between 1962 and 1970, nearly 1,350,000 of them were sold, challenging the Volkswagen Beetle in its home market, and while Iacocca did not regret its demise in America, there were some who did.

One of them was an English chassis engineer working in the United States named Roy Lunn, formerly with Aston Martin, who was sure the mechanical components of the Cardinal could provide the basis for a small American sports car. He had allies among the engineers at Ford's transmission plant in Livonia, Michigan, who had designed the trans-axle. A front-drive car puts its power on the road by driving the wheels through a forward transaxle, and the layout provides considerable flexibility for the designer, for it is also possible to locate the engine behind the driver's seat and propel the rear wheels through a back-mounted axle.

Early in 1962 Iacocca asked his vice-president in charge of styling, Gene Bordinat, to undertake some studies that might lead toward a new Thunderbird type of two-seat sports car, and Bordinat assigned four stylists to the task. Two of them—John Najjar and Jim Sipple—working with Lunn, came up with a midships prototype using the Cologne V4 engine and the Cardinal transaxle. At this time also—since the gods were still smiling on Iacocca—Herb Misch, the vice-president in charge of engineering, was looking for a show car with which to impress the enthusiastic press at the 1963 new-car introductions. Bordinat suggested the car Najjar and Sipple were developing, and Lunn was asked to build a drivable car, and he did by October 2, a considerable achievement by anybody's standards. The car had not been given a name during its development, but Najjar—without any of the heavyweight research that name hunting usually involves—suggested Mustang. The Mustang he had in mind was the famous fighter aircraft of World War II, not, as is generally believed, any kind of four-legged animal. The derivation was, however, no more than an academic concern; such a special car had to have a special badge, and the design staff crafted a small, high-stepping stallion that suited its own conception of a Mustang and the car it had produced.

This Mustang—which now, when it is remembered, is referred to as Mustang I and resides in the Henry Ford Museum—was unveiled at the United States Grand Prix on October 7, 1962, and driven around the Watkins Glen circuit by Dan Gurney, reaching a speed of 120 mph on the straight. It was an immediate sensation and received enormous press coverage. That December it was impossible to pick up an automobile magazine on any American bookstand that did not have the Mustang on the cover. *Car and Driver* called it "the first true sports car to come out of Detroit." The fascination quickly crossed the Atlantic, and London's *Sunday Times*—whose motoring editor, Maxwell Boyd, was not given to thoughtless extravagance—declared it was "quite the most exciting vehicle of its class to have appeared for years."

Ford dealers began to cope with some unusual human traffic jams in their showrooms and had to explain that the Mustang was "not available yet." The truth was that it never would be, for Mustang I was never intended for production. It was considered too expensive to be manufactured in volume and likely to address itself—as had the earlier Thunderbird—only to a limited and relatively affluent market. Mustang I was taken to Watkins Glen to whet the appetite of young America for the real Mustang, which was still under development. I was always very sorry that Mustang I never went into production; almost as sorry as Roy Lunn. It was a thoughtful and technically advanced design for its time. The famous European sports cars—from Alfa Romeo, Sunbeam, MG, and Triumph—all had engines at the front, and not only was Mustang I faster than all of them, including the rear-engined Porsche 1600N, but it had the most delightful road manners and handled beautifully. It was nearly five hundred pounds lighter than the Porsche and, in appearance, years ahead of all its competitors. The seats were fixed; the pedals and steering wheel, adjustable to the driver. It could even be made to fit the towering Dan Gurney like a handmade glove.

Its enthusiastic devotees in the company, however, had no counter for the more practical considerations that argued against production. Ford had no place in its larder for exotic dishes; it was in the bread-and-butter business. Mustang I had an importance as a symbol, a statement of intent, and a design exercise, and it was a more significant ingredient of "Total Performance" than even most of its aficionados knew or came to understand. But it was not what Ford or Lee Iacocca was looking for.

Iacocca knew what he really wanted from the first day when he was given the Ford Division, although to begin with, he could not have described it in specific terms. What he wanted was excitement, and soon after his appointment he put together a small group of executives who met regularly in the evenings—and sometimes on weekends—at the Fairlane Motel. Under the leadership of Don Frey, his principal product planner, the Fairlane group was charged with the task of using the mechanical components available in the Falcon and creating a sports car for the masses. Mustang I might, at best, have become a cult car for that limited market that had earlier taken the Thunderbird to its heart, but the Fairlane group was looking for something with an annual volume of perhaps a hundred thousand, a car that would have four seats and not require unorthodox design or excessive investment.

Any doubts about their being on the right track evaporated in 1961 when General Motors' Chevrolet Division introduced a sporty version of its rear-engine but plain-Jane compact Corvair, called it Monza, and gave it bright bucket seats and a lot more horsepower than the Corvair had. Its introduction intensified the already feverish tempo in Ford's design studios, and Gene Bordinat began to unveil more and more fashionable creations with more and more evocative names: Allegro; Stiletto; Avanti; Avventura. The company's three design studios— Advanced, Ford, and Lincoln-Mercury—were set to compete against each other, and they did in conditions of enormous secrecy, keeping everything under lock and key when they went home at night (if they went home at night). Henry Ford II went to look at all the models presented for consideration but was lukewarm toward most of them. Eventually, however, Joe Oros, the head of the Ford studio, produced a design that had been completed by his principal assistant, Dave Ash. It was essentially a reconceived Falcon with a long hood and a short trunk, and Iacocca, along with everybody else who saw it, knew that the contest was over. Oros and Ash had won. The car, Oros said, with conviction and insistence, was called Cougar. Some years later, when we were discussing the considerable mythology that had grown up around the Mustang, Henry Ford II told me: "Anybody could see it would be a hit. I had argued for a couple more inches legroom in the back, and that was done, but apart from that, I was happy. So was everybody."

But even with Henry's support, it was not that easy. I have spent many hours in Ford design studios all over the world, falling in love with full-size modeling-clay designer dream cars, wishing they could be in production right now. Everything in the cloistered temples of automobile studios always looks more exciting than the real things in showrooms. But the road between is a hard one, and it was no primrose path for Iacocca.

Arjay Miller, who had succeeded John Dykstra as president, was enough of a car man to recognize a winner when he saw one—even a dark horse—but the company was already committed to enormous expenditures for other cars in the range in both divisions, including some fundamental mechanical improvements, and he was concerned with overspending and with what car men call cannibalism. There is little point in any motor manufacturer's introducing a completely new member of the family if it does no more than eat its brethren. Sales serve no purpose if they merely substitute for existing cars that might otherwise do better in the marketplace. Miller, moreover, for all his enthusiasm, was not going to commit himself to an Edsel no matter how much he was persuaded by its design and likely appeal. He never forgot that the Edsel had gone into production without proper staff analysis and he therefore submitted the Cougar to the kind of detailed review now taken for granted. The Falcon was relatively hot in the market, and a new car called the Fairlane had been developed from it—to appeal to customers wanting something bigger—and here was a sporty version. A further consideration was that Arjay was not yet sure of Iacocca; when Iacocca killed the Cardinal program, Arjay had been forced to write off $35 million. Iacocca, who wanted to be free to work on his own projects, was not amused and thought Miller's attitude typical of a "true bean counter," but Arjay wanted to be sure, and the information he was initially provided contained no substantive reassurance.

The Market Research staff, during the review process, estimated an annual sales figure of ninety thousand, but when Iacocca presented the program on September 10, 1962, he was below that figure. He was asking for $40 million to bring the Cougar to market, and he had figures to show that it would be satisfactorily profitable with an annual volume of seventy-five thousand. It was a sensible approach. Frugality is the key to success in product planning, and Iacocca was not without caution at this stage of his career.

The longest period in a car man's life is the one between program approval and "job one," the start of production, and Iacocca was impatient. He was firing on all cylinders, and the excitement he generated produced extraordinary dedication throughout his division, giving even the most dour executives a sense of mission. Freed from the prohibitions of the AMA ban on racing, William Innes, chief engineer of the Engine and Foundry Division, and his boss, Charles Patterson, vice-president of the Power Train Group, spent millions on new and more powerful V8 engines. Charlie Patterson, who had graduated from Scotland's Edinburgh University and joined Ford in 1927 as a diemaker, believed passionately that Ford's casting and engine technology were drag strips ahead of its rivals, and both men were determined that "Powered by Ford" would mean high-powered. In this era of "Total Performance," no car was left untuned.

Iacocca's young men—their desks piled high with new ideas—then decided to enter the 1963 Falcon in motor rallies, and since the Monte Carlo Rally was the most famous of all, that was where they would start. Others took the slow, learning route to the top; not Ford. With more powerful engines, bucket seats, and a richer interior, the Falcon was dressed up for a party and brought to Monte Carlo in 1962 with a planeload of American motoring writers. Aristotle Onassis took Iacocca to the Monte Carlo Casino, and everybody had a good time. It was clear that the faster Falcons, intended for the rally itself, would not stop at the speeds they were now able to attain unless their drum brakes were replaced, but that was no problem; the Ford Division promptly built ten thousand with four-wheel disk brakes. It, incidentally, made Ford America's disk brake pioneer, and it was not long before disk brakes were available on other Ford and Lincoln-Mercury cars.

Ford of Britain's own motor racing program, which I thought was coming along nicely under my own contented control, played a worthy part in the Falcon's success in the rally. We found the drivers, mechanics, and even an elegant young woman to run the control center in Monaco, and it was no surprise to us when the Falcons won the top class in the event in January 1963. Ford's Swedish driver, Bo Ljungfeldt, was the first driver since the Monte had started in 1911 to record the fastest time on every open-road special stage of the rally. A few months later bigger Fords with aerodynamic "fastback" bodies were unveiled for American stock car racing—with a new 450 hp engine—and began to dominate the high-speed ovals where young America gathered to watch the good ol' boys at play. There was also good news for Colin Chapman. I took the Ford Division's racing boss, Leo Beebe, to Colin's Lotus factory at Cheshunt to work out the contract that was to give birth to the Lotus-Fords and internationalize Indianapolis.

This frenzy of activity—together with the steadily increasing collection of trophies that graced Ford's Dearborn headquarters—did wonders, too, for the Cougar program. The reputation of the company was on the increase, and the approved production of seventy-five thousand a year was increased to two hundred thousand with the conversion of a second factory at San Jose in California; a third plant was soon added, bringing investment to $65 million. Full-size clay models of the car—still without a name—and mock-up interiors were shown across the country to prospective customers at hush-hush research clinics, although the secret could not be kept and people in the know began to call at dealers and place orders. Even more reassuring was the reaction to price. Those who attended the clinics were asked to guess what the car would cost, and the estimates fell encouragingly between $3,500 and $3,800. Some went as high as $8,000 and did not seem deterred by the prospect.

In the middle of 1963, when the J. Walter Thompson advertising agency got its hands on the first complete prototype and began to shoot film, the car was still nameless. Three different horse emblems had been designed, and they had been admired on the clinic cars; but Thompson's first promotional film was called Torino, and there were some who thought this a good name; it might appeal to Iacocca, whose parents were Italian-born, but he thought it too European. Cougar had gone away, despite Oros's protestations. The one name that kept coming to the top of the list when market researchers canvassed potential buyers was Mustang, and Mustang it had to be. The emblem was redesigned so that it came to look like the badge on Mustang I: a stallion galloping across a background of three stripes—red, white, and blue. There may have been a whiff of nostalgia about it, for it was not too far removed in concept from Ferrari's famous prancing horse. I suspect the eventual design won the day, as did the name, because both looked and sounded so right on Roy Lunn's Mustang and had become familiar with the passage of time.

It is easy to scoff at the elaborate and often passionate mating dance that confers names on cars. Henry Ford II always thought it important, and no car—built anywhere in the Ford world—was ever given a name without his personal approval. He did not like them all, and he would occasionally complain that we had too many damned names and would confuse the public; but he never criticized the ritual. Manufacturers seek to give their cars personality, and owners often take the process a great deal farther. Henry had no fixation about the procedure. When a name was up for discussion and the arguments were mounting, he would say: "If I came to you and said I had a hell of a name for a new car— Oldsmobile—what would you say?" Yet I have seen new car programs costing $1 billion or more go through more easily than the choice of a name.

The Mustang went on sale on Friday, April 17, 1964. At the World's Fair opening in New York the previous day, Walter Hoving, chairman of Tiffany's, gave Henry Ford II the Tiffany gold medal for "excellence in American design." He might well have invented an award for value for money. The factory price of the Mustang was set at $2,368, and it sold 418,812 in its first year. Henry's mailbag was full. The only complaints came from people who could not buy one. He was delighted with the congratulations he received and generous with those he bestowed on the people who made Mustang happen, but Lee Iacocca deservedly received a greater share of the glory. The April 17 edition of *Time* magazine put his picture on the cover and provided inside an appreciation of his endeavors that would have been enough for most mortals. Three days later he was the cover story in *Newsweek*, thereby achieving a unique double in U.S. media history.

The mesmerism that the Mustang induced took Ford's share of the American market from 23.9 percent when the car was launched to 27.1 percent in six months. Two months before its second birthday, it passed the one million sales mark, and profits from its happy customers exceeded $1 billion. In the late fifties Ford had tried to sell function and safety while its competitors crept out their back doors to go racing and promote performance. America did not want to buy safety, but a handful of years later Ford had beaten them at their own game.

In January 1965 Henry Ford II appointed Lee Iacocca head of the car and truck group for both Ford and Lincoln-Mercury, and in May Iacocca was elected to the board of directors. He had ridden his own prancing horse to the starting line for the last big trophy: the top operational job at the Ford Motor Company. He was still only forty years of age, the time, it is said, at which life really begins.

The Mustang was the sales success but by no means the high-water mark of the "Total Performance" years. Thirteen days after it was launched, Ford announced a sports program designed to carry its name across the last unexplored frontier.

The Monte Carlo Rally and the Indianapolis 500 were only two of the legendary mountaintops in the gazetteer of motor sport. The Twenty-

Four-Hour Race at Le Mans was a test of endurance that had come to be accepted as a special kind of challenge, and those who conquered its long, straight, and sweeping curves—in sun and rain and through the long, long hours of the night—were a breed apart. It was also different from Indianapolis and even the Grand Prix in one other important regard. People tended to remember the names of the drivers who won at Indy and in Formula One; Le Mans was a test for machines. Bentley and Aston Martin, Ferrari and Porsche had gone to Le Mans and left tired but taller and with powerfully enhanced reputations. Had the Ferrari deal gone ahead, victory at Le Mans might have gone to a Ferrari-Ford and would have been a great deal more certain, for Enzo Ferrari—in his fastness at Modena—knew all there was to be known about long-distance racing. Many of the people in Ford did not even know where it was, just that they had to be there.

Thirteen days after the launch of the Mustang, therefore, Ford announced its assault. On April 3, 1964, Ford unveiled one of the most beautiful racing machines anybody had ever conceived. Its looks were clearly derived from Mustang I, but it was more masculine and meaningful, and its destiny was racing pure and simple so there was no need to hunt through the dictionaries for a suitable name. It was called the Ford GT40. Its body had been designed in Gene Bordinat's advanced styling studio in Dearborn in October 1963, but the prototypes had been built in total secrecy in England.

It is a curious fact that of all the countries in the automobile-racing world, England should be the most resourceful and innovative, and while others have learned and the imbalance is now less obvious, this was certainly true in the sixties. Most of the Indianapolis chassis to this day are made there, and small racing enterprises seem to flourish around every bend in the road. So it was to England inevitably that Ford's Leo Beebe went in the summer of 1963 to hire Aston Martin's wise and dogged Le Mans expert, John Wyer, to mastermind the GT40 program and to enter into an agreement with Eric Broadley for engineering development. Broadley's Lolas were very similar in mechanical configuration to the GT40 and promised to be the perfect test beds for engine, transmission, and suspension. A small brick factory was rented on a new industrial estate at Slough, and Ford Advanced Vehicles Ltd. was founded with John Wyer as managing director. When I was invited to become one of the other three directors of this enterprise, I promptly canceled my summer holiday so that I could be in at the beginning. Bruce McLaren, a young New Zealander—one of motor racing's greatest development drivers—and Roy Salvadori agreed to lend their talents to the effort, and arrangements were made for testing at the Brands Hatch, Snetterton, and Goodwood racetracks in Britain and Monza in Italy.

Development would have been a great deal more efficient, and John Wyer's patience would not have been the principal component under test, had racing been the only objective. But the GT40 was also a marketing program, and when the first production GT40 was finished on April 1, 1964, it was immediately flown across the Atlantic to appear as the Ford centerpiece at the New York Auto Show. And it arrived back only in time to complete four sessions at the Le Mans test weekend in April. It had looked stable enough on the stand in New York, but at 150 mph on the Mulsanne straight generated enough lift to become airborne, scattering bits of fiber glass and veering off the road when it landed. The driver, Jo Schlesser, was unhurt, but the car was written off.

The first race was the One Thousand Kilometers at Nürburgring in Germany—the twisting fourteen-mile circuit in the Eifel mountains— and Phil Hill, America's only world champion driver, who was sharing the car with Bruce McLaren, was second fastest in practice but retired after eleven laps. That June at Le Mans, where three cars were entered, Phil Hill set up a lap record before retiring. Two cars were put out by gearbox failure, and the third caught fire early in the race. Two weeks later three cars were entered for a twelve-hour race at Rheims, France, that began at midnight. None was running by dawn. At the end of 1964 Leo Beebe and his men in Dearborn surveyed the wreckage of their high hopes, several cars, and certain reputations and decided to hand over the racing program to Carroll Shelby. Ford Advanced Vehicles would continue building GT40s for sale, providing development assistance and support for private teams. The change seemed more than justified when the GT40 won its first race at Daytona in Florida, but Le Mans was again a humbling experience.

The issue in 1964, which was debated when we returned to the team hotel for the official wake, was essentially reliability. Races can be won only if the cars finish, but the discussion was directed entirely toward horsepower. The 289 engine of the GT40 had a capacity of 4.2 liters, and Ford had a 427, or 7-liter, engine in the cupboard and was using it to good effect in the United States, where its stock cars were winning everything. American racing men are born with the belief that there is "no substitute for cubic inches."

I argued ineffectively against the big block engine because the car itself was already far too heavy, but I discovered how small a minority of one, or perhaps two, can be. John Wyer kept his own counsel, but he also knew that reliability was the issue. Shelby went back to America, and Ford established a workshop in Dearborn under the control of Roy Lunn, producing a couple of Mark II GT40s with the big 427 engine and a new Ford gearbox. The cars were run around the company's desert test track in Arizona. When they proved themselves capable of 200 mph, Shelby tucked his stopwatch back in his jeans and shipped the two cars to the 1965 Le Mans with a gaggle of other entries. The Mark IIs qualified for the race first and fourth, but neither lasted more than a quarter distance, and all the others failed to finish. At this postrace inquest I again argued that power alone would not win Le Mans. The Mark IIs had undoubtedly been impressive. I stood in the trees that fringed the Mulsanne straight and watched them go by at 195 mph. It was the kind of experience that argued against conservatism, yet I was still not convinced. Big engines never have to work as hard as smaller ones, but the car still has to be reliable enough to put the power on the road and keep going. Shelby had been ambling around Le Mans under a large Stetson, and he shoved it on my head. "You'll come around," he said, "because we're gonna make the mothers right." I said racing, not testing, was what got race cars right.

Shelby went back to America and built three new Mark IIs and a further two for the Holman and Moody team, which was based in Charlotte, North Carolina. John Holman, who raced everything, including boats, had been very successful with Ford production cars in NASCAR events, where big money was at stake, and he had a reputation for knowing what he was doing. The five cars were entered by the two teams for the Daytona Continental in 1966, and I was delighted to hear it, for the organizers had come to a decision that seemed to me of crucial importance. The race had been extended to twenty-four hours so that it would serve as an important test of durability before another Le Mans. On paper the Mark IIs were bound to win, for there was little opposition; the works Ferrari team had been withdrawn, but that was not the point. The only thing anybody wanted to know was whether or not the Mark IIs would finish, and there was much relief when they did: first, second, third, and fifth. Only one retired. Le Mans, they said, here we come.

The annual Le Mans test weekend of 1966 was set for April 1 and 2, and it was wet and nasty. Ferrari had kept his cars away. Both Shelby and Holman told their drivers to take it easy, for there was nothing to prove; nobody could learn anything in these conditions. Everybody was resigned to going home when Walt Hansgen lost control of his car on the approach road to the Dunlop bridge, and I stood by its side for twenty minutes while they got him out. Nobody else could speak any French, so I volunteered to take Walt to the hospital in an ambulance that had difficulty with crowds of spectators, and I stood in the operating room for the longest hours of my life and watched his life ebbing away; he died five days later in the U.S. Army hospital in Orléans. The GT40 was a strong car and built with driver safety in mind, but it was not strong enough; perhaps nothing could have been. The older of the two surgeons who worked so hard to save Walt asked me: "Did you know him well?" I said no, we had just met, although he had driven in five previous Le Mans races. "Those who come to Le Mans know what they risk," he said, and I supposed it was true, although drivers never do believe in their own vulnerability. When I got back to the hotel, I had a drink with John Holman. Everybody else was in some other place, and I was glad to be alone.

Two months later, when Shelby and John Holman came back to Le Mans for the race itself, they were better organized in every way and looked like winners. The cars were beautifully prepared. Ford had always known they were an advertisement for the company and expected an immaculate turnout. John Holman shipped over the biggest truck I had ever seen on a European road with a completely equipped workshop built in the trailer. Henry Ford II came over for the race and he and his second wife, Cristina, were staying nearby with Giovanni Agnelli.

Cristina, the Italian-born divorced wife of a Canadian navy officer, had been married to Henry for sixteen months then. Since she first met and talked to him at Maxim's in March 1960—at a dinner arranged to honor Princess Grace of Monaco—she had been the other woman in his life until February 1964, when Anne, his first wife, sued for divorce. Cristina and Henry had married before a judge in the Shoreham Hotel in New York City on February 19, 1965, and I had met them both when they landed in London early the following morning. At that time she was easy to please, invariably punctual, forever asking questions, learning, she said with a laugh, to be Mrs. Henry Ford II. Her tawny hair, green eyes, and high cheekbones made her striking in any company. By 1970 the marriage was virtually over—at least in Henry's mind—for she had not succeeded in her learning and had, I thought, a view of Henry that accorded more with an imagined personality that so often cropped up in the newspapers than with the man himself. I was occasionally sad for her because Henry was married to the Ford Motor Company, and marriage to him was always a form of polygamy.

The Italian magazines loved writing about Cristina as an Italian Cinderella. Probably the most accurate of them said merely that she was the grandchild of a "poor stonebreaker," the daughter of a "housewife and shoemaker," born in Grancona on November 27, 1929. A persistent reporter from Bologna wrote: "Actually it seems she was a babysitter, then a model in Milan, various languages, well chosen friendships, the marriage with an officer, on familiar terms with Giovanni Agnelli, a lot of vivacity, and an intelligent femininity wisely divided between Italian tenderness ('a woman can do a lot for a man when it's dark') and the matter-of-factness of the pioneers of the West ('equality, equal rights and privileges, I believe in the future of womanhood')." She had been christened Maria Cristina Vettore.

What is beyond doubt is that she had great fortitude and an instinct for self-preservation. She had starved in the later months of the Second World War. "You have no idea," she once told me, "how hungry we were." She was lamppost slim, and I observed that she still was not eating very much. "But that," she said, "is for different reasons." She got on well with Charlotte, who was petite and shy, because she made an effort to charm Henry's children as she had their father.

Cristina had never attended a motor race and was fascinated by everything at Le Mans, and before she went home, she was able to share the winner's podium. Bruce McLaren and Chris Amon won the race with Ken Miles and Denny Hulme second. The Mark IIs had come home in the first two places—twenty meters apart—and Ferrari had been vanquished. The triumph lingered for a long time.

To show that the victory was no mere accident of dollars and determination, the GT40s came back again in 1967 and repeated the victory with Dan Gurney and A. J. Foyt in the winning car. But the second victory failed to impress the chairman of the Ford Motor Company. Henry never had any doubt about the true value of motor racing to an automobile company, and he knew that his grandfather had built a racing car before he had built the company. He continued to love fast cars. Every time he landed in London he would ask, "Well, what have you got now?" and I would have delivered to his house the latest and hottest car from our European stable.

But his ardor for racing had begun to cool. On one trip he had found himself sitting in a first-class seat in a BOAC Boeing 747 next to a gregarious fellow who had made a lot of fuss on boarding the plane with a large flat brown paper parcel, which had been carefully stowed at the back of the cabin. On planes Henry preferred to read the latest whodunit and sleep, but he had a curiosity about people and things that demanded satisfaction, and could not resist asking his companion: "Is that your parcel at the back?"

The fellow traveler said: "Yes, Mr. Ford. Actually, I suppose it's yours." He went on to explain that he was ferrying a windshield for a GT40 to Europe since one had broken in practice. Henry asked him where he had come from, and he said California; he was working with Carroll Shelby.

Later at the airport, as we waited for his baggage, Henry said to me: "Have you ever flown a racing car windshield first class across the Atlantic?" I confessed that I hadn't. "Have you ever heard of anybody who has?" he went on, and I said no. "Neither have I," he said, "and what's more, it's not going to happen again."

It was a cold morning, and these were icy words. In 1965, as part of Ford of Britain's equally successful performance activities, I had entered into an agreement with Colin Chapman of Lotus and a young genius called Keith Duckworth for the production of two racing engines, including a new V8 for the Formula One Grand Prix. I had extracted the then enormous sum of $323,000 from the Policy Committee in Dearborn—where I had been given the blessing of no less an oracle than Ed Lundy—and the car and engine were due to make their appearance in 1967, more or less at the same time as Le Mans. After one day's acquaintance with the car—he was then a "tax exile" living in Paris to avoid the high U.K. rates—Jim Clark later went out to win the Dutch Grand Prix, the first race in which it was entered, and although this was still in the future, I had my own ambitions and did not want them disrupted.

"I am not talking about you," Henry said. "You can do what you want, and this is Europe, and things are different over here. Over there I suspect all this stuff is getting out of hand." It was a judgment based on little evidence; I was sure he had no idea how much was being spent on "Total Performance;" but his twenty-two years in command of the company had tuned his instincts, and when he felt the first stirrings of doubt on any subject, he had one inevitable response. "I poked my finger in" was the way he usually put it.

Henry's unease was shared by others in the upper echelons of management. "Total Performance" had been a marketing recipe, a calculated response to bring excitement to a "stodgy" company or at least one with that kind of superficial reputation. America was young, and young America wanted excitement, so it made apparent sense to swing with the sixties. The business and government leaders outside the United States, however, who entertained Henry in their executive dining rooms and, now and then, sat round his table were seeing different omens on their horizons. Every year he was away from Detroit for long periods and increasingly preoccupied with more fundamental issues than domestic American sales statistics. Ford had nearly 26 percent of the U.S. car market in 1965, and was gaining one point of penetration a year, but these statistics gave him less reassurance than might have been expected.

Despite the improvement in American roads brought about by the Interstate Highway Act of 1956, road deaths were on the increase. More and more inexperienced drivers were being let loose with no requirement to prove their driving abilities. Anybody sixteen years of age could jump into a car, and the more powerful cars available were an evident temptation to speed. In 1964 the federal government imposed safety standards for all motor vehicles purchased for government service. Congressional committees were not impressed by the performance of automobile company executives who were called before them to testify on safety matters and were scandalized by General Motors' campaign to discredit Ralph Nader, whose book *Unsafe at Any Speed*, published in 1965, had questioned the safety of American cars, specifically GM's Corvair. Private detectives working for General Motors interviewed scores of Nader's friends in an apparent attempt to cast doubt on him, and a book that might otherwise have passed as pamphleteering became a public issue. GM's president, James Roche, went before Senator Abraham Ribicoff's subcommittee on March 22, 1966, and was forced to apologize to Nader in person and on national television. Nader was later awarded $425,000 in an out-of-court settlement after he sued GM for invasion of privacy, and by then he was a martyr-hero. Lyndon Johnson gave his presidential backing to the National Traffic and Motor Vehicle Safety Act of 1966, which established a National Highway Traffic Safety Administration, with the power to set safety standards for new cars beginning with those produced after October 1967. Its first standards set out requirements for impact-absorbing steering wheels, seat belts, standard bumper heights, and the padding of interior extrusions.

California had declared its own special concerns about the automobile in the fifties; its unique topography together with the emission of pollutants from car exhausts had created a difficult smog problem. It was not true that you could see forever on the West Coast, not even on a clear day. California insisted hydrocarbon emissions should be reduced beginning with the 1963 models, and exhaust control devices, which would further limit the emission of oxide of nitrogen, carbon monoxide, and lead, became mandatory for autumn 1965. All U.S. manufacturers fought the imposition of these costly regulations and could fairly insist theirs were not the only products contributing to smog. They were nevertheless the most obvious, and nobody felt remorse about imposing new burdens on "Detroit." The manufacturers argued even more vigorously about the proposed extension of Californian standards to the rest of the country. Why should the citizens of Denver, Colorado—with their heads in the clouds and their lungs full of pure mountain air—have to pay through their own untainted teeth because of a geographical fault in California? But Nader had more environmental allies than he knew, and the Motor Vehicle Air Pollution and Control Act of 1965 brought Californian standards to the entire country.

Detroit argued that Washington did not understand the problems. Reducing engine emissions was a bit more complicated than putting a filter tip on a cigarette, and a great deal more expensive. Catalysts to soak up and consume pollutants required costly ceramics and platinum. Some engines could never attain the required standards considering the primitive state of the technology. Detroit had a point. Government officials often imposed standards without reference to, or consideration for, the considerable technical demands they were making. Nor did they provide enough time for the changes to be made. The only solution to some emission standards was new engines, and nobody in modern times has ever designed and put a new engine on the road in fewer than three years. Unfortunately, the public voices which might have been sympathetic—particularly those of members of Congress whose constituencies housed substantial automobile manufacturing—were not helped by the words from Detroit, and they, too, suspected that the arguments were no more than alibis. The truth was that they were not prepared to spend enormous amounts of capital and go back to the drawing board.

It was not only the car that was coming under siege in the United States. Race riots were spreading across the country, threatening stability and social order. The threat from imported cars was growing, and the Volkswagen Beetle was not far behind the Mustang in American sales volume.

Then uniquely—so far as Ford was concerned—Henry Ford II was only too aware of the perhaps larger challenges in the rest of the world. On June 6, 1967, Egypt closed the Suez Canal, and the Six-Day War with Israel broke out. Everybody would lose the war, for the oil tankers would now have to go around the Cape of Good Hope. It has to be said that Henry had no quick or immediate remedies for the growing social and political pressures upon the Ford Motor Company in the United States, although the conversations we had at the time persuaded me he had a better feeling than anybody else for the climactic change that was coming over America. "Total Performance" was a heady recipe for instant success but not nearly a sufficiently all-embracing strategy for the future he was beginning to see with greater clarity. He was also impatient with the progress the company was making in Europe, and there he knew precisely what to do. A few days after the triumph at Le Mans, I met him at the Plaza d'Athénée in Paris—always his favorite hotel—and he had separately summoned John Andrews, the general manager of Ford Germany, and Stanley Gillen, his opposite number in Britain.

For nearly twenty years—since his seminal postwar voyage of discovery—Henry had worried about Ford in Europe; not merely the progress of the business itself and its fast-developing markets but, more specifically, with the way it managed and exploited its growing resources. From 1962 onwards his impatience with the way things were became increasingly evident. He attended long meetings in France, Britain, and Germany, and great mountains of paper were consumed in the most detailed studies—conducted on both sides of the Atlantic—in an attempt to bring order, deliberation, and some sense of urgency to the affairs of Europe and to arrive at conclusions. In 1964 he asked John Bugas to create an International Operations Committee and it met for the first time, with Bugas as chairman, on February 2, 1965.

It seems odd, to reflect in retrospect, how entrenched and even claustrophobic were the managements of Ford in Germany and Britain at this time. They had grown up as virtually independent fiefdoms and their appetite for sustaining the differences communicated itself throughout their separate establishments. Both companies needed better products and more of them, but straightforward resolution of simple issues was repeatedly sidetracked by microscopic analysis of purely peripheral considerations and by the evident fact that there were few devotees of a one-Europe approach. The principal by-product of the sixties was optimism but Ford's international finance office was decidedly wary. In one of its papers it concluded bluntly: "The possibilities of a rapprochement between the UK and the EEC seem very remote." Ergo, it made sense to have Ford Germany manufacture within, and sell to, the five EEC markets while Ford Britain satisfied itself with the same sort of approach in EFTA. There was an apparently sound justification for this point of view. In 1964 the costs to Ford in tariffs and other duties in selling cars and commercial vehicles across the various national borders were more than $40 million. Ford Germany began to look expansively for new factory sites and went as far as Nantes, Nancy, Calais, and St. Etienne in France.

Some analytical minds were urging partial forms of cooperation. The two companies, it was argued, could share components and use the same engines. Perhaps German products could be assembled in Britain and vice versa. There was much talk of different "product identities" for the two separate dealer networks with different names, but Henry said he only had one surname and it was Ford. John Bugas frequently seemed lost in the maze that was growing up around him. It became a paper chase—dollops of detailed opinions were forever being rewritten—and even brilliant men were lured, like Childe Harold, into byways and dead ends from which they often beat hasty retreats.

It was difficult not to respect the tenacity with which John Andrews held to his point of view, what he called the "two fishing lines" approach. He was all for better planning and the pooling of resources, but he would not be shaken in his determination to preserve what he saw as the different character of Ford in Britain and Germany and, more to the point, the characteristics of their products. He had an unswerving respect for German engineering and was also persuaded that the countries of Europe would always sustain their individual, even chauvinistic, preference for German as opposed to British products despite the lingering prejudices and passions which had been kindled by the recent war. Loyalty to one's country, he argued, is not at all the same as brand loyalty. Andrews never did or said anything that was foolish, and there was some substance to his point of view.

Henry would have none of it. In 1964 and 1965 he took the chair at product committee meetings in England and Germany—often in shirtsleeves—and insisted that Ford in Europe needed common products and a combined effort to satisfy the growing number of European car owners. "Because that's the point," he said to me one night at dinner. "Our people are thinking too much about what they already know. What I know is that people want better products and the best way to do that is remember there is only one Ford Motor Company and we don't have the resources to do everything twice over."

In April 1965 he appointed Robert Stevenson to replace John Bugas of what was then called Overseas Automotive Operations, and the same day John Andrews was made vice-president in charge of the European Group. John Bugas became a consultant to the company and remained on the board of directors until 1978, but 1965 marked the break in his long working relationship with Henry although their friendship endured until John's death.

The changes of 1965 brought about the beginnings of a new way of doing things in Europe. German and British executives began to work in each other's offices and factories. I was sent to spend some time in Germany "to effect a change in their introspection," as it was grandly put. But such progress in brotherhood as we all made was not nearly dramatic enough for Henry, and it was at the Plaza d'Athénée in Paris that summer of 1967 when his patience came to an end and he made the crucial decision himself.

"What we need," Henry said, "is a Ford of Europe to knock a few heads together and make things happen faster." Ford could not rely on the American market where so many strange things were happening. The Middle East was "up for grabs" and the Japanese were going to dominate the Far East. In Europe, on the other hand, the Common Market was working and people were prosperous; Britain could not stay out of the EEC much longer. He had heard all the arguments but the time for argument was over. "And it's no use looking to Dearborn," he told John Andrews. "They have enough on their plate. You have got to do it yourself. Make Ford of Europe."

I had a drink with Henry in his suite that night. There were two books on a side table: Ernest Hemingway's *A Moveable Feast* and one by Martin Luther King Jr. which had been given to him in Detroit and inscribed, I think, by the author. It's title was *Why We Can't Wait*. I thought it very appropriate.

I spent another day with Henry and decided that changes would be made when he returned to Dearborn if only in the "Total Performance" campaign. Toward the end of the year there was one obvious retrenchment, although this was a consequence of success and not a portent of new strategies. John Wyer, whose own GT40s had never finished a race, was told that not Shelby or Holman or any other Ford U.S. team would be returning to Le Mans, and he was offered Ford Advanced Vehicles Ltd., which included the remaining unfinished cars and the inventory of components, at a modest price. A successful English Ford dealer named John Willment, who also owned a construction company, offered to help finance the takeover, and J. W. Automotive was formed under Wyer's control. With substantial help from Gulf Oil, Wyer redeveloped the GT40 with smaller engines, a decision that was, in any event, enforced by the Le Mans organizers, who were becoming concerned at the speeds of the big-engine sports cars and motivated by the fine nationalistic instincts of the French and Italians, who were only too happy to see the Yanks go home and stay there.

With as much support as I could muster from Ford of Britain, John Wyer took his beloved GT40s back into racing despite the many people who were calling it a historic car. He had something to prove, if only to himself. But there was some reason for the suggestion that he was no more than the master of an antique sports car company. Ferrari was again on the rampage, and the Porsche 917s were going down the Mulsanne straight at 217 mph. As a farewell present, Ford had paid for changes in the circuit that enabled the introduction of a chicane before the pits, intended to slow everybody down, but regulation in motor sport is inevitably surmounted by the ingenuity of its competitors. One look at the Porsches, even on a slower circuit, was enough to convince anybody but Wyer that the GT40 had had its day. John Wyer, as ever, said little and kept his own counsel and one GT40—number 1075 because it was the seventy-fifth to be produced—wrote as fine an ending to "Total Performance" as anybody could wish, giving me the greatest motor-racing day of my life, twenty-four hours of pure, self-indulgent pleasure.

Pedro Rodriguez and Lucien Bianchi drove 1075 to victory at Le Mans that year, and then in 1969 the graceful, young Belgian driver Jackie Ickx—whom I had started racing with Cortinas when he was only sixteen years of age—recovered sufficiently from an accident to take over. Ickx and 1075 went on to win the 1968 BOAC 500, the Spa Thousand Kilometers, the Six Hours at Watkins Glen, the Twelve Hours at Sebring, and Le Mans again in 1969. Wyer won the world manufacturers' trophy and promptly gave it to me for my modest services. It was an unexpected bonus because the last race at Le Mans was its own reward.

Ickx knew, I think, that it was the end of an era the day the race began.

He refused to join the driver scramble across the track in the traditional Le Mans start. He walked across the track in a leisurely fashion and took time to fasten his seat belt, by which time the rest of the field was virtually out of sight. After one hour he was placed fifteenth, and the Porsche 917s looked dominant. By halfway—as thin flakes of cloud began to wind themselves around the moon and I waited for the relief of dawn—1075 was fourth. Ickx was sharing the car with Jackie Oliver, and they drove like men with a mission. By the twenty-first hour the last of the Porsche 917s had gone, and 1075 was in the lead; but Hans Herrmann (and Gerard Larousse) in a Porsche 908 were soon within meters of Ickx. For three hours the two cars were almost wheel to wheel, separating only for pit stops and coming together again in a duel I shall never forget. In John Wyer's pit nobody spoke, and I don't think I was breathing. When the race reached its end, 1075 was 120 meters ahead, and Ford had won its fourth and last and finest Le Mans. Some said the GT40 should be in a museum, and now it is: in Harley Cluxton's private collection in Scottsdale, Arizona. In its lifetime 1075 covered 12,000 racing miles—20,000 altogether including testing—and brought an era to an end.

The next year Ford formally ended its American motor sport program (and was to remain out until I brought it back in 1980). Henry and his company had other things on their mind.

I expected change when Henry went back to the United States after the 1967 Le Mans, but it was nevertheless unexpected when it came. On February 3, 1968, Arjay Miller returned from a visit to Latin America and was given a message when he landed asking him to meet Henry in the office. He knew something of significance was about to happen, for it was a Sunday. Henry told Arjay, without preamble, that he had been talking to Bunkie Knudsen and Bunkie had accepted the presidency of the Ford Motor Company. Arjay would become vice-chairman and chairman of the Finance Committee. Henry had been thinking about it for a long time.

It was a difficult and unwelcome thing for both of them. Arjay was a friend and a confidant and one of the trusted architects of the revival of the company. But Henry was increasingly concerned about the way Ford's U.S. cars were being designed and manufactured, and he thought Arjay perhaps was too fine an intellectual and financial mind to cope with the increasing political, social, and economic pressures that Ford and the rest of the industry were obviously facing. Arjay accepted the point and was too much of a gentleman to argue. He accepted the vice-chairmanship, for he had no clear plans for his own future. He had anticipated many more years as president, and his dedication to that responsibility was never in doubt. Henry, for his part, was well aware of Arjay's qualities, and Arjay remained a valued member of the board of directors and a close friend long after he had decided to yield to his old yearning for academia and leave Ford to become dean of the business school at Stanford. When Henry, many years later, came to write his will, he was to give an extraordinary expression to his regard for the man who had served him so well.

The man Henry chose in his place—Semon E. ("Bunkie") Knudsen—seemed to offer what Henry felt he so badly needed: another Ernie Breech, a man with all the qualities. And it did not hurt that Knudsen carried with him the unmistakable aura of General Motors or that like Henry Ford II himself, he was the scion of an auto dynasty.

Bunkie's father, William S. Knudsen, had been one of the two "great Danes" in Henry Ford's corps of principal lieutenants. It was Knudsen senior who had been sent to Europe in 1919 to bring some order into Ford's European operations after the First World War and build factories across the Continent. In 1921 he had quarreled with old Henry and joined General Motors to become, within a month, the $50,000-a-year vice-president of Chevrolet. In his eleven-year reign as head of that division, he had forced Henry Ford to abandon the Model T. He had risen higher to become president of GM, commissioner for industrial production in the Second World War, and a lieutenant general in the U.S. Army.

Bunkie was close to his father and had added to his inheritance with the best education that money could buy and a degree in engineering from MIT. He, too, had gone into GM. He, too, had run Chevrolet, and he had also made Pontiac the hottest GM nameplate with his own brand of total performance. After Henry Ford II had offered the presidency of Ford to Ernie Breech, who proved hard to get, he invited Bunkie to consider it.

Henry was also aware that Bunkie had a conscience, and he liked that. Bunkie's niece had been badly injured in a Corvair accident, and he knew of others who had been killed. The Corvair had inspired Ralph Nader's unremitting attack in *Unsafe at Any Speed*, and before its publication Bunkie had gone to the GM Executive Committee and threatened to resign unless he was permitted to design its rear suspension, as he did for the 1964 model. It was an action that may well have crippled his ambitions to follow his father into the presidency of GM. What is certain is that when Henry approached him, he believed he had gone as far within GM as he ever would, and he immediately accepted the Ford presidency.

I developed a contented relationship with Bunkie Knudsen, brief though it was. It began with our mutual interest in performance cars. We, in Britain, had invented an inexpensive formula for single-seat racing cars which we called Formula Ford, and I flew one across the Atlantic to Bunkie and got a very quick Mustang in return. In 1969 I asked him to come over to Copenhagen because we were celebrating the fiftieth anniversary of the plant there, a plant—I reminded him—that had been founded by his father. He came with his wife, Florence, to whom he was devoted, and the Danes made a great fuss over him, which was both a pleasure and a relief. In Dearborn he was an outsider from the day he arrived. He was a gentle man and had no friends in the company, and nothing in his character or his experience gave him weapons sharp enough to withstand the fine Italian web Lee Iacocca wove to secure his departure.

There is no doubt that Iacocca could weave spells and command exceptional loyalties from his own people, but it was not always easy or comfortable to be one of his chosen. Partisanship of this kind inevitably leads to the conviction that security consists not so much in how well a job is being done as in for whom. What, if anything happened to Lee, would happen to his familiars? It was an anxiety Iacocca learned to use to his advantage.

He declared war on Bunkie immediately. Lee felt he was the product man, and didn't need a president who would get up at dawn to be early into the design studios. Arjay Miller had never behaved that way. Bunkie had brought no allies with him from GM save a stylist, and he was not welcome either. On a visit to England Bunkie had thought a new Cortina, then in the design stage, was sitting too high on its wheels and lowered it two inches. Lee was told that Bunkie had "screwed up" the program by forcing unnecessary mechanical changes, but I thought it looked twice the car after his intervention. I also found it refreshing to have somebody in the presidency with a high regard for the technology of the motorcar and for innovation under the skin. Iacocca told his minions that they had no future in the company if Bunkie survived. He talked about all the outside offers he was getting, and then he told Henry that his people did not want to work with Bunkie. If it was not an ultimatum, it sounded like one.

The company Henry was trying to bring together at this time was facing difficult external problems and the last thing he wanted was internal upheaval. Henry himself was introspective and uncertain about what to do. He did not believe Iacocca's threats of a wholesale evacuation by North American management had any substance; but he could not be sure, and he could not take the risk. Moreover, he was not short of respect—even admiration—for many of Iacocca's achievements as a supersalesman. On the other hand, he felt he could leave the Ford Motor Company in Bunkie's hands and sleep at night. With Iacocca in charge, he would have only bad dreams.

Henry was also influenced by the one or two others with whom he discussed the impasse. His brother Bill was staunchly for Iacocca, and so were other key members of the board of directors, even some who had welcomed the broader vision they thought Bunkie would bring. And so it was. Wanting to save Bunkie the unpleasantness of a formal sacking in the office, Henry asked Ted Mecke—the vice-president in charge of public affairs—a man of sound judgment and humanity, who was on good personal terms with Bunkie—to go to his house and break the news gently. There was no alternative. I served much later with Bunkie on a small group planning the arrival of Grand Prix motor racing in the streets of Detroit and was persuaded that he was in no way soured by the experience, which, I thought at the time, he must have seen as inevitable. A lesser man might justifiably have felt betrayed.

On Thursday, September 11, 1969, therefore, Bunkie Knudsen— nineteen months president of Ford Motor Company—went into honored retirement. If Iacocca thought the departure would bring him the presidency, he was mistaken. There certainly appeared to be no other choice from within the company, and Henry had discovered what happened when outsiders were taken aboard. But he was unwilling to endorse what seemed suspiciously like mutiny by handing Iacocca the prize, and Henry genuinely doubted that Iacocca had the resources or the character to deal in a comprehensive and statesmanlike fashion with the problems the company was facing and that were so plain to see. He therefore decided upon an awful compromise and appointed three presidents: one for North America, who was Iacocca; one for International Operations, who was Robert Stevenson; and Robert Hampson, to whom he gave the so-called Diversified Products. He knew that a tripod is the least satisfactory form a table can take, and one leg, he also knew, was out of joint.

His earlier hopes for McNamara had gone with the wind of change in Washington. His hopes of another wise man had been frustrated by Lee Iacocca. The problems remained. He didn't know who would tackle them.

CHAPTER FIVE

Traveling Man

A note in my 1986 diary records that in the ten years from 1976 I spent 1,952 hours—more than eighty whole days—in the air and flew well over one million miles on business. Unlike Prufrock, I measured my life not in coffee spoons but by airport departure lounges, where feminine voices spoke softly but not to me. Most of my earlier diaries, covering the first five years of the seventies, were mislaid in the move to the United States, but I certainly traveled as many miles each year in that period of time. When I went through the travel diaries of Henry Ford II after his death, I began to suspect he had covered a greater distance and wondered—as I often had during his lifetime—where his stamina came from. Even a brief recapitulation of some of his constant voyaging from 1970 to 1972 provides important insights into his character. From 1970 onward he was continuously on the move, talking to governments, presiding at management meetings, handshaking his way through factories from Australia to Singapore, Moscow to Bordeaux, restlessly enlarging the resources of the Ford Motor Company outside the United States. He dragged the board of directors behind him, and between July 1970 and August 1971 Lee Iacocca made six trips to Europe and tiptoed gingerly into a world Henry had made his own for more than twenty-one years.

On December 10, 1970, after months of difficult deliberation, Henry granted Iacocca his ambition, appointing him president and chief operating officer. The troika—the obviously temporary and, as it turned out, unworkable caretaker regime of three presidents that had come about as a result of the Knudsen fiasco—was never likely to last for long. "It was a mistake," Henry said, "a dumb, damn thing to do." And he took the burning brand in his hand and knighted Iacocca. Apart from the inevitability of it, Henry felt the move had a certain logic. Lee knew comparatively little about the company's international operations; but he gave every evidence of being assured where the American market was concerned, and it was at least possible that once his ambitions were satisfied, he would get down to the mounting problems in the United States so that Henry could achieve his own self-appointed task of building the final ramparts in the dominions overseas.

Earlier that year, after we had returned from the Soviet Union, where Henry had been invited to explore the possibility of Ford's building a truck factory—unsuccessfully, as it turned out—Henry preoccupied himself with a summer board of directors' tour. The tour took them to the dedication of an enormous new factory in the German Saarland, to another comparatively new factory at Genk in Belgium, to Bergamo in Italy, where Philco-Ford had a subsidiary making refrigerators, and to Rome, where Cristina was in her element. Henry did not neglect the United States, where Senator Edmund Muskie's amendments to the Federal Clean Air Act were passed by Congress, imposing a further reduction of almost 90 percent in vehicle emissions and where the safety lobby was hell-bent on redesigning the automobile itself. Accompanied by Lee Iacocca, he had a secret meeting in the Oval Office in April 1971 with President Nixon and John Ehrlichman at which they discussed the probable impact upon the entire industry of ill-considered legislation, but although Washington was only one hour's flying time from Detroit, the gulf between the administration and the automobile capital of the world was beginning to look a great deal wider than that.

The contrast between Henry's reception abroad and in his home country always seemed to me bizarre, for European governments were usually part of the solution, not the problem. Government edict, however, was not the only danger threatening Detroit. In 1950, of the 7 million cars built in the world, 85 percent came off the long assembly lines in North America, but twenty years later—when worldwide production reached the figure of almost 22 million—59 percent were being built outside North American plants. The Japanese motor industry, brought back to life by the demand of the American occupation forces for military vehicles—and given a further rewarding impetus by the even larger demands of the Korean War—built more than 3 million passenger cars in 1970, and the leaders of the European industry, more prescient than those in the United States, could see that it was not only the sun that rose in Japan. They were losing their Far Eastern export markets. The pattern of demand was also changing toward smaller cars, and Ford, in both Europe and the United States, had empty shelves in its dealerships, for it had nothing to offer at the lower end of its product range. The Cardinal might have been small enough for the United States—had Iacocca not killed it—but in Europe there was a growing, classless market for minicars in which Fiat was the evident leader. The trouble was that minicars seemed doomed to make miniprofits, and many a mini—or B Car, in the product-planning language of Ford— had threatened to bring its maker to bankruptcy.

We had long struggled with the problem in Britain. A week or so after I joined the company, Sir Patrick Hennessy took me to see a small front-wheel-drive prototype which was both roomy and nimble and for which he had great hopes until the "numbers" pronounced its stillbirth. After 1968, however, when Ford of Europe had been given substance and organization by the tireless evangelism of John Andrews, the Product Committee decided to give its own young European lions $200,000 and its blessing to go away and search for the clues that would make a B car possible. An influx of American executives to Ford of Europe, including Joe Oros, whose Dearborn studio had fathered the Mustang, made it possible to plan more ambitiously. The gathering together of all of Ford's fifteen European companies into a single, happy—if, occasionally, quarrelsome—family made it easier to plan one car for the entire European market, and the Americans needed no reminding that there was also the United States to think of.

Joe Oros was distinctly irritated to discover that the B car task force had no need of his abilities. He was used to a country where the shape came first and the unseen mechanical components arrived in due course. But Ford of Europe's task force was not concerned with how its B car would look. If the concept worked, there would be no shortage of designers; what had to be proved was that it would make financial sense, and after twelve months the task force was convinced it had the answer. Existing B cars had been bought from competing dealers and taken apart; every single piece was arranged on floors and walls like a jigsaw, and the task force believed it knew how to arrive at better engineering solutions and more efficient methods of manufacture. In February 1971 we sat around a long table in the British Research and Engineering Center at Dunton in Essex and took Henry Ford II and Lee Iacocca through the arguments, but the task force was less prepared when it came to answer the question of where its baby would be built. The sales analyst on the team had reached general agreement that European dealers could sell perhaps 150,000 of the B cars a year, but there was no capacity in the existing plants for a production increase of that magnitude. And for a company that is in the business of mass production, 150,000 cars is not an ideal capacity; 250,000 is more like it. Ford and Iacocca, however, were not discouraging. Henry liked small cars and drove them regularly on holidays in the south of France, and Iacocca was about to father the Pinto, essentially a small runabout, in the United States. It was agreed that the work so far was promising, and the discussion was encouraging. Iacocca took away some of the concept sketches that had been presented to him, and Henry departed for a six-week tour of Ford Asia-Pacific. Ford had 450,000 employees on the five continents, and although some were oceans away, there was no subsidiary too small to be excluded from his all-embracing interest.

Ford Asia-Pacific was under the control of a handsome, black-haired, deep-voiced American who had been born in the tough environment of Chicago's South Side. William Oliver Bourke—who used the O but not the Oliver—had started what might have been an ill-fated management career with Ford as manager of the Edsel distribution department in 1956 but survived its demise and was scattered along with most of the others in the division, some to the ends of the earth. He soon became general sales manager of Ford Canada and was posted to Ford Australia as assistant managing director in 1965. Henry's conviction that Ford of Europe was the right way to coordinate the European subsidiaries had led him to invoke other similar forms of organization on the other continents, and in the autumn of 1970 Bill Bourke was appointed the first president of Ford Asia-Pacific with a territory that extended from Wellington, New Zealand, through the islands of the Pacific to Malaysia. These territories still bore the scars of Japanese aggression, and Bourke was the first Ford executive to be called up in the new economic war against the Japanese. Because the markets in the region were small and often primitive and scattered, Bourke's appointment had not been thought important enough to merit Henry's involvement, and Henry had never met him before he arrived in Australia.

They soon became friends. Bourke was an open man with no disposition to keep secrets, which made him amusing company but occasionally led him into trouble, for his deep baritone voice was penetrating and his indiscretions were not difficult to hear through several office walls. He was not nervous in Henry's presence. Gregarious and full of anecdotes about the strange characters and people in his cosmopolitan markets, he quickly impressed Henry with the cohesion, sense of purpose, and clear strategic vision that he was bringing to his task. Henry also liked his wife, Elizabeth. Bourke was married, for the second time, to a charming, irrepressible, and matey Australian—as forthcoming as her husband—and her companionship proved relaxing for Henry and Cristina, who had been brought along on this long and tiring tour of inspection. Henry took his pleasure in the evenings, but the days were filled with government and dealer meetings and a demanding schedule of formal luncheons—and occasional dinners—with business leaders. Ferdinand Marcos, who had been elected sixth president of the Philippines in 1965, took the Bourkes and the Fords on the presidential yacht to the tip of the Bataan Peninsula, only a couple of jumps away from Corregidor, where the great American guns of war were rusting in their bunkers. Marcos was desperate to build the Philippine economy on foundations more secure than sugar and cheap labor, and Henry and Bill Bourke agreed to establish a stamping plant on Bataan that would supply other Ford factories in the Pacific. Australian engineers and their families had to live in tents and work in an unforgiving sun to make the plan a reality, and Henry promised to express his thanks to them when he came back for the inauguration, as, alas, he never did. (Illness tied him to a hospital bed at the time, and I went along with Philip Caldwell, the vice-president in charge of international operations, in his place.) From the Philippines Henry and Cristina went on to Singapore, and the tour finished, after forty-two days, in Japan, where Henry was made aware of the still-unappreciated industrial imperialism of the country and did not like what he saw.

Five days into the New Year 1972, Henry called me from Detroit and wanted to know if I thought he should go to Israel. It should have been an easy question but it was not. The Palestine Automobile Corporation, a privately owned and autonomous company, had been selling Ford cars through two world wars and had encountered no more than the usual problems until the state of the Israeli economy brought increased taxation and made it unreasonably expensive to import finished cars, as it had always done, from Britain. A wiry gnome called Joe Boxenbaum, who was now in charge, therefore decided to ask for the cars to come out as components—in what carmakers call KD, or knock-down, form—so that he could assemble them on the spot at a new factory in Nazareth.

John Andrews asked me what I thought of the enterprise, and I pointed out that it had to be a risk. The Arab boycott offices in the Middle East were alert and alive to companies setting up in Israel, and I thought the prospect of Ford's being put on the boycott list could probably be taken for granted. I quoted other companies, some of them household names, that had thought discretion the order of the day and had closed subsidiaries in Israel to protect their bigger and more profitable Arab markets. There was no Mercedes assembly in Israel, and no Volkswagen, only—so far as I could tell—a modest effort by dealers putting together Chrysler trucks and cars from the then British Motor Corporation.

Andrews had taken my opinion with him to Dearborn, where he had gone specially to discuss Joe Boxenbaum's request, emphasizing the obvious business dangers, but Henry would have none of it. He was acutely conscious of his grandfather's anti-Semitism, and more important, he was unwilling to have anybody tell him how to run his company and where to sell his cars and trucks. When he telephoned, I repeated all the arguments, but he said it was all narrow-minded. Weren't we a world company? He said we had too many fearful people around and repeated his conviction, which I had often heard before, that business conscience made too many cowards. I said, "I thought you were calling to get my opinion," and he laughed. "I guess you've made my mind up," he said. This day happened also to be my eldest son's eighteenth birthday and we all went to the theater to see Alan Bennett's *Getting On*, with adultery, homosexuality, two shits, and a fuck, and my wife and eleven-year-old daughter remained pretty cool, all things considered. My wife said the world was a funny place, but I knew that.

On January 21 Henry called again—this time from La Réserve at Beaulieu in the south of France. He was obviously contented. Nobody had met him at the airport. He had encountered no difficulty renting a car. Nobody had made a fuss. Everything was fine. Two days later he came to London, and three days after that we left for Belgium because he wanted to see the tractor plant. Tractors never figure very largely in any of the books about Ford, but the company's first manufacturing plant in Europe—established in Cork in southern Ireland in 1917—was put there solely to make them, and before that the first Henry Ford had shipped boatloads over to England at the request of Britain's wartime premier, David Lloyd George, who was anxious to increase food production. The distinctive blue Fordson (later Ford) tractors have since plowed millions of acres of land, cut down forests, and harvested everything from potatoes to grapes. The Antwerp tractor plant was a major operation, and there were fears of its closure since Europe's farms seemed to have all the tractors they required and the farmers were not, on the whole, interested in keeping up with the Joneses or chrome plating. If it worked—and Ford tractors did for a long time—why replace it?

We went to the marvelous medieval rococo town hall at Antwerp for a formal reception by the burgomaster, at which Prince Albert presented the order of the Crown and Leopold I to the managing director of Ford Belgium, Rik Daems. The next day Henry and Cristina were invited to lunch in Brussels with King Baudouin and Queen Fabiola. In the afternoon we went to Ostend, a journey that was to emphasize an aspect of Henry's complex character. As we left the Brussels hotel, he saw a man standing by the door in the midst of the bustle of baggage. Cristina never traveled lightly; my wife was with me, and Mrs. Daems had joined her husband. "Who is that man?" Henry asked, and I said he was helping with the luggage. It had been decided that we would fly to Ostend from Brussels airport, and when we arrived at the hotel in Ostend, the man who had aroused Henry's curiosity was again by the door. "Who is he?" Henry asked again, and I said once more that he was helping with the bags. "Do baggage handlers usually carry guns?" Henry asked. The man was in fact a Belgian government security officer, and I had accepted his presence because the government had insisted, although I knew Henry could spot security men a mile away and hated to feel he was being protected. It was a war I fought for twenty-five years and never won. "Let us agree," he said, "once and for all, that we don't go around with armed bodyguards." On other occasions when I was prepared to overrule his insistence, I did my best to avoid argument by insisting I was concerned for my own security, and this obvious subterfuge sometimes brought about a sort of truce between us, but it was many years in the future before he took the threat of kidnapping seriously, even though businessmen of less stature in countries such as Germany and Italy were driving around in armored cars and some of his friends had been held for ransom.

In Ostend at the evening function Henry shook the hands of three hundred dealers and their wives, and we came back to Brussels late at night, staying up—Henry and Cristina, Elizabeth and I—in a nightclub at the top of the Hotel Macdonald called Le Gong. He had been given a little gold whistle for Christmas, which he blew in the plane coming back to prove that he had his own security alarm. Elizabeth, who Cristina said was *molto simpática*, danced with Henry, and Cristina steered me around the small dance floor, and it was 4:20 A.M. when we felt tired enough to go to bed. In the last half hour Henry had grown reminiscent and talked about moving permanently to London in two or three years' time. He thought Iacocca might have proved himself by then and the trips to Europe would give him experience. At least, he said, he hoped so.

We returned to London on January 29 but not for long. Henry and Cristina went off to Haarlem in the Netherlands to stay with John Loudon, Chairman of Royal Dutch Shell, and I met them in Madrid two days later. Cristina showed me some press clippings that said that Aristotle Onassis had quarreled with Jackie Kennedy at London airport because he wanted to marry Cristina, and Cristina was obviously delighted with this nonsense. "They say," she said dramatically, "that he *larves* me!"—then burst into laughter that made her eyes wet with enjoyment.

Despite the continuing presence of Cristina, the visit to Spain was in pursuit of serious business concerns. The marriage had begun to fail almost as soon as it began because Cristina, naturally enough, had expected a more social life once she became Mrs. Henry Ford II, and she found that—in Detroit anyway—Henry was away all day at the office and only interested in the evening to come home to a hamburger and a book or television. She tried to talk of business, but her ideas, although charming, were based on an almost total misunderstanding of what Henry actually did. He therefore began to take her on duty trips, believing that the different places would give her more to do and that she would enjoy the mixture of business and pleasure that filled most evenings.

Madrid had been chosen for a meeting of three thousand European Ford dealers invited to the introduction of a range of new British Ford cars, and some top brass from Dearborn were invited. Lee Iacocca's arrival was delayed by the illness of his father, Nicola, who had leukemia and died at the age of eighty-three the following year. Henry said he knew that they were a close family and Lee, no doubt, would join us if he could, although he found it harder to understand why the other American executives who were expected also failed to turn up. Iacocca's praetorian guard liked to travel with him. "Were all their fathers sick?" Henry asked.

The remark was not as unfeeling as it sounds. Ford of Europe had long had its eyes on the Spanish market. The first Ford cars—five Model As—had been exported to Spain from America in 1907, and by 1933, when Ford had a factory in Barcelona, one car in every three sold in the country was a Ford. The civil war had made life impossible, and in 1954 the tents were folded and Ford Spain was no more. But much had happened since Franco had taken over, and there were some people in high places with even higher hopes for the future. The boom in tourism, which eventually brought thirty-two million tourists a year to a country with a thirty million population, was beginning to hasten its economic development. The Spanish fishing fleet was the largest in Europe; wine and citrus fruit production was growing. The government spoke of a million-a-year car market by 1980, and in December 1971 the minister of industry, José María López de Letona, had been invited to meet Henry Ford II in Dearborn to discuss his government's ambitions. In Madrid on February 2 López de Letona, anxious to take the relationship farther, asked Henry to luncheon with his principal officials.

Late that night, after a dinner at the Jockey, we sat with our shoes off in Henry's suite at the Ritz Hotel and wondered whether Spain could be made to work. Iacocca had added some of his American troops to the group trying to develop a workable program for the B car, and it was beginning to look as if the prospect of Spain and a new market—plus the evident enthusiasm for the car as the numbers began to make sense—might eventually prove to be a bold, even daring stroke, but Henry said there was another consideration that nobody talked about: Who was going to manage such an enterprise? With the aid and inspiration of some Dom Pérignon, I reminded him of the three maxims of the bullfighter—Style, Mastery, and Timing—and said I preferred Style, Courage, and Execution and that should be our motto. Henry found a piece of paper and wrote the three words down, and we went somewhat joyfully to bed.

The following evening Henry and Cristina went to dinner with Prince Juan Carlos and his wife, Sophia. Juan Carlos, whose father had once worked for Ford in Detroit, was being cautiously groomed by General Franco to become king of Spain in a revived monarchy, and Henry had known him a long time. They enjoyed a common passion for shooting the fast and frustrating Spanish partridge. It was essentially a social evening, but the prince wanted to talk only about the prospect of Ford's coming to Spain, promising his support even to the extent of recommending knowledgeable Spaniards who could make it easier for us to solve the many problems involved in building a new plant and new cars in a new market.

Cristina went off the next day to Rome to a party with Roberto Rossellini and Sophia Loren, and I flew to Marbella on the southern coast to check a route along which several hundred motoring writers would soon arrive to test the new cars. I drove the 409 kilometers to Granada and back and went to bed at eight and began to think that my children would soon find it difficult to recognize me.

On February 6 I got up at 6:00 A.M. and flew to Madrid to pick up Henry, who was decidedly shamefaced about admitting to a hubbub at a Madrid party during my absence when the Spanish police had arrested an intruder, whom they were convinced was set on kidnapping Henry. We were escorted to the airport by Spanish police, to whom, on this occasion, he made no objection. The following day, in Cologne, Henry had a private meeting with the German industrialist Dr. Herbert Quandt, who came to the Excelsior Hotel with an offer to sell 25 percent of Daimler-Benz, which meant Mercedes, for $450 million, and Henry was profoundly torn by the visions their conversation opened up. Dr. Quandt said he would offer his own holding together with that of the Flick family, and while this would not mean control (because that was out of the question), it was nevertheless a good investment. When Dr. Quandt, who was virtually blind and walked hesitantly with the aid of a stick, left the meeting on the arm of his aide, Henry sent for tea and asked me what I thought. That did not mean that I had any special qualifications for answering the question but rather that he wanted to think aloud about the enticing prospect of what the deal could mean for Ford in general and in Ford Germany in particular. It was not an easy decision because the investment might have led to a sharing in technology and even perhaps some cooperative product development.

Henry's dilemma—and he knew it—was that he wanted Spain very badly indeed, and he wanted the B car, and he also knew that Ford did not have the financial resources to invest in Daimler-Benz and continue to build its own resources. Ford profits had reached a record high of $703 million in 1965, but a long United Auto Workers (UAW) strike in the United States in 1967 had brought them down to $84 million, and although they had climbed back to $657 million in 1971, the business of automobile manufacturing is as demanding of money as it is of labor. Each year that passed made the $65 million investment for the Mustang one of the bargains of the century. He sat on the offer, however, for the best part of the month before he called Dr. Quandt and said he felt that Ford could not make the commitment.

Henry went to Jerusalem on Valentine's Day, and people said it was symbolic. His grandfather's professed anti-Semitism had been no mere laughing matter; it was a family shadow Henry always found difficult to live with and even to understand. Being left-handed, he said, made him levelheaded, but whatever the reason, he was certainly free from prejudice of any kind where people were concerned. Max Fisher, one of his closest friends over many years, was a leading figure in the Jewish hierarchy of America, and they had worked side by side to address the problems of Detroit, particularly after the 1967 riot. Henry had breached single-handedly the prejudiced fortifications of the Detroit Club, which did not admit Jews to membership; he proposed Max Fisher and fought the application through. They both were pragmatic men who liked sitting at firesides late into the night considering the affairs of the day, and Max's petite wife, Marjorie, an accomplished hostess, was always an understanding ally. Apart from friendship, there was another bond. Leaders of large companies and small ones, like tennis players, need walls against which to practice and see if their ideas rebound. In the larger company it is very often difficult to bounce some ideas against working colleagues particularly if their own future or status is involved; the need is for the uncomplicated, even distant man with no prior knowledge or particular prejudices. Max Fisher was such a wall, and he was not uninformed about the Ford Motor Company since his first friendships with its elite had been with John Bugas and Ernie Breech.

He was also a Zionist, not, in any sense, a zealot or even a missionary but simply a humanitarian, and therefore, being a Jew, he worked for the Jews. He was chairman of the Jewish Agency, influential in the Nixon administration, and a key man in the activities of the United Jewish Appeal in New York, and there has probably never been a larger fund-raising enterprise. Through the seventies the Jewish Agency had something like $500 million a year to spend on humanitarian Jewish causes; two-thirds came from the United States, and 10 percent from Britain. One of the things the agency did with the money was buy people. At one time it was providing the Dutch embassy in Moscow with enough to pay $1,100 a head for each Russian Jew who was allowed an exit permit. The

Russians were flown to Vienna and put in a camp and were later ferried to Israel for resettlement. The agency had paid as much as $10,000 a head to the Romanian government, and similar sums had been handed over in North Africa, notably Morocco. It is a nasty modern business, and it is not confined to Jews; the West Germans have paid large sums across the border in recent years to purchase people from East Germany. Few people discuss the traffic, and Max Fisher never did; but when Henry talked to him about his own intended trip to Israel—so that he could see for himself and make up his own mind about Joe Boxenbaum and his vehicle assembly project—Max Fisher said he would like to go along.

So it was that in February 1972 Henry and Cristina Ford; Max and Marjorie Fisher; Irving Bernstein, executive vice-president of the United Jewish Appeal in New York—with me bringing up the rear—took off from London Airport in a Ford Gulfstream II to make the acquaintance of the Promised Land. Cristina crossed herself on takeoff, and Henry laughed and said we were going to Israel, not Rome. There was the usual shirtsleeved gathering of reporters when the plane landed in Tel Aviv. One television reporter seemed to think that our briefcases contained plans for a major industrialization of the country, but Henry said he had merely come to see for himself; he had always found it the simplest way to obtain information. The TV man, who had been doing his homework on the Ford Motor Company, said that Ford's annual turnover was greater than Israel's annual budget, the implication apparently being that it would not miss the odd million or so, whereas even modest investments would make a great difference to a country in which car ownership was beyond even the aspirations of most people. But Henry never made promises he could not keep, and the reporters were clearly disappointed. One asked me if it was "only a tourist trip," and I said it was a bit of both: some business and, I hoped, some pleasure.

It was with tourism that the visit began. Teddy Kollek, who had arrived in Israel from Vienna thirty-five years earlier and was, for a time, deputy to David Ben-Gurion, came to the King David Hotel in Jerusalem to collect us. He had been mayor of the city for five years and gave the impression that it belonged to him, a personal possession to be loved and cherished and fought for. Jerusalem then was still warm and welcoming despite the bitterness generated by the Six-Day War of 1967 and the Israeli annexation of the old parts of the city. The ethnic mix of the country consisted principally of Jews from Central Europe and the Middle East, but there were also a lot of Americans, and as we wandered

about, several of them recognized Henry and stopped him to chat about
the Ford cars they had owned and the pleasure they had derived from
them. Teddy Kollek was keen to show off the new children's library and
the new flats built with some of the millions Max Fisher had collected in
the United States, but he could not long be kept away from the archae-
ological excavations. In the continuing restless search for their own
identity, just about all Israelis, it seemed to me, were digging beneath the
sands and coming up with astonishing artifacts that were held to prove
that the Bible, and therefore Israel itself, were a historical fact and not to
be argued with. This sense of history demanded a visit to the mosque
built around the enormous rock upon which, it is said, Abraham was
ready to slay Isaac—or, if you are a Muslim, from which Muhammad
ascended to heaven—and which is the holiest place in the Muslim world
after Mecca. Cristina wanted to go to the Wailing Wall; when we did,
she made a wish and would not tell Henry what it was. We drove around
the old city walls to the Citadel, not many years earlier the headquarters
of the Jordanian Army and now restored as the seat of the Armenian
bishop of Israel, a young, vigorous man who had an Israeli air hostess for
a friend and was pleased to lead us through the souks to the Church of
the Holy Sepulcher, which was also being renovated. The church,
which stands on the supposed site of Christ's crucifixion—really nine
churches in one—is administered by Armenians, Catholics, Franciscan
friars, and the Greek Orthodox Church, among others, and Henry said
they must have worse management problems than he had. After lunch
we went to Bethlehem, parking in Manger Square, and more Armenian
priests took us to the Church of the Nativity, where Cristina stayed
awhile to pray—"Did you pray for Walter?" Henry asked—and then we
had to visit the Good Shepherds' Gift Shop, where Cristina bought
Crusader crosses for Henry's two daughters and he patted her rump. I
bought some pressed-flower bookmarks for my daughter, whose birthday
was ten days away, since they seemed to me the only pure and pretty
things in the place. In the late afternoon Henry said we had been tourists
long enough and we should go back to the hotel and change for the
dinner party that was being given for us by Golda Meir.

It was a simple dinner—for fourteen people—in the middle-class
house Golda Meir had inherited from Levi Eshkol, the previous premier.
Mrs. Meir's sister, a typical U.S. matron from Milwaukee, was there,
along with Shimon Peres, then minister of communications and transport; Zeev Sherif, the minister of housing; and Walworth Barbour, the
ample American ambassador. Mrs. Meir was in a reminiscent mood at

first and talked of her time as Israeli representative in Moscow, when she and Nehru's sister, Mrs. Vijayalakshmi Pandit, were the two leading ladies of the diplomatic set, and Irving Bernstein told a funny story about the Jew with a stutter who failed to get a job as a radio announcer and complained of anti-Semitism. Henry complained that his deafness had grown worse in recent years and said he had a permanent ringing in his left ear that the specialists said was due to shooting. He could not tell if the ringing would stop if he gave up shooting, but he was not going to and was resigned to using the other ear. But when the main course arrived, Mrs. Meir talked Arab oil politics and little else, and Henry said it was the subject he had come to Israel to consider, for it concerned him most and he thought the United States government foolishly indifferent to its likely impact.

The next morning, leaving the ladies asleep, we left the King David and drove five minutes to the Knesset buildings, where an army Bell 205 helicopter was waiting to fly us to a kibbutz at Kfar Ruppin on the border with Jordan—three hundred people and two thousand acres with an electrified fence and air-raid shelters. David Nahari, a colonel who had grown up among Arabs and spoke fluent Arabic, reflected, as did most army officers at that time, a respect and something of a liking for King Hussein and his Bedouin. "Brave men and the only ones who really fought," said Nahari, who believed, as did many others, that they still had a chance of coming to peace terms with Hussein. After a couple of hours we flew to the Golan Heights, low over the old Turkish railway line Lawrence of Arabia used to blow up in an earlier and more gentlemanly war, and by midday we were in Nazareth, shaking hands with Major General Mordechai Gur, the officer commanding the northern region of the country who became a Jewish hero when he led his paratroops to capture Jerusalem. His wife told me that he had made general at forty years of age, "actually thirty-nine and a half." It might have been surprising anywhere else, but the entire Israeli Army was young (the helicopter pilot looked about seventeen). Gur was an interesting man who had written and published two children's books about a heroic dog and was now writing another. In one story the dog's collar is fitted with transmitters, and he infiltrates himself into Egypt, where he is taken up by Nasser and broadcasts all the secret news back to his master in Israel. Gur seemed to have as many women soldiers as men, all in khaki miniskirts and also absurdly young. "This is the kind of army to be in," Henry said. We flew back from Nazareth along the coast, dropped Irving Bernstein in Tel Aviv, and came back to Jerusalem. I was told I had a couple of hours before dinner with Abba Eban.

The Ebans' dinner was different from the one with Golda Meir, and his table gave every indication of being the hub of Israel's artistic and intellectual coterie. The house was larger, with good paintings, a library, a courtyard, and the inevitable collection of antiquities, which I was vain enough to think not as good as my own, largely Greek collection in England. And because of my own interest in archaeology—although no more than amateur—I was delighted to find Yigael Yadin among the guests. Yadin had been Israel's chief of staff but was now professor of archaeology at the Hebrew University. It was he who had excavated Massada and had brought the Dead Sea Scrolls to Israel. Over dinner he told me the extraordinary story of their recovery. An advertisement offering the scrolls for sale had been spotted by a newspaperman in the *Wall Street Journal*, and after that it was all Sherlock Holmes and the Jewish underground; he had not been chief of staff for nothing. Marjorie Fisher told Yadin that Saturday was the Fords' seventh wedding anniversary, and he asked me if they would like some antique lamps as a gift; it must have been a successful present, for I saw them later in the house in England. Isaac Stern, who spent a great deal of time in Israel playing to large and small audiences—sometimes to very modest groups in the kibbutzim—arrived after dinner and had dinner on a tray while we finished the coffee, and Henry adjourned with Eban and his wife, Susie, the Jackie Kennedy of Jerusalem, to discuss "matters of state."

All his life Henry extracted almost everything that was important to him from people rather than from words on paper and seemed to be able to forget or remember at will, throwing out of his mind things he either did not want to remember or felt he did not need to, and he assimilated information quickly. As we drove home from the Eban dinner, he said: "They have to be more realistic. This isn't yet a country of three million people, and they will never have enough volume for auto manufacturing. What they need is high-value products because the volume isn't there for anything else. But they don't know it yet. They seem to think that they can ignore the economics. I told them the trouble we are having with the B car and a volume they could not reach in ten years."

The next day we were due to go south into the war zone of the Suez Canal, and Henry called at 6:00 A.M. to say Cristina would not be coming although the previous evening she had objected to being left behind. I called Max Fisher with the news, and he said: "Now you have given me a great shock." Nobody that I knew had ever seen Cristina before 10:30 A.M., and even that was early. Henry, who was invariably punctual, got into the habit of automatically excluding her from everything that took place before luncheon, and for that she was often late. So we went to the Knesset again without her or Marjorie, and the four of us—Henry and Max, Irving and I—boarded a twenty-eight-seat French Frélon helicopter with an escorting officer and headed for the canal. We were over the Sinai Desert and still some distance from the army base that was our destination when the helicopter shuddered as though it had met bad weather and then began to gyrate as if wounded. Henry fastened his seat belt; I was torn between the desire to do the same and get my camera out. I managed to do both before we hit the sand with an almighty thud. When I was learning to fly in Southern Rhodesia (as it was called then) during World War II and made a bad landing, digging the nose of a training aircraft into the ground, a Royal Air Force instructor told me my reactions were slow, and I was furious then and later; but he may have been right, for the helicopter incident did not bother me. Nor, apparently, had it shaken Henry. He undid the lap belt and said, "Well, since we're here, we might as well go for a walk," and we piled out of the Frélon onto the Sinai, which was covered with shells of some snaillike creature and stretched forever. The pilot seemed baffled by the incident and took off the engine covers, but we eventually discovered that a large end section had come off one of the rotor blades. "Max will now look for oil," Henry said. The pilot radioed for a relief helicopter, and after some twenty minutes or so a light aircraft came over, attracted to our position by smoke flares, which had been stuck in the sand, and we resumed the flight to the Sinai Command Base, where Major General Dan Laner, the deputy commander, said: "You have had an experience." Henry said it had been no trouble: "When your number's up, it's up, and today it wasn't."

General Laner had about a dozen bases along the seventy miles of the canal, which was fringed on the Israeli side with bunkers and banded with endless coils of barbed wire—a garland of thorns dotted with small blackbirds. Men moved between the bases in mobile patrols without noise in the almost oppressive silence that only a desert can create. "We are one to ten in men and one to twenty-four in guns," the general said, calculating as he had so often before the odds against Egypt. We had driven through Qantara, a deserted, shell-shocked, ruined town— unrecognizable from the place I remembered from twenty-five years earlier, when I had been briefly based there en route to Southern Rhodesia. Henry stood looking at the canal, remarking several times how clean it was. We had lunch with the brigade commander, but the return to Tel Aviv was delayed because the second helicopter had also developed a fault and we had to wait for another.

We flew back over the Gaza Strip and the crowded refugee camps of the Arabs displaced by the war, and I ran into one of the only two quarrels I ever had with Henry. Cristina, when we met her again at the Tel Aviv Hilton, to which we had transferred from Jerusalem, was enchanted with the story of the drama in the desert. Eyes bright, she said it would appear on all the front pages and Henry would be a hero. I said he would not. I had called the Israel Defense Forces contact I had made on an earlier trip and asked him not to release the story. "Why?" asked Cristina, waving her emphatic, long fingers. "When Teddy Kennedy crashed in a helicopter, it was on television. Everybody talked about it." I said that the entire trip to Israel had been a political hazard, and the Arabs might not boycott Ford for an ordinary business safari; wandering around a war zone was a different matter. "It would be good for Henry," she insisted. "People think my husband is a playboy. Now they will see he is macho." I said nobody thought he was a playboy except people who read fairy stories in American gossip columns, but by now the argument had grown heated, and Henry was having a bad time.

"Do what she wants," he said.

I let the story go against my will, and it still rankled the next morning, when the minister of industry was due at the Hilton to talk business. I had been invited to the meeting but sat in the Hilton and sulked. Eventually a page came to find me and said, "Mr. Ford would like you to join him in his suite," so I took the elevator to the top floor and joined the meeting but remained mute. When the minister had gone, Henry said: "What's the matter with you?"

"We had a row yesterday," I said. "Don't you remember? You were shouting, and Cristina was shouting, and I don't have to put up with that."

He looked at me with what seemed to be complete wonderment. "But that was yesterday," he said. "It's over. What's it got to do with today?"

We went off to Joe Boxenbaum's assembly plant at Nazareth—"turn left at Mary's Well," Schlomo, the driver, had been told—to find a small, neat factory with thirty-five different nationalities and two Russian Jews who had been in Israel only two weeks and spoke nothing but Russian. Since the army called up all men for three years with up to eight weeks a year on the reserve, the average man working in the plant put in about eight and a half months a year. I discovered a sheet of paper on a notice board which must have come from somebody's heart. "When the Americans rush off in a new direction," it said, "wait for a while. If they don't come back, follow them."

There were many other meetings and discussions still ahead. Mandy Rice-Davies, who apparently knew Max Fisher, came around to his suite in the evening. She had arrived in Israel six years earlier in the wake of the Profumo scandal in London. She was taller than I remembered, and younger—still only twenty-eight. She said Rabbi Weitzmann still believed she could become a "proper Jewess," and she was working on it. Schlomo said that everybody in Israel liked her because nobody worried about anybody's past. There was a dinner in Tel Aviv with Isaac Stern, who was staying in the palatial guesthouse of the Israel Philharmonic, before which he took me to his bedroom, where his two Guarneris (circa 1737) were lying on the bed. He picked one up fondly and played "The Stars and Stripes Forever." He is a splendid raconteur, and later at night, when Henry insisted he was going to bed but said Cristina wanted me to take her to a discotheque, Stern volunteered to come along. I got to bed at 2:15 A.M. and was tired the next day at a meeting with Shimon Peres, who predicted 1.5 million new arrivals in the country in the next ten years, a subway in Haifa at $16 million a mile, and many other wonders. He talked about the developing aircraft industry and a new top secret tank. Henry said we did not make tanks, and the aircraft industry was there for defense purposes; motorcars were down-to-earth economics, and Ford was not going to make any kind of military equipment except in the United States or maybe Britain if Britain was at war.

The one encounter that has remained in my mind—and has come back to me with almost immediate presence many times in later years—occurred when we went to see David Ben-Gurion in the house he had built in 1913 but had later given to the state. He had come some distance to see us since, at eighty-five years of age, he chose to live and end his days in a kibbutz. His hands were bad. The eyes had not lost their twinkle but must have hidden his thoughts, for he had to endure a visit from his doctor every evening. The house was one vast library with one room full of books on the Greeks and others with shelves of Russian and Chinese texts. He could read in eleven languages. He talked, as we wanted him to, about the creation of the Jewish state and predicted that five million more emigrants would come. He was alert to current events—gratified by Nixon's visit to China—but feared the next war would be about oil and that Israel's own fight for survival would last for generations. Old age does not always bring serenity, but it evidently had for this thin-haired old prophet in sandals and open-necked shirt. He had no regrets about the past and no impatience with the future. Hadn't the Jews waited for centuries to return to their land? Why expect a less patient tomorrow?

The Dynasty. Composed for the photographer in the company's boardroom, with portraits of their father and grandfather: Benson, Henry, and William Clay Ford.

The most formidable of the Ford women: Eleanor and husband Edsel in the twenties, braving the cold winds on the Great Lakes.

THE FORD FAMILY

The Young Tycoons. Henry and Benson on the SS *Aquitania* on their first visit to Europe and their grandfather's growing dominions.

Tall in his first ambition. Henry with his grandparents, on the broad lawns of his parents' house in Grosse Pointe, upon being commissioned into the United States Naval Reserve.

Dear Henry –

Your letter came this morning, and am writing at once, to let you know how we feel about the news, we have loved you devotedly, since the day you were born and the girl you take for your life companion, will share in our love, we are all protestants and it will be strange to have a catholic in the family, but we will take it as we should, I have many friends who are Catholics, Father Coughlin

who is so disliked by so many we count among our friends, years ago, when your father was younger than you are, I thought of this same thing, and I decided that it would be right, be she catholic or protestant, all we wished was that he would love her, and that he would be happy, and I feel just the same about you, we want you to be happy, I do not remember having seen Anne, but your father and mother have told

us about her, they both love her, so am sure it will be all right, you were very sweet to write and tell us about it, and we will be very glad to see you both as soon as it is possible, we are not going south before the 10th of Feb, as Granddad has promised to be here for the first showing of the Edison Picture in Port Huron on 9th with all our love, dear Hens

Callie + Granddad

Blessings on a mixed marriage. One of the very few personal letters that Henry did not consign to the shredder.

THE SECRETARY OF THE NAVY
WASHINGTON
July 21, 1943

My dear Mr. Ford:

    I acknowledge your request of July 17, to be placed on inactive duty. I just forwarded your request to Admiral Denfeld of the Bureau of Personnel with the suggestion that this request of yours be granted. No doubt you will hear directly from the Bureau through the Commandant in the near future.

    I think the action you are taking is thoroughly justified and understandable, and that the services you will render as a private individual will surpass any work you could possibly do in your present position.

    I wish you all kinds of good luck.

Yours sincerely,

Frank Knox

Lieutenant Henry Ford II, USNR
Headquarters Ninth Naval District
Great Lakes, Illinois

"My dear *Mr.* Ford . . ." It was a letter Henry kept all his life, and when he was furnishing his house in England it was framed and given a place of honor in his bathroom.

The fourth generation comes of age. Henry and Anne with their children at Charlotte's twenty-first birthday party. Left to right: Anne, Charlotte, Edsel, Henry, and Anne.

Henry with his son, Edsel, and Edsel's wife, Cynthia.
Their son was inevitably christened Henry Ford III.

New car, new president.
Henry with Bunkie Knudsen and Arjay Miller.

Pupil and old master.
Henry with Ernie Breech,
who brought order to chaos.

THE MEN WHO RAN THE COMPANY

The one who went away. Henry Ford and Robert McNamara,
the whiz kid who was beckoned to Washington to march to a different drum.

French leave. Carl Levy, managing director of Ford France, Lee Iacocca, Philip Caldwell—later a brilliant chairman of the company—Bill Bourke, and the author at Arromanches during a break from a directors' inspection of the plant in Bordeaux.

He used to say Ford was a people company, and nobody walked more factory miles or met as many people as he did. Henry and fellow workers in Detroit.

Chairmen Three. Three of the four men who took Ford to the peak of its prosperity. Henry with Red Poling and Don Petersen, both of whom went on to become chairmen of Ford Motor Company.

The third lady. Henry and Kathleen Duross about to be married in a very quiet ceremony in Carson City, Nevada.

First marriage.
Henry and Anne McDonnell
on their wedding day.

THREE WEDDINGS

Second marriage. Henry and Cristina with witnesses on their wedding day.

JUST HENRY

First venture into management.
Henry at Yale, where he had just
become manager of the rowing crew.

A matter of destiny. Henry Ford II in the arms of his grandfather: the time is 11:58 A.M.
on May 17, 1920. Young Henry is two years and eight months old, and he has been given the honor
of starting the new blast furnace at the Rouge.

Reflection in a mirror. Kathleen Ford was—and is—never far from a camera; and Henry was a patient subject, even in what was otherwise a reflective sanctum.

Test driver. Henry at the wheel of a new European Ford car on the German test track. He had an eye for detail and a heavy right foot.

The moving finger. Golda Meir has a word for the wise in Tel Aviv.

With Detroit's long-serving mayor Coleman Young and Leonard Woodcock of the United Automobile Workers. They had Detroit in common.

TRAVELING MAN

LBJ and HFII. They were partners as well as friends, and Henry's regard for Lyndon Johnson was a prime cause of his continued votes for the Democrats.

The king who became an ally. With Juan Carlos in Valencia.

Illness kept Henry away from China when the first invitation was issued; but Deng Xiaoping came to see Ford operations in the United States, and Henry was able to repay his guest with a later visit to the People's Republic.

Old friends, new saddles. John and Joan Bugas with Henry and Kathy on the Bugases' ranch in Wyoming—the nearest, John used to say, anyone can get to Heaven.

PRIVATE MAN

Gentleman's dreamboat. The *Southern Breeze* at anchor off Nassau.

Henry rode horses in Wyoming with the Bugases and in England when he was at Turville Grange. He is shown here on a quail hunt at the home of his sister, Dodie.

Santa Maria II with Captain Ford on the bridge, cruising the Detroit River.

The Henley Ford. Henry on his way to do a little shopping at Henley-on-Thames in England, keeping resolutely to the left of the road.

Yes, it does sometimes happen to the men who make them. Henry with jack and flat tire on the road near Turville.

TURVILLE GRANGE

A man and his dog. Henry and Teal—who was a good gundog but spoiled with too much loving—taking tea together on the lawn at Turville Grange.

Turville Grange—a royal favorite's "dear, little house"—which belonged to Jackie Kennedy's sister, Lee, and her husband, Prince Radziwill, before Henry bought it as his home in England.

Kiss for a faithful servant.
The master of the house
bestows his blessing
on the butler,
Tomasz Szarek—
one more photo
from Kathy's private album.

The last portrait. It was taken by Kathy at Turville Grange in Henry's last months. He said it was true to life and made him look a lot better than he felt.

I stayed up that night and wrote a brief—and, I thought, comprehensive—report on the trip for Henry to give to the Policy Committee in Dearborn. It had been agreed with Boxenbaum and his partners in detailed business discussions that Ford of Britain would ship components to the Israeli Automobile Corporation (as it was now called) for assembly in Nazareth. Henry was not convinced the agreement would make economic sense for Israel or Ford, but he was not prepared to have anybody stop him from carrying on the nonpolitical everyday business of the Ford Motor Company. There was to be no direct Ford investment in Israel, and he had come to that decision because it did not make economic sense; politics had nothing to do with it. He read without comment the section in which I expressed the opinion that Ford would nevertheless be placed on the Arab boycott because the Arabs could not be expected to see the difference between investment and supply. The cars would still carry the Ford oval. And six weeks later it was. The boycott office in Baghdad said Ford was now included among those companies with which Arab states could not do business, and it was fifteen years before the boycott was lifted. By then the fluctuations in the Israeli shekel and the heavy duties that remained, even on components, had brought the boxes from Britain to an end, and Boxenbaum had to rely on components made in his own besieged country.

I was more than ready to go home but still not able to do so. We took an El Al Boeing 747 to Paris for a meeting on the Philco-Ford plant at Bergamo, which was losing money and having difficulty surviving. Henry slept for a couple of hours on the plane and read Yadin's book on the Dead Sea Scrolls. There were briefcases piled high in the Plaza d'Athénée suite when we got to Paris. He was never out of touch with Dearborn, and the papers never stopped. The agenda for the March meeting of the board of directors—Ford has no board meeting in February—was packed full as usual, and the backup papers were two inches thick. He held them in his hands late at night and asked me a question that was an echo of one he was asking himself. What did I think his role in the company ought to be in the future? I said he was the chairman, the father of his family, the third generation of the automotive dynasty; what choice did he have? He stuffed the papers back into one of the cases. He said he could still choose to be what he wanted to be, and I said he was dreaming. He liked the word and repeated it; it was no bad thing to dream occasionally. What, for example, should the Ford Motor Company be, where should it invest, who should run it? I said he was only fifty-five, no age to be thinking of inaction, and he insisted that retirement was not seriously on his mind as something that would happen soon. He would like more time to himself, time—as he put it—to live a little. In any event he would have to die one day, and others, and probably men from outside the family, would have to run it. These were the things on his mind, and they required a lot of thought. I rose to go, and he said he had one last request: Would I write a memorandum for him on the subject? I said I wouldn't dream of doing such a thing. "It's only for me," he said. "It would help me to think."

I went back to England and picked up my wife, who said this was not what was called living, and took her to Marbella, where the European motoring writers were now gathering to drive the new British Zephyr and Zodiac, which had been shown first to the dealers in January. They were publicly unveiled at the March Geneva Show, and I went there, too, to discover among other things that Princess Anne had told Jackie Stewart she wanted to drive his Grand Prix car. On April 20 at Silverstone—surrounded by some very complex secrecy—she did. I went to Ireland for a car introduction and was not very surprised to get pneumonia for my birthday, the first time I had ever been ill. Henry called from Dearborn when I was walking wounded again and said his mother was coming to England and would I rent her a dog because she liked to have a dog about the place and the rented house was without one. I had never hired a dog before, but it proved not too difficult. I went to Monte Carlo for one Grand Prix and Spain for another and came back to pay attention—as my wife put it—to my family, dining with my son's housemaster, watching both boys in a school performance of *Julius Caesar*, worried how well one of them would do in a cricket match against Eton, planned an extension to the house—since I was running out of space for my books—and then took my sons to Le Mans, where—GT40 days long past—we were running some Capris in the production class. It was still only June.

In July I went to Southern Rhodesia because Dearborn had asked me to see if I could discover what was going on there. Ford had a small but highly efficient factory in Salisbury and was the principal marque in the country when UN sanctions were imposed and we closed it down. The political diktat threw fifteen hundred blacks out of work, but the company was always scrupulous in following the letter of other people's laws. There had nevertheless been rumors that the Rhodesians had found a back-door method of resuming production. I tried to discover just what was going on the polite way and spent a couple of days trying to be subtle. Eventually I decided that the best way to find out was to walk into the factory and see for myself. James Bond wouldn't have hesitated; I did but need not have been so timid, for I found myself welcomed with broad black smiles and urgent entreaties from the small group of white managers to bring Ford back as soon as possible. They were assembling Alfa Romeos, Fiats, and Renaults with about three hundred employees, but I never did discover where the sanction-busting components came from.

Salisbury was dead, and the white residents were unable or unwilling to understand why the world chose to misunderstand them. It was the only country in Africa where blacks and whites attended the same university, and the other blacks, they said, were being "brought along" as fast as any reasonable human being could expect. The worst thing about Salisbury, however, was not its insularity but the fact that nobody laughed all the time I was there. Sanctions were not biting deep enough radically to alter (or threaten) the whites' way of life. Tobacco and other exports still found their way out of the country, albeit at a reduced price, and a regular airlift ferried Rhodesian steaks to eager customers in Switzerland and other countries who were not going to let sanctions change their lives. The only sympathetic person I met was a game warden from the park near the Victoria Falls who said that if the poachers were not stopped, there would soon be no wild animals left anywhere in Africa, and when I got home and summer had arrived, I emptied my bank of its balance and took the entire family to Kenya—the last magical country on earth—and hired an aircraft for what I was beginning to think of as the last safari. Henry was enormously envious and later went there himself, growing a beard and looking extraordinarily like Ernest Hemingway, even—despite the admonitions against the shooting—bagging a lion. At that period in 1972, however, he had other things in his sights.

The B car project, which was certainly conceptually on track, was gathering momentum, and the continuing success of the British Mini, which had been introduced in August 1959 and was by now creating a new awareness that small was beautiful as well as functional, was ever more evident on the British roads and in Continental Europe, too. At one of the European management meetings Lee Iacocca had given a bravura performance to the top seventy-five members of Ford's European management and talked for sixty-three minutes. He had a talent for bringing audiences to their feet, although his rallying calls were not always appreciated for their sensitivity. At a Claridges meeting he told the managing group, "There are only ten chargers among you," but went on to say, "What the hell, I'd hate to have seventy-five people like me!" The truth was that there were a lot of chargers in the European operations and no lack of individualists. The B car program had started with a group that had bypassed all normal company procedures and was prepared to "buck the system" any way it could to bring a small car to market. It was more than prepared to charge but not in every direction; nor did it want to leave the valley littered with the bodies of horses or flog them to death. The Mini had been introduced by the British Motor Corporation (BMC); but the detailed financial analysis of the kind Arjay Miller had demanded for the Mustang had not been done, and it was widely believed that BMC was making a profit of no more than £15 a car. The Ford B car group believed that, apart from the lack of basic financial planning, the Mini had been priced too low on introduction and was convinced BMC was probably losing money on every one that was built. This analysis—revealing as it was of a competitor's discomfort—was no cause for celebration. The Mini was alive and well, and its uneconomic selling price, bad though it was for BMC, had conditioned car buyers to such an extent that Ford had no choice but to match it and yet be profitable. The B car would demand a larger investment than any European Ford so far because the car itself and every component in it had to be new. There was no set of existing mechanical components that could be used. The smallest available engine might be converted for marriage with a transaxle, but it would still have to be made smaller.

The October management review of the program was certainly going to be crucial, and Henry Ford II knew it as well as anybody. I had had little contact with him since my departure on holiday, but the introspection evident in Paris—nourished, I dared to believe, by the memorandum on his future, which I had, after all, duly completed and dispatched—had taken him farther than I anticipated. In July 1972 Philip Caldwell was appointed chairman of Ford of Europe; Bill Bourke was summoned from Australia as president; and Harold Poling was appointed, three months later, as director of finance. They were the three most talented and accomplished executives Ford had ever enjoyed in Europe, and their posting was the single most prescient and daring management move Henry had made since Breech and the Whiz Kids.

The development of American business overseas was much less vigorous than is often imagined and was not really significant until after the Second World War. Professor Mira Wilkins, a distinguished and pertinent American historian—who worked on a history of the Ford Motor Company with Allan Nevins and Frank Ernest Hill—once pointed out that "it was counted a proud achievement when the first American manufactures (the Singer sewing machine, the Yale locks, the McCormick reapers and mowers) were exported in quantity to Europe." But the impetus that made these American products household names in many different languages often came from European entrepreneurs and distributors who had ready-made markets for ready-made goods. The war, however, brought battalions of uniformed Americans to Europe, and the Marshall Plan itself was administered largely by men with business experience. By 1961 more than three thousand U.S. companies were doing business abroad but only a handful—and few of their executives—had any real familiarity, or experience of, working on the other side of the Atlantic. For one thing, there was no economic imperative to force U.S. companies into the export business. The enormous domestic market in North America was readily able to absorb its own manufactured goods, and the only surpluses that necessitated sales overseas were those for agricultural products. The Britain that was made bankrupt by the war—in common with the other shattered economies of Europe—was forced to export to obtain foreign currency, and there was a time when the quickest way to the House of Lords for any company chairman was through prowess in foreign markets.

There had, of course, been Americans in Paris for 150 years, from the time of Benjamin Franklin, before the Lost Generation, as Gertrude Stein called it, invaded the Left Bank in the twenties, but their commerce was art and literature. The business executive felt with some justification that he was going to be a lot safer at home. Young men on the lower rungs of corporate ladders were only too eager to step into the offices of those who were sent abroad out of sight and mind and fearing to be passed by in the race for promotion; many, it has to be said, who crossed the Atlantic found it was indeed a longer journey home and sometimes there were no jobs awaiting them. This state of affairs was partly due to the fact that the brightest and best resisted deportation—which was frequently the way they saw it—and only the second-class citizens had to submit. Few of them spoke any language but their own, and they were apprehensive, as were their families, of strange places, habits, and customs. One American in Europe, who once brought a group of executives to France from a Ford subsidiary in the United States, told me ruefully: "My gang only feels safe in the hotel. They think the Red Indians begin at the end of the Champs-Élysées."

Henry Ford II knew that for a variety of urgent reasons, he had to change these attitudes within the Ford Motor Company from the top to the bottom. The time was fast approaching when half the automotive business of the company would be transacted outside the United States, and his apprehensions about the state of America persuaded him that the balance might shift farther. He was now convinced that the B car could be made to happen. He knew, too, that a new commonality was coming to the world of the motorcar, and what was good for Boston, England, was also likely to appeal to Boston, Massachusetts. He felt that technical innovation and new approaches to car design were more to be expected from Europe rather than America. And he knew, he said, in his bones that Philip Caldwell, William O. Bourke, and Harold A. Poling were the men to prove him right.

Apart from their unquestioned ability, Ford of Europe's new ruling triumvirate had one other thing in common: None of them had been born with any special privileges, two had lost fathers at an early age, and all had to work their way through college and company to their present positions in the hierarchy. Caldwell was fifty-two years of age and had been the highest-ranking civilian in the U.S. Navy during the war, responsible for a vast and complicated supply network for American forces in the Pacific. He had joined the company in 1953 as manager of its procurement planning department, bringing his considerable naval expertise to Ford at a crucial time in its history. By 1972, he had enormous experience of the science of automobile production, having worked in Engineering as administration manager and in Parts as assistant general manager, and as vice-president and general manager of Trucks he had made Ford's commercial vehicle operation into the most profitable group in the company, completely transforming the market appeal and integrity of its products. When the Philco-Ford Corporation ran into trouble in the cutthroat market for washing machines, refrigerators, and radio and television sets, he was posted to its headquarters in Philadelphia and calmed its troubled waters, saving from the storm a so-called aeronutronic division that went on to become Ford Aerospace—a world leader in the production of communications satellites and the communications mastermind behind the U.S. space program. He had then become responsible for all Ford's U.S. manufacturing. None of these jobs had he held for long, and this, in a sense, was the measure of the man; he could get things done quickly. In person, he was lean and precise, immaculate in dress, contentedly married with three children to a wife who had been the eleventh child in her family. He had a private passion for early American furniture and collected wisely and with deliberation.

He was something of a tyrant to work for in that he never seemed to have enough information on any subject and would force his executives down to the tunnels of the earth to excavate the facts and figures with which he would deliberately come to his own conclusion. "I know I make you mad," he once said to me when I was doing something for the umpteenth time, "but it is the only way I can work," and I came to see the method behind his insatiable appetite for knowledge.

Harold Poling was called Red because his hair was rust, but he, too, was a well-oiled working machine. He had joined the company in 1951 from Indiana University with an M.B.A. in his knapsack as a cost analyst in the Steel Division and had gone on to various finance assignments in the Transmission and Chassis Division and the Engine and Foundry Division, ending up as controller of the entire Product Development Group, in which position he revolutionized the time-wasting business of model changeover, eliminating much of the complexity and shrinking the time between the phaseout of one model and the introduction of another. Just before his appointment to Europe he had been given a grandfather clock for being the most valuable executive in North America, and I had an idea at the time that it would always be right—to the second.

There wasn't one surplus ounce of fat in his body. He was a scratch golfer and did his daily dozen, as we used to say, with the observance of a monk. We built a gymnasium on the top floor of the Brentwood offices in England, where Ford of Europe had its headquarters, and he played squash there each lunchtime with a young butler from the penthouse dining room. One floor below, in his office, he spread the gospel of financial responsibility with a frugal regard for the consequence, and I fought many guerrilla campaigns against him over my share of the cake and felt victorious when we broke even. I work best when I feel free and left alone with my own ideas, but I enjoyed working with all three men, within the disciplines they brought to us, and found that I was not denied my freedom.

With Caldwell's command of detail, Bourke's unquestioned flair for product and selling, and Poling to keep the score, Henry Ford II thought he could look forward to great happenings and fast progress, and as it turned out, he was right in his expectations. Caldwell hauled down the Stars and Stripes and ran up his own European flag the day he was appointed. Called to a meeting in Dearborn by Lee Iacocca, he said he could not afford the fare, and what's more, he hadn't the time to spare. He telephoned Henry Ford II and said that if he was going to run Europe, he was going to run it from Europe and meetings with top U.S. management should also take place there. I had recently persuaded Henry to buy a Georgian town house in Mayfair as a London office. He had lovingly overseen its restoration and chosen every piece of furniture and equipment down to the cutlery, and it was never difficult to persuade him to come to London. So began a routine, which continues to this day, of three management meetings a year, with deliberations in the design and engineering centers in Britain and Germany, and it is probable that nothing ever gave Philip Caldwell a more certain feeling about the support he would have in getting things done.

The B car program was accelerated, as it began to make more and more sense, and emissaries were sent to travel Europe and prospect for sites upon which new factories might be built. Spain was a hinge to the enterprise, and we went to look at places in Algeciras, Pamplona, Barcelona, and Valencia. At a private meeting with French President Georges Pompidou in the Élysée Palace in Paris, Henry promised that Ford would build a new plant in France, where it no longer had a manufacturing presence. It was necessary to look outside Britain, for in those years of full employment we were running out of people and the German factories were kept working only by the continued employment of thousands of "guest workers," who were brought up from Turkey in Boeing 747s and lodged in company apartments and living quarters. Spain had people in abundance, but there were some political concerns. General Franco was an old man, and his body could hardly support his advancing years. What sort of transition could be expected, and what sort of environment could we anticipate from a new and presumably democratic government? I wrote a report on the subject prophesying an orderly and even expansive future for the country and for Ford, which was added to all the other plans and predictions.

In November I spent a week in Madrid with Henry and Philip Caldwell, since the October meeting had decided that the B car program was ready to be blessed and submitted to the board of directors. Some concerns remained, and Lee Iacocca and Philip Caldwell decided that the last remaining doubts could be removed only by Henry himself in discussions at the highest level in the Spanish capital. "I am beginning to like it down here," Henry said as we arrived. "I've got a good feeling about the place." We went to the Jockey restaurant the night before we came home, and Caldwell, who did not drink, watched us dispose of three bottles of wine. "I hope," he said, halfway through the third bottle, "that you know what you are doing." I said I thought I did. That year I had had a lot of practice.

CHAPTER SIX

The Younger Statesman

H enry Hamill Fowler sat in his wooden house overlooking the sweep of New England's Pleasant Bay and said with due consideration that if you were asked to name the business statesman of his time, you would have to nominate Henry Ford II. And his time goes back a long way. He was born on September 5, 1908; one day earlier, and he would have shared his birthday as well as his christian name with Henry Ford, although nobody—not even his wife, Trudye—had ever called him anything other than Joe. The nickname derives from his days at Roanoke College in the twenties, when the favorite student rendezvous was a restaurant run by two Greeks who spoke little English and found it difficult to remember or pronounce the names of their young customers. They called everybody Joe, and when Henry Fowler entered Yale University, he carried on the tradition; since everybody was Joe to him, he was soon Joe to everybody, and the familiarity has a proper sound to it, for Joe Fowler is a small, bright-eyed, bow-tied Democrat who makes friends easily and enemies not at all. He is one of that rare breed of dedicated public servants who now seem virtually extinct. He was appointed counsel to the Tennessee Valley Authority by Franklin Roosevelt in 1934 and rose to become undersecretary and secretary of the United States treasury for John Kennedy and Lyndon Johnson.

When Kennedy was elected president of the United States on November 8, 1960, the American economy was sliding into its third recession in six years. At the end of the Second World War, the productive capacity of the United States was larger than that of the rest of the world combined. Some 52 percent of the gross national product emanated from America, although this state of affairs was, to some extent, a consequence of weakness overseas rather than bold management in America. Jack Kennedy brought no special talent for economics to the White House, but he learned a lot on the job and quickly. He immediately tried to stimulate the economy with a 1961 bill that increased depreciation allowances and introduced a new device for investment tax credits. Both moves were intended to encourage investment in plants and equipment. Unfortunately he was diverted from domestic affairs by a disastrous summit meeting with Premier Nikita Khrushchev in Paris at which the Russian leader threatened to hand over Berlin to the East Germans, and Joe Fowler, the principal evangelist of tax reform, was shuffled off to Europe with Secretary of State Dean Rusk to plan political and economic countermeasures against this threat.

Kennedy ran into a Berlin Wall of his own making at home the following year. A confrontation with the steel companies over prices threw the stock market into panic, increasing the fears of the many businessmen who were already suspicious of the Kennedy administration. The White House decided to respond with a "quickie" tax cut, and the president made a speech in the late summer arguing that taxes were too high and a burden upon corporations and individuals. There was little doubt that taxes were indeed too high. The Korean War had run up the highest marginal tax rate on personal incomes to 90 percent, and the corporate rate was 52 percent.

Joe Fowler and the Treasury argued against quick fixes, demanding instead a permanent modification of the tax system, although they were only too well aware that this would be difficult to achieve. The Ways and Means Committee of the House of Representatives and the Senate Finance Committee were resolutely opposed. Their opposition may seem difficult to understand against the background of our present experience; Ronald Reagan, Margaret Thatcher, and Helmut Kohl all have been standard-bearers in the cause of low-tax economies, and we have become as used to their arguments as we have to the apparent inevitability of budget deficits. The accepted American wisdom of the sixties, however, was different. At that time the United States had a deficit on its internal account of between $5 and $6 billion, which seemed huge at the time, and Congress found it hard to understand how Kennedy could think of reducing taxes in a major fashion and remaining fiscally responsible. It is an argument that is still in fashion.

Kennedy decided that he needed allies to carry his crusade forward and invited Henry Ford II to the White House, where he asked him to accept the chairmanship of a new Business Committee for Tax Reduction. He told Henry that he had "the name most people recognized" and felt that if the young Mr. Ford could be persuaded to campaign for this apparently daring initiative, the battle might be won. Henry accepted the chairmanship; his friend Sidney Weinberg of Goldman, Sachs was co-opted along with six or seven others to serve on the committee, and they got down to work. It soon became apparent to Henry that the appointment was no sinecure, and work was indeed the nature of his assignment. Even among businessmen there was opposition. The railroads and the steel industry were generally in favor, but many other influential business leaders were as worried as Congress by the probable consequences of even larger budget deficits. The Cuban missile crisis that fall added to their apprehensions.

Henry began to see that he would convince his colleagues in the business establishment only if he could prove that tax cuts would not plunge the country deeper into the red, and he therefore argued that the tax proposals had to go hand in hand with a balanced budget. If they were combined with a promise to reduce government spending, he felt confident of bringing American business to the party. He was soon able to reinforce his argument by additional recruits to his committee, which was soon three hundred strong. This group met for luncheon at a hotel in Washington, where the president argued his case but was tragically denied the chance to fulfill his campaign pledge to "get the country moving again." In November 1963 he was shot and killed in Dallas, leaving much unfinished business in the empty office that was now to be occupied by Lyndon Johnson.

The day after the assassination Johnson came back to Washington, and Joe Fowler sent him a memorandum describing the continuing deadlock with the Senate Finance Committee and adding his belief that Henry's committee was beginning to make substantial progress. Henry had a good relationship with LBJ, which developed into something much warmer under the pressure of their common interests. "He was," Henry once told me, "the last president I was on close terms with and the only one with whom I could talk man to man and feel I was being understood." Liking him as a president and a man, Henry increased his efforts, and the Business Committee for Tax Reduction grew to have three thousand members, all of whom declared themselves for a tax cut and willing to lobby their own representatives.

In January 1964 Johnson brought in a budget which was below $100 billion—the magic figure—and wore it as a badge of his commitment to control government spending. The bill passed the Senate and became law the following month. The top rate of tax came down to 65 percent, the lowest to 14 percent, and the United States went on to enjoy what Joe Fowler recalls as "six years of halcyon growth." When I sat in Joe's parlor a few days before his eightieth birthday—when he was long retired—and refought these battles of long ago, he said: "Henry was the only thing that got it through. Without him we'd have been sunk. The Senate committee was a real bloodbath. And I'm not sure we'd ever have gotten it through the House if it had not been for Henry's insistence upon a hold on spending." Johnson never forgot his debt. "The last time I saw them together," Joe said, "was in 1971 or 1972, a couple of years before LBJ died. They were at the Johnson ranch together with five or six other people. Henry had found a Model T and sent it down there, and we went out and rode in it for half an hour. I think it's still there." Henry never sought to dramatize or elevate his own role in these affairs of state. He would insist that he had a lot of "good guys" with him. Some had been seconded from the Ford Motor Company to provide staff support. Both Kennedy and Johnson were reinforced by some fine minds in the Treasury, who were themselves committed to tax reform, and when Ronald Reagan in more recent years began his own tax reduction campaign, he reminded people that he was not the first president to embark on the policy; Kennedy had been there before him.

But there was a larger significance to Henry's learning steps in the corridors and smoke-filled rooms of power. Together with his easy and intimate relationship with Lyndon and Lady Bird Johnson—a person of some consequence in her own right—they gave him in his mid-forties a postgraduate course in the ways of government and its functions.

Henry was not new to Washington. In August 1953, the month of the Korean War armistice, Eisenhower, the only other president with whom Henry had an understanding, appointed him an alternate United States delegate to the United Nations. Henry accepted the six-month assignment without hesitation, knowing—as he told me later—he was "naive as hell" in these matters but anxious for every new experience that might advance his understanding of the world beyond Detroit.

The appointment was not without challenge. His first duty was to explain United States policy to the UN Committee on Technical Assistance, and the following month—on Thanksgiving Day—he found himself saddled with an impromptu rebuttal of an attack on America's peacetime policies emanating from no less a polemicist than Andrei

Vyshinsky, the Soviet deputy foreign minister. Vyshinsky had asserted that the United States was happier with a war economy since there was more money in guns than butter and that a reduction in defense expenditure would bring about economic collapse.

Henry summoned up a vigorous off-the-cuff response. "The U.S. businessman would much prefer to have a full peacetime economy," he insisted, "if for no other reason than he can make more money and the U.S. businessman is in business to make money." He thought the federal government could put more money into the building of schools and roads, "which I am personally in favor of because it will help my business." The exchange gathered few headlines and drew little comment, but the fact he had let nobody down was, for Henry, reward enough. He was not permitted to bring helpers or advisers with him to Washington and, at times, felt very much on his own. He nevertheless grew in confidence and was brave enough to tell John Foster Dulles that Red China should be admitted to the United Nations and confess he was looking forward to the day when Ford could sell its products in Moscow.

He was a pragmatist in politics. At one of the meetings of the Technical Assistance Committee he had a tailor-made platform to translate his own views into American policy. "We are not interested," he said, "in exploiting anybody. We are interested in the mutual advantage which flows from an unfettered exchange of skills, goods, and ideas with other peoples. This is neither altruism nor imperialism—it is simply enlightened self-interest." Henry truly believed what he forcibly expressed on this occasion: that the technical assistance program of the UN and the activities of its agencies—UNESCO and UNRRA, for example—accounted for eight-tenths of the UN iceberg and, although often submerged from public view, provided the broad base of international cooperation. "To millions of people who never hear of political debates," he said, "these activities are the United Nations and upon these grassroots functions the United Nations may stand or fall. The world needs the best skills it can get"—and there spoke the maker of motorcars.

In November 1961 Henry had his first chance to address the General Assembly when he presided at the dedication of its new library. His previous experience, and the fact that the Ford Foundation had provided $6 million to make it possible, made him the obvious and tactful choice. UN Secretary-Generals Trygve Lie and Dag Hammarskjöld lobbied hard for the benefaction, and Henry was in agreement because at that stage he believed the UN was not just "an inconclusive debating society."

I have friends in Washington who began to believe at this time—and later, when he was involved in the tax committee for Lyndon Johnson—that Henry was seriously contemplating a political career or, at least, seeking a larger role in the affairs of the United States. Some did see him as an emerging younger statesman. But they didn't know Henry, and he, as ever, chose not to let them know him. He had given his heart and his life to the service of only one country, and it was called Ford. And it was to Ford that his increasing store of knowledge would be applied.

His friendship with the Johnsons endured until Lyndon Johnson's death. It gave him the opportunity to take off his jacket in the White House—and wander in jeans on the Johnson ranch—and from this privileged standpoint he increasingly saw the bleaker side of political authority and shed most of his remaining political illusions. Coming back from one trip there, Henry told me bluntly: "He has less power than I have."

There is some evidence of his regard for the Johnsons—and theirs for him—in the letters Lady Bird wrote in 1972 and after January 22, 1973, when Johnson died of a heart attack in Texas. On December 15, 1972, four years after her husband had vacated the White House to Richard Nixon, she wrote:

1972 has been—in an odd, inverted sort of way—a wonderful year for us. It began gloriously with a long month on the sunny coast of Mexico. We settled in quietly at the ranch, and I've got to say, surprisingly, it turned out to be a beautiful time—lots of sitting under the live oaks in the front yard, driving around the ranch to see the deer, antelope, crops, improvements—sometimes picnics and boating over at Lake L.B.J. I think of it as the summer of our sweet content (apologies to Steinbeck). The wildflowers were never more glorious, in fact everything in nature flourished.

Lyndon Johnson had had a severe heart attack in April; but he had got over it, and Lady Bird looked optimistically to the future. "Now Lyndon is feeling better each week, and it seems we are once more stepping up the pace—football games on the weekends, and even one fantastic 'Cinderella Ball,' all glitter and glamour—and now, just ended, the Civil Rights Symposium here at the L.B.J. library, a crescendo of work and reminiscences with old friends." Having signed the letter "Fondly Lady Bird," she added in handwriting: "We hope to see you in '73. Our 1912 Ford sits in the L.B.J. library and draws the eager interest of young and old."

Two months later she was writing again after her husband's death.

Dear Henry,

It was dear comfort to read your handwritten note. Your name has been threaded through our lives over the years, and always it was woven into a fine tapestry of appreciation and achievement. Lyndon so much admired you for your patriotism and was enduringly grateful for your support. And, some of our happiest memories were of the times we spent with you and Cristina at the White House and at the Ranch. Though I am quite sure that at sometime in the future his loss will come crashing down on me in deep sadness, for now my thought is one of appreciation for the thirty-eight years we shared. He had sixty-four years of accomplishment and a life that was rich in the fullness of its days. They would have been less, however, without the strength and friendship of those who were his partners in his trials and his triumphs. I am so proud—as I know Lyndon was—that your heart and your help were his for a while.

It was one of the few letters Henry kept into his last years.

<hr>

The year 1972 had been wonderful not only for the Johnsons but for the Ford Motor Company, too. During the twelve months the company had sales in excess of $20 billion—having produced 5,702,000 cars and trucks—and a return on assets of 8 percent. There was a world market of 32 million cars and commercial vehicles. These were by no means the statistics of disaster. Yet Henry was uneasy. He was impatient with the time it took to get things done and critical of what he called short-terming—the superficial, or Band-Aid, approach to both problems and opportunities. He had been surprised in Washington by the insularity of many American leaders in business and politics, and he thought Washington a dangerously introspective town. His restless travels overseas gave him access to both ends of the American telescope. He began to believe that the system, which allowed American presidents only two terms of four years apiece, was no way to run so large a railroad. The first year was devoted to learning, and the last to campaigning for reelection. A second term was really only one of three years since the last twelve months in office reduced the president to a lame duck. He sat with friends in Washington and wondered what hope the United States would have of changing to a system of one six-year presidential term; this, he believed, would encourage longer-term planning. He was sure his own company was suffering from the failure to look far enough into the future and doubted if enough attention was being paid to the basics of the business and the fundamentals of its future prosperity. He began to see with increasing clarity that politicians would seek to shrug off their own responsibility for the management of social change and the growing demands of a television electorate—within Marshall McLuhan's global village—by demanding more of business. The trip to Israel had reinforced his concern about oil—Golda Meir would have convinced the most myopic optimist—and the probing in which he engaged with government leaders on his various journeys convinced him the time had come to sound the alarm within his own company and force some urgent consideration upon everything from cabbages to oil kingdoms. "I don't think we're together," he said, "on the big things."

In February 1973, therefore, he summoned Ford's worldwide management to Boca Raton in Florida for a management conference intended to open eyes and ears and initiate some action. Boca Raton is an enormous hotel and conference center on one of Florida's inland waterways, a fishing line or two away from the ocean. It is one of corporate America's favorite convention centers since it is possible to temper the weightier affairs of business with the lighter pastimes of golf and tennis, swimming in big clean pools, or hunting for wahoo and kingfish in the deep waters offshore. Lee Iacocca had an apartment in one of the high-rise condominiums nearby. When I arrived from London, Henry was putting the finishing touches to a state-of-the-company address, over which he had been laboring for some time, using a thick felt-tipped pen to underline in red the more emphatic arguments in the text.

When he delivered the speech, raising his eyes from the podium and peering over his half-frame spectacles as if to be sure of an attentive audience, he left no doubt about the number or complexity of items on his agenda. He ticked them off one by one, listing the problems and suggesting remedies: The steady growth of government regulation throughout the world would be demanding of time and money but would require timely and responsible reaction; it was therefore necessary to anticipate sooner and more intelligently. There would be environmental pressures, wider anxieties about vehicle and highway safety, restrictions in the use of cars, and the voice of the consumer—individually and in pressure groups—would get louder. He elaborated his concern for sensible "human engineering," a phrase he began to use in the forties—perhaps echoing Walter Reuther—and talked about the changing expectations and character of people at every level in the company, urging a sustained effort to promote more women and blacks into management. He had no doubt that there would be an energy crisis of sorts and predicted gasoline rationing and the prospect of its price rising to $1 a gallon in the United States by 1980; overseas car owners were already paying substantially more than that. Everything pointed to an enhanced demand for cleaner, quieter, safer, and more efficient vehicles of all kinds, and he predicted that half the U.S. market would be represented by small cars within six or seven years.

It was not the speech of a pessimist; he could see opportunities for growth and achievement particularly outside the United States but also within provided that management came to grips with its problems and had the foresight to deal with them in a timely fashion. I thought it an incisive performance although, in my opinion, he never spoke best from a prepared text. There was more wit and mischief in his delivery when he spoke off the cuff, but if he wanted to be certain nothing would be left out, he invariably stuck faithfully to his script. And on this occasion he was determined to be comprehensive. Ford, he said, had to be innovative in engineering new products and in the processes which produced them, and there had to be new families of engines before the end of the decade. Old recipes and warmed-up dishes would not provide sufficient nourishment. He called for greater and more intelligent use of Ford's international resources, including less duplication, more common products, and a closer relationship with suppliers. "Personal mobility is our principal product," he said, "and if we do not find ways of making better products, our competitors will. We must have more respect for new ideas and less for tradition. We must not become victims of change; we must capitalize upon it." And where people were concerned, social responsibility was not enough. Social responsiveness had to be the order of the day.

Henry Ford II never said anything he did not believe—in public or private—but sometimes he could be as wrong as the rest of us, and he was wrong about one thing during this address. He was concerned about the state of America's balance of payments. The net inflow, or "positive balance," was $300 million in 1968, he recalled—perhaps with some sense of personal remembrance and satisfaction—but in 1972 the situation had reversed, and there was a net outflow of the same amount. This, he insisted, would require more care in committing the company to programs involving the importation of cars or components, and I thought this an interesting sidelight on his continuing conviction that the cars America bought should be built in America. He was resolute on this issue and angrily refused even to buy Japanese steel. He denied Lee Iacocca the opportunity for a liaison with Honda when that company was merely emerging as a car producer. He later changed his mind about joint ventures with Japanese companies, but his view of life, as it was expressed in Boca Raton, persuaded the company's senior management, I believe, not to think seriously enough about the coming invasion from Japan.

Perhaps it would be more precise to say it was one reason. It was not the only one, for Boca Raton in 1973 was a world conference in name but still remarkably insular in reality. Overseas executives—some of whom had crossed datelines and taken days to get there—felt that they were guests at a strictly American happening and that too many of their Detroit colleagues still had a modest appreciation of the nature of Ford beyond the boundaries of their own country. There was another participant in the conference, whose contribution persuaded me that Americans' excessive reverence for market research and the punditry of the pollster may also have been a factor in the state of their unreadiness for the unrevealed future. Lou Harris was a guest of honor at the conference, and Mr. Harris was one of America's most respected opinion research gurus, but it seemed to me then—as it has, subsequently—that his kind of expertise can be dangerous since its conclusions are so often based on what people think as a result of their past experience.

When I was responsible for the organization of a later Boca Raton conference, I invited a brilliant young pollster who had played a major part in Ronald Reagan's election as president, and he was able to show with accuracy why the majority of Americans had voted his ticket to the White House. But neither he nor any of his brethren could have predicted the success or failure of any candidate—known or unknown—for the election four years ahead. Yet that is what the car business is about, and many other businesses, too, and although there is said to be safety in numbers, I have often thought that there is no daring to be found there. It was fortunate for the Ford Motor Company, at this time, that its chairman had considerably more vision in the seat of his pants than all but a handful of others in the industry and that other people at Ford were prepared to fight for their own convictions, for the most daring initiative in the company's history was about to be taken, and the world into which it was adventuring would demand confidence in the future rather than comfort from the past.

For the first time at any world management meeting, a number of new and still-unborn cars, including the Pinto, were on display at Boca Raton for inspection and comment, but the only project the European contingent wanted to talk about was the B car, which was now endowed with a code name and called Bobcat.

The B car initiative had come a long way since the small Ford of Europe task force in Britain had started it off. Lee Iacocca had appointed Hal Sperlich, a product planner he also regarded as a "charger," to accelerate the studies and see if it could be made to happen. Philip Caldwell and Bill Bourke were as keen to bring the idea to reality as anybody, but both knew the immediate need was for a new Escort, a modern version of the smallest Ford offered in Europe and a proven success in the market. They were happy to see American resources engaged in the B car but had to put Escort first. They were also beginning to believe they could add Spain to their own part of the empire with or without a B car. Caldwell kept his top European group at long meetings in the Brentwood boardroom, some of which lasted— without break and often without refreshment—all day and finally produced to his own satisfaction a program code-named Eagle for a Ford factory in Spain employing initially sixty-three hundred people—rising to seventy-six hundred—to lift European capacity to a level where the company could expect a commanding share of the European market. He presented the program to the Policy Committee in Dearborn in September 1972 and came away well pleased and with approval to take it farther.

In October Hal Sperlich showed Henry and Lee three full-size models of the B car for what he now called the Bobcat program and was given $1.3 million to spend on what I still believe to be the most thorough "ask-the-customer" program ever undertaken. One of the models had been designed in the company's Ghia studios in Turin, Italy, and the other two had come from Gene Bordinat, the design *supremo* of the Mustang. They were sent by air to the Palais de Beaulieu in Lausanne, Switzerland—a deliberately neutral environment—and seven hundred men and women volunteers from Paris, London, Milan, Düsseldorf, and Madrid—in roughly equal numbers from each country—were flown to Geneva, bussed to Lausanne, and asked what they thought about the models. Four existing B cars, made by Fiat, Peugeot, Renault, and Honda, were painted the same anonymous off-white, and over two weekends the jury of seven hundred considered the seven cars, inside and out, and said what they liked and did not like, after which they went home entertained and rewarded. When this exercise was over, the three Ford models were flown to San Mateo in California and matched with an assortment of small American and Japanese cars

and submitted to seven hundred Americans. After that they went to
Brazil. The research showed beyond any doubt what car buyers said they
wanted. It did not prove that Ford could provide it.

Philip Caldwell and Bill Bourke stayed close to the work that was
being done on the car but were preoccupied with their own research into
Spain. Dick Holmes, a big, burly, effervescent American who was in
charge of business development for Ford of Europe, had been told to
apply himself specifically to the task of making Spain happen, and he
began to commute in a Hawker Siddeley 125 from Stansted to Madrid
and other Spanish landing places and, in the company of a Spanish
government official named Carlos Pérez de Bricio—who became something of an intimate with Henry Ford II—to call upon ministers,
mayors, and lesser dignitaries in pursuit of acres and acquiescence.
Spain at that time was closed to foreign goods of many kinds; if they were
not specifically banned, they were effectively so as a result of prohibitive
customs or other duties, and this was one of the first barriers Holmes had
to remove. He made good progress; on December 7 the Spanish government published a decree (which is known as the Ford decree but was
applicable to any other manufacturer who was interested) insisting on 66
percent local content but substantially lowering customs rates and duties
on imports of machinery and components. It made obvious economic
sense to Dick Holmes, but it was every bit as advantageous to the
government; Spain was sure its destiny lay within the European Common Market yet knew it had to build an infrastructure of its own that
would at least enable it to stand up to the industrial might of the other
countries in the European Community.

Holmes, searching for sites, was tempted by Pamplona but eventually
was more convinced by the logistics of a small community of 3,657
people at a place called Almusafes, ten miles from Valencia, three miles
from the Mediterranean and potential port facilities. Almusafes was no
more than a village, but it was not lacking in pride, and the mayor gladly
gave up his siesta to show Holmes what Pérez de Bricio called a parcel of
land—640 acres upon which he felt there was more than enough room
even for Senor Henry Ford. The site—bigger, I think, than Almusafes
itself—was a sort of confederation of allotments, a small countryside of
orange trees and onion fields, and it looked promising. The problem,
Holmes decided—at least one of the problems—was that the 640 acres
had 636 different owners, and not all even owned land; some of them
merely had rights to the thin waterways that provided irrigation. Some
owners agreed to sell immediately, and others, more wily, held out for

the riches they were convinced their holdings would bring; but Philip Caldwell felt confident enough of their ultimate agreement to drive the Eagle program toward a final landing.

By January 1973 it seemed that everybody in Spain knew that Ford was coming, and many people continued to offer sites within their own boundaries of authority. Justiniano Luengo, the mayor of another community, called Talavera de la Reina, near Toledo, rallied the entire neighborhood, and Henry received in Dearborn nearly seventy-five thousand cards from townspeople urging the delights of their own vacant fields and assuring Senor Ford of the warmest welcome. Some reminded him that there was a Toledo in Ohio just down the road from Detroit, and what could more effectively revive the memory of *los conquistadores* than a new imperial venture in reverse? Henry dictated a reply, and seventy-five thousand letters, all bearing his signature, were delivered to the Talavera post office on January 29 and through the town the following day. I had gone to Madrid and hired the most good-humored Spaniard I have ever met—the then director of a government newspaper group—to handle these delicate affairs, and Don Abilio de Quiros was able to reassure me on February 1 that Henry's consideration had been much appreciated. I gave Henry the news in Boca Raton the following day.

In May 1973 a formal meeting took place at the Design and Engineering Center in Merkenich, Germany, and both Henry and Lee Iacocca concluded from the discussions that it was now possible to weld the Eagle program and Bobcat together and go for Spain and the B car at the same time.

Ford of Spain was established on September 26 with the help of Antonio Garrigues Walker, a Spanish lawyer whose father had been ambassador to the United States and who was also a personal friend of Henry's. Antonio was one of the few people who called him Henry rather than Mr. Ford. Bourke and Jack McDougall, Bourke's successor, had, if anything, accelerated the pace of an enterprise that had now taken hold in Europe and was beginning to assume the character of a crusade. The early work on clay models had been completed in the United States; Uwe Bahnsen, Ford of Europe's presiding designer in Germany, and Jack Telnack, whom Bourke had brought over from Australia, had worked in the British studios, producing two variations on the accepted theme. The

Telnack model finally won the vote, and on October 2 Iacocca stood before a meeting of some one hundred managers in Germany and delivered a speech that I had written for him and that I, at least, thought would encapsulate the matters in hand. Iacocca used written texts the way Leonard Bernstein uses musical notation and invariably added his own variations. He could always captivate an audience and he did on this occasion. "You have one thousand days," he said, "one thousand days to bring this dream into reality. Actually one thousand forty-nine days and you will be spending six hundred thousand dollars a day. Bobcat is yours. I know you will do a great job." I had the arithmetic wrong because by the time the Bobcat-Spain program was ready to go to the board of directors for final approval—it had already agreed to the plan so far—it had been decided to add a second plant on the Blanquefort site near Bordeaux, for the production of the Bobcat transaxle and the investment required for the program had increased to $900 million.

After this milestone meeting Henry went off to Bordeaux. He had promised to dedicate the first Blanquefort factory—now beginning to produce automatic transmissions—but he also wanted to make sure that we were going to be good neighbors. Some inevitable rumblings had been provoked by this new venture. Bordeaux and the stony soil on both sides of the Gironde River had been the prestigious heart and headquarters of the alchemists who produced France's most famous wine for five hundred years, and the power of the princes of the vine, who guarded their small but rich estates from the fastnesses of splendid châteaux, was immense. Jacques Chaban-Delmas, the prefect of Aquitaine, was himself a force in the land and, at one time, prime minister of France itself. Pollution is a natural enough anxiety for people whose living comes from the soil or the oceans; but modern factories, properly planned, should not be a threat, and I know many Ford plants where the water they draw for their own use is more polluted than that which is pumped out.

Henry had made a friend of Pierre Tari, the proprietor and caretaker of Château Giscours, but for the Blanquefort dedication, he stayed at Château Lafite with his older friends, Élie de Rothschild and his baroness, engaging himself one night in a doughty and competitive tasting with venerable vintages from Lafite and those produced by Philippe de Rothschild next door—some of them as old as 1890. Henry assured them both that he would make himself personally responsible for the good citizenship of Ford in Bordeaux, and he repeated the undertaking at the dedication to Chaban-Delmas, to whom he confided the prospect of a further Ford development in his domain. He later brought the board of directors to Bordeaux and threw a big party at Château Giscours, and Lee Iacocca was inducted as a chevalier of a distinguished local order of wine connoisseurs.

In June 1973 Henry sent Philip Caldwell back to the United States, promoting him to executive vice-president in charge of all Ford's international operations in Europe and the Far East, Latin America, and South Africa; he was also elected to the board of directors. He had been chairman of Ford of Europe for fewer than two years, but I doubt if he had had a day off in that time—at least a day without some self-imposed business task—and Henry had been astounded by the amount of work he had done and the quality of his judgment. I argued with Henry against the move; there was still so much to be done to bring home the Spanish venture and the B car. Despite the effort put into Bobcat in the United States by Hal Sperlich and many other people, both programs were an enormous additional imposition upon the never less than demanding day-to-day conduct of the business in Europe. I said that we always moved people too quickly, but Henry was adamant. He did not disagree with my point of view. "I know we do," he said, "but we have good people to take over, and Phil will still be in overall charge. It may even be helpful to have somebody as committed as he is to push the numbers through the staffs in Dearborn."

Bill Bourke was promoted in Philip Caldwell's place as chairman of Ford of Europe, and a diminutive and immensely practical manufacturing man, Jack McDougall, was brought over from Dearborn to succeed Bourke as president. McDougall, who had been a plant engineer on the Liberator bomber assembly line at Willow Run during the war, stood about five feet in height but twice that in energy. He was a quick learner, and the rhythm of progress was not interrupted. He began to have shirtsleeves meetings in his office at 8:00 A.M. every Monday—which meant coats off and all cards on the table—and he gave the impression he was enjoying every minute of every day, as I am sure he was.

This was the single largest project in the company's history, and the challenge was enormous. The Almusafes plant alone would require nearly seven miles of overhead conveyors and sixty-three presses. The buildings would stretch along a new highway from Valencia to Benidorm for two and a half miles. It would create seventy-nine hundred new jobs, and the task of training was a formidable undertaking by itself. It was fortunate that the automobile factories in other European countries had a substantial proportion of Spanish workers who had gone abroad to find work, and they wrote job applications saying how pleased they would be to take their expertise home again for work nearer their own doorsteps. Two little girls dispatched a letter to Henry Ford II when hiring was under way, and their large copperplate handwriting brought him much pleasure. "Thank you," they wrote, "for bringing Daddy back to us."

Any poll of motor industry executives that asked them to name the one event that most changed their universe would probably come to one conclusion: the oil shock of 1973. On October 6, Egypt and Syria attacked Israel in the middle of Yom Kippur, and two weeks later the principal Gulf states joined in an oil embargo, prompting Richard Nixon to forget Watergate long enough to sign an oil allocation law, lowering the speed limit on American roads to fifty-five miles an hour, and to suggest that gas stations should close on Sunday. The effects were worse in Europe: Britain went on a three-day week. The war was still raging, and the ominous consequences of the Arab embargo were daily fare for newspapers and television the world over when Philip Caldwell and Bill Bourke finally went to the board of directors. A project of nearly $1 billion might have been difficult to sell at any time, but even Caldwell, who understood better than most the possible consequences of the Middle East conflict and the growing pressures on the world economy, felt he might have to fight very hard if he was to secure approval. Henry Ford II intended the project to succeed, and he and Lee Iacocca were still in tune where Ford's overseas operations were concerned. Henry had extraordinary faith in Caldwell and Bourke and in the thoroughness of the analytical job they had done. "Bourke's gung ho," Henry said to me, "and Phil's on board." Caldwell got his approval. It was a courageous thing for the outside members of the board to do, and they did it bravely. As they looked around the automobile world to see what others, including General Motors, were doing, they could see no similar plans for growth, no ventures into unknown territory, and they were wise enough in the business to know that few had succeeded in successfully launching a new product, a new factory, and a new labor force at the same time. "OK, it was daring," Franklin Murphy said to me, "but it made sense." In addition to his position as a member of the Ford board of directors, Franklin was chairman of the board of the *Los Angeles Times-Mirror* Company and chancellor of the University of California at Los Angeles, and his influence was of signal importance to the decision.

In January 1974 there was a ground-breaking ceremony at Almusafes as the bulldozers moved in. In March Henry went there himself and stood for a long time looking down on a scale model of the proposed factory, learning its layout in detail, and asking questions of the small group of men—a mixture of eighteen different nationalities—who had been given the task of growing a new crop on the onion fields. I picked oranges from a grove of trees nearby, and Henry said, "Nobody will ever build anything like this again, not in my lifetime," and I supposed it was true. When we came back a couple of months later and stared at the 640 acres of cleared land with not a tree or a bush standing, I remembered what he had said and reminded him. "Some people are thinking we're damn fools," he said.

Ford would never have marched along the long road to Valencia without Henry. It is a statement that takes nothing away from the young executives in Europe whose determination had led the way toward a B car or from those in North America whom Iacocca directed to join the battle. It does not minimize the commitment of the battalions of "bean counters" who made financial sense of the plans in six different currencies at a time of fluctuating exchange rates. Yet it was Henry's growing stature as ambassador to Europe and the warmth of the welcome in chancelleries and palaces that provided the reassurance upon which such enterprises depend. Confidence has to walk on two legs; marriages may be made in heaven, but they survive only with the common understanding of two people. And Henry paid personal attention to all the constituencies of his new country. His relationships with the Spanish government and its ministers were warm, and his friendship with Prince Juan Carlos reinforced the growing sense of partnership.

Some of the developing links were fragile but interesting; one of the distinguished Spaniards appointed to the board of Ford España was a descendant of Christopher Columbus. General Franco, who had ruled the country for thirty-five years, had been kept informed of the Ford project; but by then he was an old man and senile, and it was not to be expected that he would become involved. It appeared, however, that the Spanish establishment was anxious to provide the final seal of approval, and Henry was invited to meet the generalissimo in the palace he occupied on the outskirts of Madrid.

Henry was told that he would have to wear morning dress: striped trousers, long cutaway jacket, and waistcoat. The meeting would be formal. He should not expect Franco to say anything. It would perhaps be no more than an ushering into the presence. This was the last full year of Franco's life, and it was rumored that he had lost the power of speech. The meeting presented only one problem to Henry, for he did not possess a morning suit; he was in America when the invitation came, and he had no alternative but to go to a local tailor. His regular and trusted cutter in London's Savile Row would have understood the requirement but was never asked. Henry intended to wear the outfit for only one day, so it was ordered by telephone, and he received only one fitting. The morning of the Franco reception, I was standing outside the Ritz Hotel enjoying the warmth of a spring day when Henry emerged—resplendent in his new clothes—and asked me if I would mind carrying his handkerchief and glasses. It was an odd request, and I must have looked surprised. He grinned. "Do I look right to you?" he asked. I said he was every inch a grandee. "Can you see anything wrong?" I said he was immaculate. "Well, I can tell you," he said, "this suit has no pockets, not in the pants, not in the vest, not in the jacket." I leaned against the car and roared with laughter. So did he. "I never looked at it when it arrived, and I never put it on until this morning." I said I doubted if the general would notice.

The audience—for that is what it was—lasted longer than anybody expected. Henry had thought it would be entirely one-sided and intended only to say that he was pleased with the cooperation of the Spanish government and, in particular, the practical and speedy response from its ministers and civil servants—notably José María López de Letona and Carlos Pérez de Bricio. He was surprised when Franco delivered a brief speech of his own. "We are delighted to have you here in Spain," he said, which was the sort of sentiment that might have been expected. What was not expected and of special pleasure to Henry was his additional comment: "Ford, we know, is a company that can be trusted to keep its promises."

Henry also remembered his duty to his new neighbors and clambered one morning up the narrow staircase in the Almusafes town hall at the beginning of what can only be described as a triumphal progress. The narrow streets around the center of the village were thick with people shouting, "Viva Henry Ford." The women held up their children to be kissed, and I took one photograph of him leaning across the roof of a car with his arms outstretched and hundreds of hands around him as if in salute. Cynics might say that anybody who would so emphatically assure the future of this sun-dried little community of fewer than four thousand people would be assured of such a welcome, but there was no mistaking the genuine warmth and excitement that the visit aroused. Equally there could be no mistake about its impact upon Henry.

There was never any difficulty in persuading him to return to Spain, and I often thought he watched our progress there more closely than anywhere else and took more pleasure in it. Years later, when we celebrated our tenth anniversary in Spain, Juan Carlos and Queen Sophia came back to Valencia and posed for newspaper and television photographers with the latest products from the plant. The king put his arm around Henry's shoulders and said: "Well, Henry, did I sell enough cars for you today?" His interest was remarkable. When the four-wheel-drive Scorpio was introduced, he took his chauffeur and the existing two-wheel-drive model to the snow-covered sierra beyond Madrid and conducted his own handling test. When the Scorpio was voted Car of the Year by a jury of European journalists, he received them in his palace and talked learnedly about the four-wheel-drive system.

By this time Ford was Spain's largest automotive exporting enterprise and accounted for more foreign earnings than tourism. Ford operations were even more significant for the economies in West Germany and Britain. The operations in Genk and Bordeaux were pillars of the Belgian and French economies. When Spain entered the European Common Market, it was able to point to an industrial infrastructure that enabled its government to look its richer neighbors in the face. And the brass band at Almusafes had been equipped with new instruments by courtesy of Ford. Its people had some reason to blow their own trumpets.

CHAPTER SEVEN

Affairs of the Heart

It was 1975 when Henry Ford II decided the time had come to replace Lee Iacocca as president of the Ford Motor Company. Perhaps it is more accurate to say that it was the period in his life when he again began to have misgivings about the quality of its management. It has become commonplace to suggest that Lee and Henry never got on with each other or that Henry developed a personal antipathy—even neurosis—where Iacocca was concerned, but I do not believe that was true, certainly not in the beginning. Five years had gone by since Iacocca had been appointed president—having himself ousted Bunkie Knudsen—and Henry, to judge by results, was coming to the conclusion that he had again picked a second-in-command lacking in the right stuff.

The year had begun badly for him. Marriage to Cristina had long since ceased to have any meaning. They had never had much in common, beyond the initial sexual attraction, and he was reaching an age when companionship seemed important. Cristina found Detroit insular and parochial; it was easy to shine on so small a stage but not satisfying. There was a beckoning and more exciting world outside, but Henry did not want excitement in his private life. He liked at night to chew the common ground of gossip and experience, and he never enjoyed parties. Stendhal once wrote, "The pleasures of society are no pleasure at all for a happy woman," and my own observation of Cristina at this time led me to echo his observation. In her environment Cristina could be charming, the focus for every eye, and a decorative addition to any gathering. She brought more and more Italian friends to the house in

Grosse Pointe and loved the glitter of New York. But Henry's excitement filled his days, and he looked forward to placid evenings. Theirs was not the first marriage to fail for these reasons. I once lived next door to the chairman of a great company whose wife could never understand his aversion to the *cordon bleu* dinners she insisted on serving him during their evenings at home. He wanted sausages and shepherd's pie and something trashy on television. I have also come across neglected and beautiful women who can never understand why their husbands fall for mousy, domesticated ones who dress badly and seem unimportant. It is very often because they are more peaceful to live with.

Henry was not inclined to be introspective about his marriage. He only knew that it was over and had probably come to an end in 1970, when he met Kathleen Roberta Duross, a merry widow twenty-two years his junior. Their first meeting took place at his house on Lakeshore Drive at a dinner he and Cristina had given in honor of one of his closest friends, Evelyn de Rothschild. Mrs. Duross had been escorted to the dinner by the Brazilian consul in Detroit, and Henry was immediately taken with the self-possession and vivacity of this young woman with striking red hair and a healthy irreverence toward her host. He brought her to London with him in 1971, and she soon came to hold an important part in his life. He bought a small house some ten or twelve miles from Grosse Pointe, and they would meet there in the evenings. Occasionally he would pick me up at Detroit's Metropolitan Airport after one of my own increasingly frequent trips from London and drive me to the house, where we would sit in the kitchen and talk to Kathy while she cooked dinner. The difference in their ages was never particularly apparent. I thought her undemanding.

In February 1975, by which time they had developed an entirely private life of their own, Henry took her to California for what was supposed to be a vacation. They went out to dinner, and Henry drank more than is permitted by the California Highway Patrol, one of whose officers stopped the car as he drove back to the hotel, having concluded that he was "not staying within traffic lane markings." Henry failed the blood test that followed, and the incident made headlines. For a man of the world, he was curiously sensitive about this escapade and, back in Detroit a few days later, went nervously to a dinner of the Society of Automotive Engineers, a little like a male Hester Prynne with an imaginary scarlet letter beneath his black tie. The audience quickly removed most of his apprehensions by showing its affection, rising and cheering him all the way to his table.

Henry hated untidy situations and would have liked to resolve his private life; but his mother had been unhappy about his earlier divorce, and despite his disenchantment with his second marriage, he was unwilling to bring her further distress by going through another divorce and marrying for a third time. Cristina's friend Imelda Marcos, wife of the president of the Philippines, told her that men are like children and must occasionally be allowed to play; eventually they always come home. Kathy, whose life was, if anything, more complicated by the revelation of their friendship, said that if marriage ever came, it would arrive in its own good time.

In any event, Henry, with more pressing concerns on his mind, lowered the shutters—so far as he could—on his private life and began to concentrate on his first true love: the Ford Motor Company. When David Horowitz was researching his book on the Ford family, Henry gave him one reluctant interview and was emphatic on only one subject. He said: "The things that are not part of Ford Motor Company don't count in my life anywhere near as much as the company does. That's just without question. The company is always number one in my life." The statement should not be interpreted as callousness, for he was sensitive to other people's changing moods and considerate of their feelings. We had a butler once in the London apartment who was dying of cancer and not well off. One night Henry pressed a large sum of money into his hands, and when this was resisted, Henry said: "Take it. I won it gambling, and since you take such good care of me, you ought to share the winnings." We both knew he had not been gambling.

Henry arrived in London on June 3—four months after the California incident—wearing a light gray Prince of Wales check suit, uncrushed by its night journey. I met him at the airport and drove with him to his house in Lees Place, Mayfair, and hoped he would not keep me long. Some Lewis Carroll first editions were coming up in auction at Sotheby's, due to begin at 10:30 A.M., and I wanted to be there to bid. He looked tired but otherwise fit, and we spent an hour discussing the way things were going in Europe, Harold Wilson's beleaguered government in Britain (where inflation had reached a record inflation rate of 25 percent), and the fast-approaching tour by the company's board of directors. As I was leaving, he asked me if I thought Bill Bourke would be free for dinner, and I said I was sure he would be. "Ask him to come at eight," Henry said. "Tell him nothing formal. I shall be wearing slacks and a shirt. I just want to talk."

I had little doubt about the reason for the dinner or its importance since Henry rarely invited company executives to his homes, even on social occasions, and believed wisely that business is best conducted on business premises. But he was intent on giving me a clue anyway. "You know what it's about," he said, "but don't tell him anything in advance."

I said: "I hope you are not going to do what I think you are going to do."

Bill Bourke had been president and then chairman of Ford of Europe for little more than three years. The Spanish enterprise was approaching a critical stage of achievement. Ford of Europe under his management had become an assured, extroverted, even arrogant group, and it was good to go to work in the morning. We were at our desks at 8:00 A.M. and sometimes 8:00 P.M. Nobody was more capable of husbanding our resources than Red Poling, and we had ridden the aftermath of the Arab oil embargo better than any of our European competitors. There was another reason for my apprehension. I have always felt that there is a penalty to be paid for success. Changes in leadership cannot fail to be unsettling in some degree, and I believed then—as I do now—that it would often have been better for the company and the person concerned if he had been kept longer in his existing job. Some American managements are fearful of leaving executives too long overseas in case they "go native," and the men themselves (and their families) are usually only too willing to go home, where they believe their future lies. But neither of these considerations applied (or apply) to Ford. The only justification was the one Henry always gave when I protested one move or another: "I know. I agree with you, but we are growing fast, and we have to fill the jobs. There never are and there will never be enough qualified people to fill the jobs that have to be filled." What Henry never admitted, but was evidently true, was a growing belief that his European executives were more experienced than candidates with only American qualifications and had resources that were becoming more important to the U.S. company and its markets. Bill Bourke was not pressing for promotion. He was happy in London, and so—apart from some normal colonial differences with the English natives—was his wife. They had a grand terrace house in Regent's Park and gave every evidence of enjoying themselves. They had kept their small ranch back in Australia near Melbourne, and Bourke talked only of seeing things through in Europe and going home down under.

Bourke asked me, "What's up?" when I passed on Henry's invitation, and I said his guess was as good as mine, which turned out to be true. He arrived at Lees Place on the dot of eight. They drank several bottles of

Château Lafite Rothschild 1962, and Henry was outspoken and in despair about Iacocca. They no longer talked to each other, Henry said ruefully. Changes must be made. Iacocca must go. Bourke must become the new president of the Ford Motor Company.

I decided to go to Madrid on June 5, twenty-four hours ahead of the first arrivals for the board of directors' tour, which was due to begin in that city. The following day I joined Henry in his suite at the Ritz, and he was emphatic about his plans for Bourke. "I never feel I know what is going on," he said. Iacocca was not a team player, or perhaps the truth was that he only wanted to play—and confide—with those who were on his own private team. The existence of an Iacocca faction or charmed inner circle was evident to others in the company, and it needed no particular insight on the part of Henry Ford II to suspect that a new power base was being developed. He was suspicious of Iacocca's friends outside the company and of deals he made with them, and though none of this was particularly specific, it did not have to be. Henry was an instinctive manager, and his disquiet often began with no more than a feeling that things were not going right.

He had more tangible reasons for concern. He was worried about the financial resources of the company. General Motors was a gold mine and seemed able to finance a complex range of commercial vehicles and cars for Chevrolet and Oldsmobile, Pontiac, Buick, and Cadillac. Ford could not. It was signally unsuccessful in that middle sector of the American market, and in the last quarter of 1974 the company had lost money. Mustang sales had fallen sharply, to 150,000 in 1970, and later versions of the car failed to recapture the appeal or repeat the success of its earlier years. The European business seemed to be conducted in a more objective and resolute fashion. Henry also knew what few others appreciated: that the cars Ford sold in North America were, overall, making no money at all; profits came from other activities. And indeed, it was not until Caldwell and Poling and Petersen—a rising star in the Ford heavens—reduced the company's operating costs by billions of dollars, by judicious attention to the basics of the business, and dedicated themselves to product quality and integrity, that Ford's U.S. cars came back into the black.

As Henry roamed the suite in the Ritz, I said I hoped he had not underrated the opposition the Bourke move might create, suggesting that it might be a good idea to consult some other people. Bourke was unknown in Dearborn except as a visitor. There were other vice-presidents with ambition, and Iacocca was a street fighter. He had had no difficulty in disposing of Bunkie Knudsen by the simple process of rallying his own forces within the company. Change was fine, I argued, but revolution was to nobody's advantage.

Henry said he was not fooling himself and was not naive enough to believe that the accumulating problems facing Ford in America would or could be resolved with the departure of Iacocca, and in the ensuing conversation I began to see that Iacocca's removal was probably the linch pin for a larger reform. Henry was approaching his sixtieth birthday and had been effectively running the company for thirty years. The subject of his retirement came up more often every year, and we used to chat about the things he might do when—not if—he finally settled in England and lived his own life in his own fashion. I think he also resented the artificial circumstances imposed upon his relationship with Mrs. Duross. As midnight passed and I excused myself to go to bed, he said that he was not foolish enough to believe that Ford without Iacocca would magically become the company he wanted it to be or get down to a thorough resolution of its problems. "It's not," he said, "just him."

Henry woke with our discussion fresh in his mind, and that evening he took Franklin Murphy and Tom Taylor—two of the outside directors closest to him—to dinner at the Jockey, where they talked tactics. Both Franklin and Tom were more direct than I had been, and Henry was thoughtful the next day when the directors' tour began with an off-duty excursion to Pedro Domecq's farm at Jerez de la Frontera, the heart of Spain's sherry country. It was a day to take the mind away from affairs of state. We drank sherry with the assumed wisdom of connoisseurs, and some unexpectedly extroverted directors and vice-presidents were persuaded to risk waving the muleta at some decidedly docile bulls. Everybody, including Lee, seemed relaxed. His wife and two daughters had accompanied him to England in one of the Ford Grumman Gulfstreams, and he was meaning to pick them up again and take them to Ireland at the end of the tour of inspection. He was curiously outside the party; Henry scarcely spoke to him, and Lee made no attempt to open any conversation on his own account.

There was never any prospect that they would be buddies, although they could well have been better allies. Their personalities were very different, and neither was truly what he seemed to be. There is a public Iacocca with whom so many people feel themselves familiar. They have seen him night after night on television, and he has smiled at them from countless magazine covers. The book William Novak wrote for him has sold millions of copies, and the legend that he has created—or, perhaps, that has been created for him—has become an accepted "fact" of life. He is seen as an outward, gregarious man, but that has never been the case. His circle of friends has always been small, confined by choice to a few intimates; he ventured hesitantly into unfamiliar territory or gatherings of people and was often uncertain among strange faces.

This may not accord with the perceptions of those for whom he is a personality—a little larger than life—whose televised presence in their homes personified confidence and power. This is not criticism, merely observation. The public, when it stops to think, knows that the television screen, which so decisively shapes public opinion, can present people only at their face value. It offers, at best, a one-dimensional view. I have known not a few famous people, renowned for their fluency, their apparently impromptu speeches and ready wit, who lie awake before a big occasion and work for days on prepared texts, who still wear private armor and have to steel themselves before venturing into the spotlight. And it was not possible for Lee to meet Henry even halfway without coming halfway himself. In Spain, in the summer of 1975, I was much concerned with the concealed but unfolding drama and wondered why a man of Lee's undoubted talents could not have worked out a relationship or at least a rapprochement that would have permitted a proper concentration on the very real problems that faced the company. If business becomes a bullring, it is hard to concentrate on matters of life rather than death.

Still, on the surface the board tour was a great success. The directors went to see Juan Carlos—soon to be king—and to Valencia for the inauguration of the enormous manufacturing complex that had risen there so quickly for the production of the B cars—or, at least, a large proportion of them, for production was also planned in Britain and Germany. The first car was due to be produced at Saarlouis in May 1976, and Valencia was to start up in October; by the middle of 1975 there was more than enough physical evidence of the immensity of the investment to which the board had given its blessing. The directors returned to Madrid well pleased and reinforced in the intelligence of their decision.

When we got back to the Ritz from Valencia, it was evident that Henry had not devoted his mind entirely to Almusafes and the inauguration. One of the directors of Ford España gave a garden party in his home, and I got back to the hotel with Henry about 1:30 A.M. He said, "Let's have a drink before we go to bed," and called room service. Henry fretted around the suite until the waiter had gone and then asked me: "If you could have anybody you liked for Bourke's job in Europe, who would you have?" I do not want to elevate my own consequence where such deliberations are concerned. Very often Henry asked me questions of this kind because there were so few people with whom he felt disposed to discuss such things, but the questions he posed frequently served no other purpose than to allow him to reconsider and shape his own views. It was occasionally a dangerous game to play. My wife reminded me, now and then, of the role Thomas Cromwell had played in the life of Henry VIII and recalled what eventually happened to him. I had only two big arguments with Henry Ford II in the twenty-five years I worked for him—both over women and neither of any real relevance to business. Where business questions were concerned, I invariably avoided the direct reply and argued the broader issues, the consequences of action rather than the action itself, and I never once voted for, proposed, or lobbied for any individual appointment. Sensible confidants help their inquisitor to know his own mind rather than theirs.

In the Ritz, therefore, I again argued the common sense of avoiding confrontation unless it was unavoidable. Bunkie Knudsen was still a fresh memory, and perhaps, in Henry's mind, an open wound. Immediate elevation of Bourke to the presidency would also create the inevitable snakes and ladders elsewhere in the hierarchy, and I reminded Henry that it had been many years since Bourke had worked in the United States. He had never held senior positions there and would need all the help he could get. The discussion went on for a couple of hours and seemed to clear Henry's mind.

By Wednesday night we were back in London for an appointment at 10 Downing Street with the prime minister, Harold Wilson. The following day there was a board meeting at the London office, and it was a long and somewhat tense affair. The cash situation was poor; borrowings were up. Henry took Tom Taylor and Franklin Murphy to luncheon at Wilton's—where he was surprised to meet his daughter Anne—and over the table things came to a head. Franklin later thanked me for my "diplomacy," which I took to mean his agreement with my "softly, softly" arguments in Madrid. In any event, he and Tom Taylor had argued along similar lines, and at the Grafton Street office in the afternoon Henry told me: "I'm going to take Bourke. I'm going to give him North America. It will be a stepping-stone."

On Friday the thirteenth he returned to the United States. Departure time for his flight had been brought forward, and he had to rush to the airport, getting into the car without his breakfast or his tie. I took a week off. It was my second son's half-term holiday. We joined the party Cristina Ford gave at Mark's Club in London for Nelson Rockefeller and his new wife. Cristina came to London for the party with her friend Princess Pallavicini and told me I should persuade Henry to "do more things like this. He should meet more important people." I did not say he had other things on his mind.

With Henry gone, Bill Bourke became increasingly restless. Had Henry gone straight home and done the deed, as he originally envisaged—replacing Lee Iacocca with Bill Bourke—it might have been a quick and clean ending, but further consideration on his return journey confirmed his belief that a less radical first step toward his ambition would cause less upheaval. It seemed likely also that a more gradual approach to change would enable Bourke to establish himself among the strange faces and places in Dearborn's World Headquarters of the company. Putting Bourke into the North American job, however, required consequential appointments and consultation with other people, including Iacocca and the subcommittee of the board responsible for such senior personnel matters. The delay was unfortunate, for rumors had begun to work their own mischief.

Philip Caldwell, who had stayed in London for a few days after the board tour, took Bourke aside one day and asked what was going on. Bourke said truthfully that he did not know. He continued with preparations to pack up his London house and move to the United States, which provoked more rumors, but the month passed without an announcement. Henry Ford II finally called him on July 1. He said there had been too much talk in Europe about the plan. Other people had taken strong positions. There was general agreement that it would be a good idea for Bourke to work in the United States but not immediately, and it was not until October that he was finally appointed executive vice-president, North American Automotive Operations, and elected to the board of directors. By then the American problems facing the company were mounting, and Bourke found himself in the hottest seat in the company and working for Lee Iacocca. Some sort of miracle would now be needed if he were to achieve the presidency.

Bill Bourke had scarcely settled into his new corner office, and the workmen were still busy in the small house he had bought in Dearborn, when Henry received a reminder of his own mortality and perhaps a warning that he might not be given the time to create a management that could confidently carry Ford into its second century. Two months after his fifty-eighth birthday, he left his home in Grosse Pointe and went for a walk. It was a damp, heavy November evening. The clouds were low over the lake. He had strolled along Lakeshore Drive and had turned onto Provencal Road, kicking at the fallen leaves, when he felt in the region of his heart a sharp pain that extended down to his left elbow. He sat on the wet curbside with his head in his hands, and people from a nearby house came out to see what was wrong. He explained that he was not far from home but could not move until the pain cleared, as it did after ten minutes or so, when he returned to the house and went to bed. The next day he made an appointment at the Henry Ford Hospital and was given a stress test, which was apparently negative, for he was told to carry on normally. It was just one of those things. After all, he wasn't getting any younger.

He had always enjoyed good health, and *enjoyment* is the appropriate word. He was a big man and heavy, and he had lived hard and worked hard and—away from the affairs of business—had also drunk hard. He had given up spirits twenty-five years earlier, but he was a knowledgeable and doughty wine drinker and habitually smoked ten cheap cigars a day. He gave up Havanas when the U.S. government made them a forbidden pleasure. They were still obtainable in Europe, but he was a stickler in such matters and insisted that the cheaper varieties were better anyway. In his childhood he had twice had operations: for mastoiditis when he was two years of age and for appendicitis when he was six. But these were mere juvenile interruptions. He was a tough guy.

The stress test suggested to me, at least, that discontent with his marriage and the tensions involving Lee Iacocca were combining with the other inevitable demands of the business—and his tireless but obviously tiring travels—to produce pressures that were not easy to release. Still, I shrugged off the incident, as he did, and on November 25, when Henry was in Latin America on a business trip, I had dinner with Kathy Duross in Detroit. She was glad there had been no further alarms. "He works too hard," she said, "but nobody will ever change that." In December I kept an appointment with him at the Ford Foundation in New York, and I thought he looked tired. Wasn't it time, I suggested, for him to slow down a bit? He put his hand soulfully on his heart and said he had invited Kathy and Joan and John Bugas to Turville, his house in England, for Christmas. "We'll have a relaxed time, I promise you," he insisted. I agreed he would be in good company and in the best possible place; there was no better place for a troubled heart.

———————————

Turville Grange was the fulfillment of Henry Ford II's quest for a place of his own, somewhere that was entirely his and only his and where he could be at peace in a tranquil world. When he began to search for a small country estate in England, he was immediately charmed by this property and looked no farther. It occupied some fifty acres on Turville Heath in Oxfordshire, a few miles from Henley, the small riverside town on the Thames that is the temple of English rowing. Henry had once been manager of the college rowing crew at Yale. It was no more than ninety minutes from London's West End. Windsor Castle was on the other side of the river, perhaps ten miles away, and the narrow country roads wound through villages where it was ten to one you would be stopped by a herd of cows crossing the road and five to one by a Ford tractor. Henry had owned, for some time, a small house—little more than a cottage—in Mayfair, but it was the countryside that he liked best, and his greatest love was shooting for grouse and pheasant with friends such as Louis Mountbatten, Lord Lambton, and the duke of Marlborough. He was a trustee of the Blenheim Trust, which the duke had formed for the upkeep of Blenheim Palace—the splendid seat of the Marlboroughs where Winston Churchill was born—and he gave generously to its preservation.

Turville Grange had a romantic history. A house has stood on the site since 1700, but it was not given a name until 1887, when a certain Mr. Smith converted three cottages into one house and decided the finished creation was proud enough to be called a grange. Mr. Smith did not live there long, and its great days began when it was bought by the marquis d'Hautpoul de Seyre. The marquis had married Julia Stonor, whose mother had been the favorite lady-in-waiting to Princess Alexandra, wife of England's future King Edward VII. When Mrs. Stonor died, Alexandra, an enchanting Danish princess who met Edward at seventeen years of age and married him at eighteen, took Julia Stonor under her wing and made her a special charge. Subsequently, when Edward and Alexandra became king and queen, they continued to care for Julia, whom they loved as a daughter, and it was not surprising that one of their sons, Prince George (later to become King George V), fell in love with her, too.

She was always his "dearest Julie." The love was clearly reciprocated, but George and Julie—no matter how sincere their love for each other—could never have married. It was not merely that Julie was a commoner. The Stonor family had lived at Stonor Park, just down the road from Turville Grange, for eight hundred years, and her brother's title (he was Lord Camoys) had been created in 1415 for an ancestor who had brilliantly led the wing of the English army at the Battle of Agincourt. The long and sturdy English line of the Stonors is longer than that of the royal family. What prevented any consideration of the marriage was that Julia was a Roman Catholic.

Queen Alexandra was well aware of her son's affection for his ever dearest Julie and played her cards with great delicacy. She had some considerable practice in these matters, for her husband had been born with an eye for pretty women and some thought he had had an affair with Julie's mother. In 1891 Julia Stonor married the Marquis d'Hautpoul, a somewhat shadowy French nobleman eight years her senior, and two years later Prince George married Princess May of Teck, who had been engaged to his recently deceased brother. Julia and her husband extended the Turville Grange estate through the purchase of adjoining land and greatly improved the property, substantially rebuilding the house so that it was fit to receive the king and queen and their family, including Prince George. George, who succeeded his father as king in 1910, liked Windsor Castle and drove regularly from there to Turville Grange. On March 24, 1913, he noted in his diary: " . . . after luncheon, motored with May, Mary, and Cust to Turville Grange and paid Julie a visit in her dear, little house, she has much improved the garden now. She gave us tea and we got home at 6:15." (May was Queen Mary; Mary, Princess Mary, their daughter; and Cust, Sir Charles Cust, the king's equerry.) He did not always arrive in company. Sometimes he went alone. Turville Grange became a special place where he could shed the cares and formalities of kingship and relax in the company of the woman he had loved in his youth. When Henry Ford II bought the house and I discovered its earlier connections, I was pleased to believe that history was repeating itself.

Virtually every member of the royal family who visited Turville planted a tree in the garden, and each planting was commemorated with a metal plate thrust into the soil at its foot. The trees are tall now, and the plates weatherworn, but they hold their memories. One windowpane in the master bedroom still bears the inscribed signature scratched on its surface by Princess Victoria. Queen Alexandra stayed at the house every summer, and it was one of the first places of refuge for her sister,

Dowager Empress Marie of Russia, who escaped to England in a British warship in 1919 after the Bolsheviks had murdered her son, Czar Nicholas II.

George V died in 1935, and one of the floral tributes at his Windsor funeral was a blazing vermilion wreath bearing the inscription "From your broken-hearted Julie." The marquis d'Hautpoul had himself died in 1934; but Julia lived on at Turville Grange into her eighty-third year, and the list of guests at her requiem mass in Stonor Park Chapel on February 7, 1950, reads like a roll call of Edwardian society. Soon after her death, Turville Grange was bought by Oliver Brett, third Viscount Esher, who had coveted it for many years. Lord Esher was a large part of the inspiration in the making of the National Trust, which is now Britain's largest landowner, and presides with secure benevolence over the bricks and rolling acres of 270 of Britain's stately homes and castles. Lord Esher loved Turville Grange and with his son, who became president of the Royal Institute of British Architects, substantially remodeled the house, taking away some of its Edwardian character and giving it a much more Georgian look. When he died in 1963, an urn was placed in the garden, and it stands today, where he so often did, at the end of his avenue of chestnut trees, which blaze ocher yellow in the autumn and arch their arms together, filtering the sun. After the death of his wife, the house was purchased by Prince Radziwill, who built a large covered swimming pool in the kitchen garden, laid down a tennis court, and made other improvements. Princess Radziwill was Jackie Kennedy's sister, Lee, and they have each left on the house and its guest cottage the stamp of their own tastes in interior design.

Henry spent £250,000 buying Turville Grange from the Radziwills and perhaps as much again on his own improvements. He shipped favorite pieces of furniture from his home in Grosse Pointe together with a collection of French impressionist and postimpressionist paintings, which shattered my children, who had never before seen such splendor in a private home. Henry had bought paintings with discretion—most of them between 1955 and 1969—and Turville Grange was soon enriched by two Matisses, a wonderful Degas portrait of his father, Cézanne's *Maison de Bellevue*, and works by Vuillard, Bonnard, Derain, Pissarro, Modigliani, and Vlaminck. At one stage in his life Henry owned seven of the most wonderful nudes ever painted, including Renoir's life-size *Autumn*, which hung in his Detroit home and brought all the year long a September radiance to the entire drawing room. Kenneth Clark once said that impressionism was the painting of happiness.

There was one oil at Turville I liked very much. It was a small painting by Camille Pissarro and pictured a fête held at Stamford Brook to commemorate Queen Victoria's Jubilee. Pissarro, leader of the original French impressionists, had lived in England for a period. Henry bought the picture in 1948, and it was, I think, his first significant art purchase. It hung, I thought most appropriately, at Turville Grange, for it was as though it had come home, and it pleased me to believe that this early acquisition, so very English in the scene it recorded, was a happy coincidence, perhaps even the first indication of his affection for the country that brought him most peace of mind.

There is no doubt that England-as-home had long been in his mind when he bought Turville in 1974, although he had no knowledge of its history at the time the contracts were signed. The plates under the trees and the diamond-cut signature on the one bedroom windowpane testified to its royal connections, but it was not until Her Majesty the Queen graciously allowed me a search through the photographic albums and diaries at Windsor that its history was properly known. I made a little book with words and photographs, printed six copies, and gave them to Henry for Christmas 1976. My wife chose two epigraphs for the book. One from *Don Quixote* said, "Whom God loved, his house is sweet to him"; the other quoted Hamlet: "There is no ancient gentlemen but gardeners. . . ." Perhaps Tennyson summed it up more evocatively: "An English home—gray twilight poured on dewy pastures, dewy trees, softer than sleep—all things in order stored."

Tennyson, in a sense, reflects Henry's own view of the house, for no place was ever so important to him as this small gentleman's estate in England. Toward the end of his life he was spending as much as three months there every year, and it provided for him, as it had for King George V, the monarch of another kingdom, a contented refuge from the cares and worries that never ceased to press upon him. You could rattle in your car across the cattle grid spanning the drive and persuade yourself it was some kind of drawbridge, but it was never defense against the constant letters and telegrams, newspaper clippings, and company papers to which he had to grant admittance. Still, the lawns were green, and the rhododendrons were lush. A large kitchen garden provided bumper crops of runner beans and broad beans and potatoes and marrows and served as a nursery for new rose bushes. The greenhouses provided a mass of geraniums and gardenias and even orchids for the house. The interior of the house was bright with patterned wallpapers and floral drapes. A Staffordshire jug on one of the shelves in the study proclaimed Samuel Johnson's conviction: "When a man is tired of

London he is tired of life." The gardener kept the house full of flowers and would also loft the clay pigeons from the skeeter Kathy had bought for Henry one Christmas, and he kept a fine Labrador and, for a period, a couple of horses. And tucked away in the trees was a genuine gypsy caravan Kathy had also given Henry, although I could never quite imagine the two of them on the road together.

An additional boon Turville conferred on its owner was anonymity, coupled, I would have to say, with English reserve. He could take his car or one of the two motorcycles he had bought for himself and Kathy and cruise down the hill to Henley, browse through the book or antique shops, or wander by the Thames. Nobody bothered him. Nobody wanted anything. He liked to shop for himself and took care choosing the gifts for his small circle of close friends at Christmas, and he could do so in England without fuss. He called me one day before he was established in Turville to say he wanted a suitcase and asked where he should go to buy one. I gave him the name of a good shop in Piccadilly. "Will they take a check?" he asked. I said I thought they probably would. In Henley they took them without comment or surprise—although there was one day when an old and usually apocryphal joke came true. He went into a local dealer without check book or sufficient cash to cover a modest purchase and asked for credit. He said he was Henry Ford and lived "round the corner." And the serviceman really did say: "Go on— pull the other leg." Henry was delighted.

For all these reasons I was reassured when he promised, after his heart pains in 1975, to spend Christmas at Turville Grange. The holiday, however, was not what he intended it to be. The pain came back to his chest. He went to his bedroom and John Bugas sat with him and asked what was wrong. Bugas was a determined person and close enough to accept no prevarication from Henry, who was a turbulent invalid. John himself had recently undergone surgery for a heart condition at the St. Joseph Mercy Hospital in Ann Arbor, and he went downstairs immediately to call Dr. Ralph Brandt, director of its cardiac laboratory, and book an appointment for Henry to have a thorough checkup on his return.

Henry had no intention of going to St. Joseph's and only pretended agreement to "keep John happy." Just before he had left the United States for his English Christmas, the office of the People's Republic of China in Washington had sent him a pressing invitation to visit Peking and talk with Deng Xiaoping about the automobile industry there and some kind of Ford association for the future. Apart from India, China was the only country in the world of any significance Henry had never visited, and he was determined to go. I spent a good part of my own Christmas planning the proposed itinerary and assembling the paraphernalia that would provide a basis for discussion.

In January, with the holiday over, we flew to Paris, Brussels, Frankfurt, and Düsseldorf to talk to potential members of the Ford European Council Henry had decided to establish. We spent one night in a German hotel, and although he went to bed unusually early, he showed no signs of distress and gave no indication whatsoever of his desire to seek medical advice. On January 19 I flew to Dearborn to collect him for the Chinese trip, and at six o'clock the following morning the telephone rang by my bedside in Dearborn's Hyatt Regency Hotel. "Guess where I am?" he asked. I had no idea. "I'm in St. Joseph's Hospital. I have angina." There had been a recurrence of the chest pains when he got back to Detroit, so he had kept the appointment with Dr. Brandt. "You're going upstairs," Dr. Brandt said as soon as he finished his examination. "No, I'm not!" said Henry. "I'm going to China." But he lost the argument and stayed in the hospital for ten days. I left for China with Philip Caldwell, who had been deputized for the mission, with a heavy heart. There was one heart that was heavier. Kathy Duross had stayed in the Hyatt for one night and talked to Henry on the telephone, but she was not allowed to visit.

We had consoled ourselves with the recollection that Henry's mother had suffered from angina for many years and had lived to the age of seventy-nine. Kathy hoped Henry would see the diagnosis as an opportune and timely warning. "The poor guy's not yet sixty," she said, "and he has given his whole life to the company. He's still young. He ought to have some fun and enjoy things." It was not, however, toward enjoyment that Henry's thoughts were directed as a result of his ten caged days in the hospital. Dr. Brandt's tests and diagnosis had indicated no immediate cause for alarm, but they had made Henry think even harder about the one subject ever in the forefront of his mind: the unfinished business of the Ford Motor Company. His first attempt at reform had foundered, he decided, because he had underestimated the obstacles. He saw that he had to have allies if he was going to make such a change without disrupting the management process. He was also sufficiently honest with himself to recognize that he might not have all the answers himself, maybe not all the questions either.

He therefore began to consider the employment of outside consultants, and in March told the board of directors that he felt the time had come to have a good look at the company, and this meant seeking expert and impartial advice. There was by no means general agreement that a team of outside guide dogs was really needed to map the way ahead, but Henry threw into the discussion his desire to have his own future role in the company defined, and I suspect it was this that obtained respectability for the idea. It was proposed that McKinsey and Company should undertake the study.

Alonzo L. McDonald, a senior partner, brought Frederick Searby, the managing director of McKinsey's Cleveland office, to Dearborn to discuss the scope of the inquiry and to prepare for a long voyage of exploration in which they would travel the world and submit the company and its people to microscopic examination. Alonzo McDonald was a good choice for the job and proved his talents later in three diverse assignments: as United States trade representative in Geneva, as chief of staff at the White House, and then as vice-president of the Burroughs Corporation. No restrictions were placed upon his eventual recommendations; for once in his life Henry was not looking out the window or over his shoulder at General Motors.

Lee Iacocca called the appointment of McKinsey "a declaration of war" and decided that the enterprise was nothing more than a smoke screen to obscure his assassination. It is certainly and obviously true that Henry's unhappiness with Iacocca was an important ingredient in this initiative, but he had deeper concerns, including his angina. And the McKinsey papers, including Fred Searby's correspondence with Henry, leave no doubt that the chairman of the Ford Motor Company had a broader point of view and a wiser appreciation of its management problems than its president. It is indeed my own belief that a rational analysis of the McKinsey study confirms many of Henry's doubts about Iacocca's ability as a strategic manager.

The McKinsey team set out its intentions under three separate but complementary headings: to establish, first of all, a strong management basis for future change, which implied better leadership and more sophisticated planning; to create an atmosphere in which decisions could be more soundly implemented; and to develop an organization that would use Ford's undoubted strengths to greater advantage. It did not seem particularly revolutionary at the time, but it was not intended to be; Henry was looking for evolution rather than revolution. It must have created more internal apprehension than was apparent, though, since the office the McKinsey analysts had been given in Ford's Dearborn headquarters was broken into one night and somebody went through the files.

When Henry was discharged from St. Joseph's on January 30, Ralph

Brandt had made him promise to stick to a low-cholesterol diet with no animal fats, sugars, or carbohydrates. He was told to give up smoking, cut down on alcohol, and abstain from coffee or tea. He bought the first of his exercise bicycles and was told to do the equivalent of four miles a day. After the March board meeting, however, the angina began to trouble him again, and the advisability of surgery was discussed. This was the worst possible prospect for him. He was no more concerned than any other person about open-heart surgery, for he was pragmatic in all things, and toward the end of his life—when he had fulfilled (as he saw it) his mission—he approached his death as deliberately as it is possible to imagine. The problem in 1976 was that he did not want to be away from his office and out of touch even for a matter of weeks, for he had obvious concerns about the making of mischief in his absence. Nevertheless, he could not risk uncertainty about his health, and Dr. Brandt, therefore, made appointments for him with four of America's leading heart specialists: Dr. William Sheldon at the Cleveland Clinic; Dr. Robert Hall at the Texas Heart Institute; Dr. Eugene Braunwald at the Peter Bent Brigham Hospital in Cleveland; and Dr. Richard Gorlin at Mount Sinai Hospital in New York. Between April 13 and May 3 he went to see them all. The conclusion was that there was little risk involved in an operation but no immediate need for one. The treatment prescribed by Dr. Brandt was obviously working, and there was a demonstrable improvement in his condition. The detailed reports provided as clean a bill of health as he required, so he carried on as usual. He saw no need to be diverted from the unfinished business at hand.

Many people were sympathetic toward Lee Iacocca's position at this time and regretted the widening distance that seemed to separate the chairman and president despite their apparent physical proximity. The top floor of Ford's World Headquarters in Dearborn consists of two quiet, carpeted corridors of working suites divided in the center by the boardroom and conference rooms. Behind the closed door of each suite are a secretary's office, the principal office, and a small toilet with a shower. The building is not called the Glass House for nothing, and daylight has no difficulty getting in. A penthouse above contains a gymnasium, dining rooms, bedrooms—where outside members of the board of directors stay overnight ten times a year. Henry's corner office had its own drawing room and bedroom. But apart from an hour or so in the middle of the day, when the office doors opened and their occupants sat together at luncheon, it was not a gregarious place, and I sometimes thought Henry's office the loneliest place in the world. Few people understand and even fewer experience the loneliness of power, the isolation that faces the man or woman at the head of things. Every time I flew from Europe to Detroit, I would call his office and invite myself there for conversation and coffee (before his angina, and later, he always drank tea—endless cups of tea), and this was often regarded by others with something like awe or puzzlement. Why would anybody venture into the corner office unless you had to? Why risk an examination? I don't think it was fear, the risk of revealing a perhaps hidden inadequacy or getting the sack, that produced such thoughts. He hated firing people; that is why he did it so badly. From the day he made up his mind to replace Lee, it took him three years and an act of insubordination to stiffen his sinews sufficiently to do the deed. Nevertheless, it remains a fact that very few people, and only one or two outsiders on the board of directors, dropped in on Henry Ford II for a chat.

It has to be said, to balance the picture, that Henry himself could have made more efforts to establish informality. All his life he was fascinated by gossip—and might have inserted "conversation" in Who's Who as his principal hobby—but he engaged very little in informal discussion upon the weightier matters of management appointment or succession. To an extent this was his own fault and an unshakable aspect of his own character. When Robert Lacey was gathering material for his book on the Ford family, Henry told him matter-of-factly: "I'm very secretive. I'm very mistrustful. I don't trust anybody and that's for sure." One can say in mitigation that all the experiences of his adult life had driven home the need to keep his own counsel and to be wary of providing information that other people could use for their own ends. Throughout his life he served only the Ford Motor Company and had no doubt about where his own loyalties lay, but he was never sure how many others were as uniquely dedicated. And from the days of Harry Bennett onward, life had taught him that people who wear their hearts on their sleeves can sometimes lose their arms as a consequence. I do not discount the difficulty Iacocca must have had in breaching the barricades of Henry's personality. It was, however, a fact of life and an important constituent of their eventual separation.

Beneath their personal unease was a deeper cause for concern. It was not until 1950 that the Ford Motor Company outsold Chrysler to become the second force in the American automobile market, with a faltering share of 24 percent, little more than half of that dominated by General Motors. It averaged a little over 28 percent in the five years before Lee Iacocca was appointed president. But in the first years of his presidency it averaged less than 24 percent, and by 1976 it had fallen below 23 percent. Profits in 1974 and 1975 were—apart from the strike year of 1967—the lowest for fifteen years. The winds around World Headquarters were occasionally colder than the drifts that piled against the snow fences in winter. There were any number of reasons for this state of affairs, one of which was the remorseless increase in the sale of imported cars; by 1975, they accounted for nearly one-fifth of the total U.S. market. Management, however, was given its pay and perks to deal with such challenges, and Ford was not convincing anybody—least of all its chairman—that it had an adequate grasp of its problems or that its planning calendar contained the prospect of better days ahead. General Motors, after all, was facing the same forces in the same towns and cities, and by 1976 its market share was still above 47 percent—more than double that of Ford—and its profit performance was substantial and consistent.

Invigorated by the verdict of his doctors and generally in a more relaxed frame of mind, Henry urged McKinsey not to wait for the completion of its study but to come forward as soon as possible with interim suggestions for change. McKinsey's response, and an indication of the way it had gone about its task, are crisply explained in a subsequent memorandum:

Over the course of your tenure (thirty-one years) as chief executive officer, a pattern of executive interaction and decision making has evolved that is focused on obtaining your personal approval on a wide range of policy and operating decisions. Working within this decision-making pattern, the Ford Motor Company has attracted and retained a large group of talented executives and become one of the world's largest and strongest companies. However, this decision-making pattern will no longer be appropriate after your retirement, since your successor will assume leadership at a different point in the Company's history, and in any case will not have your unique authority as "proprietor." The most sensible response to the comment frequently made by Ford executives, "Henry Ford will be a tough act to follow," is "Don't try." Find a management system that is appropriate to the new executive team and the Company's next generation of challenges.

McKinsey's Al McDonald and Fred Searby reinforced their general argument with specific ideas, recommending a new framework at the top: an Office of the Chief Executive (OCE), which, they said, would signal "the sincerity of your intent to evolve to a less active role within the Company and begin the process of expanding top management authority to a broader group." They also recommended the creation of a Corporate Strategy and Analysis Group to support the OCE in its decision making—a sort of internal think tank removed from the day-to-day concerns of the business—and a wholesale shakeup in the product development process to emphasize the importance of longer-term planning and new technology. Henry was excited by the ideas and anxious to get moving.

The OCE was approved and established by the board of directors at the April meeting in 1977, and that afternoon all the officers of the company—the forty or so vice-presidents and senior executives—were called together to hear about it. They had absorbed the bare facts quickly and made their own interpretations of a clearly significant change. The OCE would consist of Henry Ford II as chairman and chief executive officer, Philip Caldwell as vice chairman, and Lee Iacocca as president with the additional designation of chief operating officer.

Henry was frank as ever and recognized that what he had to say would come as "quite a surprise" to most of the organization. "I have been chief executive of this company," he reminded his rapt audience, "for thirty-two years, and I am not tired of the job yet. In fact, I love it—perhaps too much for my own good and the company's!" He added: "Be that as it may." He said he knew he could not stay as chief executive forever, and the company would still be there long after he was gone, so he was committed to an orderly transfer of leadership. He confessed that he had been giving the subject a lot of thought and consideration "for a great many months." He said: "Next September I will reach my sixtieth birthday. My health is good. I have learned how to deal with the angina problem that developed early in 1976. It is my plan . . . to remain as both chairman and chief executive officer for the next three years. After that, I would no longer serve as chief executive officer but would serve as chairman until my sixty-fifth birthday in 1982. My role after I reach sixty-five is not yet clearly defined in my own mind. The world is changing faster than ever, and the environment for corporations is in a state of drastic upheaval. The complexities of running a corporation of this magnitude are far too great for any individual to cope with them alone. We must have the diversity of experience, knowledge, and perspective at the top. I have to learn to share my powers with two others, who, in turn, have to learn to draw willingly and openly upon the talents and perspectives of many others in arriving at their conclusions. My own role—more that of first among equals than primary decision maker—will not be a natural one for me, as you can all well appreciate. But I am determined to set a personal example."

He was specific about the responsibilities of his other two equals. Philip Caldwell would be responsible for strategic and business planning from people to product with philosophy thrown in. Iacocca would provide "the driving force to bring our strategic decisions to reality." All operations throughout the world would report to him.

There is little point now in trying to draw a precise map of the alleyways and one-way streets that had led Henry to this April day, although the highways of his thought processes are not difficult to determine. His unwillingness to consider Lee Iacocca as his successor had not been modified by the passage of time, but his appreciation of both men was shrewd. Caldwell, the introverted analytical workaholic with a proven record as a troubleshooter, a man who would himself delve under any stones that were left unturned, was the ideal philosopher prince. Iacocca, the extroverted salesman and battlefront general, with all of Ford's terrestrial resources at his fingertips, would be freed of the things he did less well (at least, in Henry's opinion) and able to concentrate his undivided attention on those he did best.

The world is not changed by meetings any more than battles are won by armchair generals. At best, they are a means of communication; at worst, an endorsement of status quo or rubber stamp for past decisions. At the Management Review Committee Iacocca gave no indication of personal discontent with the OCE. Explaining to the group his own position as chief operating officer, he began by thanking Henry Ford II for "the extraordinary leadership he has given our company for many, many years. I have worked for him, and with him, for thirty years now. I know, as you do, that any top job in this huge company is not easy. But the top job of chief executive officer and chairman of the board has to be the toughest of all, because the buck really does stop there."

He reminded the group that despite a UAW strike in the United States in 1976, after-tax profits had been nearly $1 billion. It was one of the reasons he felt able to say that he knew the new management structure would work. "We'll make it work and continue to make this company grow and prosper as it has in the past. I've worked with you gentlemen for a long time. You know me, and I know you. When together we understand our objectives and timetables, we do well individually and as a team."

Henry thought the meeting went well and was evidently relaxed, as he had every reason to be. And I had a new reason for some personal satisfaction: At the same board meeting during which they approved formation of the OCE, the directors agreed to my own appointment as a vice-president of the Ford Motor Company. On the evening of the following day I joined Henry and Kathy at the little colonial-style church in Greenfield Village where Kathy's daughter, Deborah, was to be married and where Henry had agreed to give the bride away. His son, Edsel, and Edsel's wife, Cynthia, were among the guests, and we later danced the night away at a party in the Dearborn Inn.

I had other more substantial reasons for satisfaction. The B car, which had been called Bobcat during its final months of development, had earlier been christened by Henry Ford II. I had been called to Henry's office one day to find him sitting with the final list of names that Bill Bourke had submitted. It had been narrowed down to thirteen: Amigo, Bambi, Bebe, Bolero, Bravo, Cherie, Tempo, Chico, Fiesta, Forito, Metro, Pony, and Sierra. "I like Fiesta," Henry said. "When you go back, tell Bill Bourke. Ford Fiesta." Fiesta it was, and Fiesta went into production in Germany in May 1976 and subsequently in Britain and Spain. In its first full year it more than justified the extraordinary faith, application, and dedication that made it possible. The Mustang had made records of its own and exceeded Ford's wildest hopes. Its first-year sales (418,812) had narrowly exceeded the previous record of the Falcon, 417,174 of which had been sold in 1960. The Fiesta did better than both. In its first twelve months 441,000 were built, including 86,400 for the American market. The growing demand of American customers for small cars—and Ford was still without an American "baby"—had overcome Henry's concern for the U.S. balance of payments and the impact upon it of Ford's own imports. A small car for the United States, to be developed in cooperation with Europe, had been agreed on; but it was still some years away, and the experience Ford would gain in American markets with a B car seemed both sensible and profitable. For the Fiesta was profitable and its success was consistent. In 1978 more than 400,000 were built, and another 444,000 in 1980, the last year of production for the United States. Sales volumes since then and to this day have averaged over 380,000 a year in Western Europe, which was something of a contrast with Mustang, sales of which declined substantially after the initial euphoria. Fiesta has remained, moreover, a reliable, high-quality, trouble-free car throughout its life, and the new model, introduced in 1989, gives every indication of continuing its place in a highly competitive market.

Comparisons may be odorous and unfair, and the climate of the American car market at this time was considerably more frenetic than that in Europe. It was, nevertheless, difficult for Henry not to reflect upon the people who, and disciplines that, had brought Fiesta to market and those in the United States, where four million Ford cars were, at various times, recalled for postproduction service attention. His American executives in Europe—Caldwell, Bourke, and Poling—had made Fiesta happen, and for the most part, their owners wrote nothing but letters of appreciation. Why could not the same disciplines repeat the success in the United States?

The answer to the question—or at least to most of them—arrived on Henry's desk in January 1978. Frederick Searby had wound up the analysis in which he and his people had been engaged just before Christmas, and on January 23 he wrote Henry a letter and attached it to a weighty report which he called "Strengthening Ford's Management System." It pointed out that Henry had created the OCE, established a corporate strategy group, explained his own intended future, and begun to plan his increasing separation from executive duties. "As you prepare for Phase 2," Searby observed, "some hard but essentially pleasant choices need to be made." For instance: "Your plan foresees thirty-five percent of your time devoted to family interests, personal investments, or to some leadership role in political, diplomatic, charitable or community affairs. Do you plan to divide this thirty-five percent among a number of involvements or to mass it against one or two important assignments? How can you ensure that you really do spend a quarter of your time on leisure and personal pursuits?" Searby said that under the OCE concept "it is perfectly reasonable that top management decisions are taken during your absence . . . and that you gradually delegate authority over major decisions. The OCE also permits the option of including other members of the Ford family in top management roles. . . ."

The questions were not difficult for Henry to answer; he thought about them every day. It was the other queries in this reasoned but critical report that were less easy to resolve. When the McKinsey study began, Searby wrote in his forthright but restrained prose, Ford had no formal plans for meeting U.S. government fuel economy standards, no explicit strategy for dealing with the Japanese competitive threat. "Ford," he insisted, "needs more than a 'me, too' approach to product planning to survive against a competitor (General Motors) twice its size, particularly when the competitor is willing to match Ford on per-unit research and development expense, has some economies of scale in tooling and facilities expenditures, and pulls through more than twice Ford's per-unit profit." There was only limited awareness that the company was likely to be capital-constrained within the next five years.

Searby pointed out that nearly three-quarters of Ford's "officer group" were likely to retire in the coming decade, and this presented an opportunity to "set in place a new generation of top leadership." Henry heavily underscored the study with thick black lines. One sentence was underlined in red: "You are seeking to institutionalize a permanent management system that encourages innovation and new ideas and allows intuition to coexist with systematic thinking."

Despite my lack of reverence for management consultancy, I have never doubted that the spectator often can see more of the game and even the need for new tactics. And there is one paragraph with which Henry was in complete agreement, one, incidentally, that continues to hold true for all business endeavor. It said:

Leadership involves more than management decision making; leadership requires providing a model for the behavioral patterns expected, including the goal of more collaboration and cooperation among managers. Leadership implies that management sets values and performance standards, rather than allowing [sic] tradition or narrowly conceived self-interest to determine "the way we do things around here." It is top management's job to shake out lethargy, to pull as well as push the organization in directions it would not move of its own accord, and to refuse to allow defeatism and pessimism to block desirable change.

It was all very well put, but not easily done, for execution has two meanings and sometimes both are necessary. And one clear problem threatened to upset the entire woodpile. The OCE was not working; at least it was not working together. Henry had taken Fred Searby's suggestion and appointed his brother Bill to the OCE, and he may have thought that this enlargement from three to four power-sharing people might bring more balance to the group. Three is always a triangle, and Bill was close to Lee and on good terms with him. The problem, however, was intransigent: The hoped-for alliance between Lee Iacocca and Philip Caldwell had never come about. Lee was convinced he was being plotted against; Henry began to come to the same conclusion.

In June Henry was able to take up his long-delayed invitation to visit the People's Republic of China. The Chinese government had made more specific requests for Ford aid or involvement in the development of its small and somewhat primitive automobile industry, and Henry was interested in seeing for himself and coming to some conclusions on the future of that mysterious market. He was also keen to have more discussions in the Far East about the economic imperialism of Japan and its carmakers. The visit resulted in the sale of seven hundred heavy Ford trucks to China, which was the good news; it also reinforced his concerns about the Japanese invasion of Western car markets.

It was while Henry was in China that Lee Iacocca decided upon a coup. The king was away in Peking. What better time for a palace revolution? Lee was undoubtedly unhappy reporting to Philip Caldwell, whose habit of turning over stones and demanding attention to unconsidered trifles and matters of moment had ruffled the egos of other people, too. Lee felt—possibly with some reason—that he had allies, and it was certainly true that there were some, including outside members of the board, who continued to admire his management style. He decided to lobby for support, presenting his own case for a higher status within the hierarchy. He took a company plane to see George Bennett in Boston and went on to New York, where he met Joseph Cullman 3d, chairman of Philip Morris and a Ford board member since 1967. He argued that Henry, still not sixty years of age, was senile and not up to the job and indicated that there were others in the company who shared his opinion. Franklin Murphy had also been approached, and he passed on the news—and his misgivings about Lee's attempt to rock an already unsteady boat—to Arjay Miller. On July 10, when Henry returned to Dearborn, Arjay told him what had happened. Henry did not believe it, but it took little detective work to persuade him that what he had heard was true. Lee Iacocca wanted to take the company away from him and, more astonishingly, seemed to think he could do it. Henry sat and talked to Arjay, who said: "You may not have thought you had an acceptable reason to get rid of Iacocca, but now you certainly do. It is now or never." There was a meeting of the board subcommittee charged with organization matters on July 12, and Henry went to the meeting prepared to make the situation starkly apparent. He was going to invite the directors to make a choice—Henry Ford II or Lee Iacocca—but it never came to a vote or even an argument. On July 13 Henry told Lee Iacocca that the Ford Motor Company no longer needed his services.

Lee did not attend the board meeting at which his departure was approved, and there was no formal vote or opposition. "He really believed he could oust Henry Ford," Arjay Miller recalled long after the incident had passed. "U.S. products were poor. We had a lousy product program. The Pinto was a disaster, and that wasn't the only one. He would not report to Caldwell, but he still thought he could oust Henry."

When Lee Iacocca's departure was announced, the formal statement included his own obituary in five sentences:

I have had thirty-two great and exciting years with Ford starting as a trainee in 1946. I look with pride and satisfaction on the progress the company has made worldwide. As I approach my fifty-fourth birthday, I have decided to resign from the presidency and from the board. Although I am leaving with many good feelings, one of the considerations leading to my resignation is the fact that I have not been in complete accord with some of the recent changes in the top management of the company. In any case, I leave amicably.

The last sentence was a little less than true. Henry Ford formally recognized Iacocca's contributions to the company and admitted the substantial differences that had arisen "on the subject of how Ford should be organized at the most senior level," which was another way of saying who should be boss. "In these circumstances," Henry said, "I believe Mr. Iacocca's resignation is in the best interest of the company and himself."

The newspapers had a field day. FORD FIRES LEE IACOCCA, said the *Detroit News*. "Lee Iacocca," it said, "is a flashy man, a huckster with style," which was true, and it added that no reason had been given for his dismissal. The *Detroit Free Press* seemed less surprised. "Lee Iacocca," it said in an editorial, "was the sort of man you would expect central casting to send around to play the role of an auto tycoon," but it added more thoughtfully: "The departure of Lee Iacocca from Ford Motor Company should not have come as a surprise. . . . The accumulating indications that the company's board and its chairman, Henry Ford II, were undertaking an intensive re-examination of the company and its directions should have told us something very much like this was going to happen."

The *Detroit News* carried an interview on the subject with Henry's brother William Clay Ford. "My brother called me into the office and we discussed it," he was reported as saying. "I told my brother my own personal opinion about Mr. Iacocca and that was that I felt he was an extremely capable and fine executive and I believed he could continue to do a fine job for us. Then he called Mr. Iacocca into the office. I think Mr. Iacocca was happy I was there because Mr. Iacocca and I have always gotten along very well. I think he believed I might have helped him. Mr. Iacocca and I have been very close. I was very sorry he had to resign." Interviews with Lee Iacocca himself suggested that Henry had said that "it was just one of those things" and had further insisted, "I just don't like you." I have a letter from George Bennett, who says he was told by Henry: "I don't like him." Henry Gadsden, another outside director, was reported as having said that Henry had explained the "body chemistry" between the two of them was wrong.

The *Chicago Tribune*, digging deeper into the sensational story, quoted a Wall Street analyst: "Iacocca's philosophy was to bring out a basic car and put a lot of fancy stripes and paint on it and sell the hell out of the styling. He doesn't believe the American public cares much about engineering." The newspaper pointed out that "things haven't been going so well for Ford in the United States" and quoted another analyst as saying: "Henry finally woke up to the fact that his European operations have been doing much better than his car business in North America."

It was not to be expected that there should be any substantial discussion in the newspapers about the less dramatic considerations leading to Iacocca's departure. Dramatizing a clash of egos is much more fun for everybody than sober analysis of balance sheets or corporate management. Henry might have avoided much of the slur and slander had he been more forthcoming. Some of the comment might at least have been tempered had it been known that he had scotched an attempted coup or averted a palace revolution. But he understood the hothouse in which he lived and was philosophical about the things that were written about him. Even in later years, when the dust of the conflict had been scattered by the winds of time, he was no more forthcoming. The nearest he ever came to public explanation—despite the fact that the book William Novak wrote for Iacocca had sold millions of copies and received wide acceptance as a true relation of the facts—was his reply to a question from the writer David Horowitz in January 1986.

He said: "There is a lot of stuff you're never going to know about me because it tears down other people and it isn't fair. Because you're going to have differences with people all the time during your life in all kinds of ways. I'm not put here to criticize people. It doesn't do me one bit of good to say 'Iacocca this' or 'Iacocca that.' Iacocca does not belong in Ford Motor Company because I didn't want him there. I think he felt he had every right to stay. He found out he didn't." When Horowitz pressed the issue, Henry added: "He was not morally qualified to be chief executive of Ford Motor Company." And that was that.

It may well be that Lee Iacocca believes his book to be true. There are many things in it that are not—untruth often exists through omission of relevant information—but even this does not invalidate the supposition that *Iacocca*, the book, truly represents the convictions of a man of great ambition and ego who was denied the one job in the world he most wanted: the succession to the throne of Henry Ford. The book is a long cry of rage, but the rage is nonetheless genuine.

I have no doubt that there were faults, misunderstandings, unnecessary fears, and much stubbornness on both sides, and I never underestimated the difficulty Iacocca found in being president under Henry's chairmanship or perhaps his frustration at always being in his shadow. Lee was a superlative salesman with an instinctive feel for marketing cars in the United States. He was lucid, swashbuckling, even spellbinding at times, but he never understood that Henry Ford II believed the Ford world to be a global world with only half its business in the United States. He never came to see that Henry regarded the talents required by its leader to encompass a sense of worldwide strategy with a proper respect for the heritage that began with his grandfather in 1903. "In terms of everything that counted," Iacocca said in his book, "I was far more important than Henry." When it came to selling cars to Americans, he probably was. In no other respect can the claim be anything other than fantasy.

There was surprisingly little conjecture about Lee Iacocca's successor. One or two newspapers began to promote the possibility that it might be Bill Bourke, but there was no board of directors' meeting in August and therefore no appointment. At the September board meeting the directors were asked to approve Philip Caldwell as president and chief executive officer effective from October 15. Henry had no doubt that his troubles were far from over. He felt, nevertheless, that he might sleep at night.

CHAPTER EIGHT

The First Good-bye

Henry Ford II gave a party at the Tavern on the Green in New York's Central Park in January 1979 to celebrate his son Edsel's thirtieth birthday. The family was there in strength, evidently pleased to have Henry's undivided attention, even for one evening. Charlotte's and Anne's children held tight to the hands of their grandfather, who gave every indication of enjoying their persistent attentions. Henry was a generous father and always willing to help with his children's problems, but the demanding mold into which his life had been set provided less time for togetherness than the family would have wished. He never forgot a birthday or an anniversary, but gifts or cards or telephone calls were no substitute for his company. Charlotte and Anne were New Yorkers—Anne with an apartment on Park Avenue and Charlotte with another on Sutton Place—and Henry was decidedly not, so there were times when they saw more of their father in Europe than in the United States.

Edsel had begun to work for the company soon after he left college, but although Henry was by no means a stern parent, he had an attitude of extraordinary rectitude toward his son's career. I never shared his point of view, and he did not come around to mine until the last year of his life. Henry was keen for Edsel to succeed in the company and wanted him to work overseas, believing that Brussels was the place for him to be. The city housed the headquarters of the European community; it was multinational and multilingual, and Henry had a job in mind there that he thought would provide training, experience, and challenge for his son. I once took Edsel on a brief tour of inspection in Germany, where he talked and lunched with the management of the German company. He went on to the Grand Prix and later wandered through the Continent with a friend before coming back to England.

Some weeks after this trip had ended, Henry said to me: "What's this about the crown prince?" I knew what he meant. Edsel had none of the swagger that is often exhibited by industrial princelings. He was naturally an extrovert, much in love with cars and motor racing, and everybody who met him said the same thing: He was a nice young man. Because of his diffidence, I had told him not to disappoint the German executives he was about to meet. "So far as they are concerned," I told him, "you are the crown prince, and you don't have to be inhibited or shy. Say what you want to say and ask the questions you want to ask." The trip obviously remained in his mind, as did my advice, and he talked about it when he got back to the United States and saw his father. Father, however, was not amused.

There are many ways of sustaining and developing the hierarchy in a family company, and few people think it strange that generations of Rockefellers or Rothschilds climb the family tree to their predestined seat in the boardroom. Nor, among Henry's closest personal friends, was the hereditary principle considered undemocratic. The process does not rule out training in the countinghouse or on the shop floor; but I have always believed there is a lot more to be learned at the top than at the bottom, and I have never known any royal princes who started in the stables unless they had a particular predilection for horses. Henry's evident mission to secure the heritage of the Ford Motor Company and lead it securely forward might well have taken into account a seat on the Ford board for his son and a career consciously developed to follow in the tire tracks of his father, his grandfather—after whom he had been named—and his great-grandfather.

But Henry would have none of it. "There are no crown princes in Ford Motor Company," he told me plainly, "and nobody gets preferential treatment because they are a member of the family."

I said: "You did." But it was not a convincing argument.

"That was different," he insisted. "Times have changed. It's not that kind of company anymore, and it's a different world. Fords who get to the top of the company will have earned that right. It would not be fair to have it any other way."

I pointed out that the family controlled more than 40 percent of the voting power of the company and might be considered effectively in control of its destiny and that this state of affairs would continue to exist after his death. People with this kind of power were not going to make informed decisions if they were never allowed outside the company cafeteria.

Henry said I was exaggerating, as usual. Brussels was where Edsel was going; he had even discussed it with the general manager of the Belgian company. There was nothing more to say. "I know you mean well," Henry conceded, "but you must not encourage him to have big ideas."

After Edsel's birthday party I went back to Dearborn to work with Ted Mecke on what promised to be the most sensitive issue of 1979: Henry's retirement or, at least, the first good-bye. The appointment of Philip Caldwell had made it possible for Henry to begin the process that would transform the Ford Motor Company from an industrial monarchy into a republic. The plan had three complementary elements: first, retirement from executive duties; second, abdication as chairman; and finally, on his seventieth birthday, departure from the board of directors. Ted Mecke, who had been appointed vice-president for public affairs in the early sixties, was a sensitive and thoughtful guardian of the corporate conscience and retained Henry's trust as securely as he did mine. We shared a common interest in books—he had a fine collection of Christopher Morley first editions—and we both were signally lacking in ambition. Ted had privately declared his own intention to retire with Henry and was urging me to consider taking his place. It was a suggestion that did not attract me, although I was glad to be able to lend a hand with Henry's retirement.

Henry himself, as ever, had firm ideas about his departure and the subsequent constitution of the management. The McKinsey papers had become thickly annotated, and when I got back to Dearborn from New York, I was bidden to dinner to discuss the first incision in the umbilical cord that had bound him to his duty for so many years. We dined at the small terrace house in Grosse Pointe where Kathleen Duross was living because there was nowhere else as comfortable or as suitable to talk freely about the things he had in mind. Cristina was still occupying his own house nearby. His mother had died three years earlier, and there was no longer anything to prevent a divorce between them, but Cristina remained convinced that Kathy was still no more than an infatuation although, after seven years, she was a great deal more than that.

Henry's own actions were certainly emphatic enough to convince his friends that the marriage was irretrievably broken. He had moved out of his home into the Edgar Allan Poe House, a self-contained cottage attached to the Dearborn Inn. His chauffeur, Tommy Shields, arrived each morning to grill bacon and scramble eggs which no kind of medical advice would ever have persuaded him to give up, on the hot plate in the diminutive kitchen, and Kathy came most evenings to cook dinners on the same basic equipment. Henry did not mind the solitude—there were times in his life when he asked nothing more than to be alone and think—but as he put it, his lodgings were "no damned place to entertain," and one weekend, when I was with him, we spent the Sunday in the pool house of his mother's home in Grosse Pointe, playing highly competitive games of backgammon and drinking iced tea, a peculiarly American habit for which I have never managed to acquire a taste. Even there he had his diary with him and was mapping out the various moves on the checkerboard of change, beginning with the annual meeting of Ford stockholders, which was due to take place in May and at which he proposed to announce formally his plans for his own future and the company.

None of Henry's campaigns was ever straightforward. The porridge would always have lumps in it. And in the spring of 1979 he still had to take account of America's most notorious lawyer, Roy Cohn. About a year earlier Cohn had brought suit in New York Supreme Court on behalf of fewer than a handful of shareholders—Bader and Bader, Rose L. Sands, and Sara Cordover—charging that Henry had approved a $1 million bribe in Indonesia to secure a contract for Ford Aerospace and that President Marcos had paid Henry privately $2 million for Marcos's agreement to a Ford factory in the Philippines. The plaintiffs were children of Cohn's partners in his New York law firm, and the shares had been purchased in their behalf to enable a conspiracy to be launched. It was a suit to which I was forced to pay attention, for in addition to the charges against Henry and other officers in the company, my own name appeared several times in the allegations as somebody who knew of these supposed misdemeanors and had apparently connived in them.

The suit also gathered together, in one improbable catalog, a list of other charges, all combining to suggest that Henry had exploited the privileges of his position by using company funds and facilities for his own private enjoyment. The nature of these charges suggested to some observers that Cohn or his informants had at least some knowledge of the inner workings of the Ford Motor Company, and the *Wall Street Journal* reported: "There is a new guessing game. Who is feeding information to Roy Cohn against Henry Ford II?"

The charges were not of the kind that would suggest a master criminal at work. Henry was accused of using company planes to fly himself and "his close intimate friend, Kathy Duross," on their vacation from London to Palma in Majorca. He was said to have caused the company to purchase a house in London "which serves no corporate purposes and constitutes an improper and illegal expenditure of $10 million." He "has the company pick up the tab for bird hunting in Scotland for Mr. Ford and his friends. Needless to say these guests further receive free room and meals during their stay. . . ." At the Ford headquarters building it was said Mr. Ford maintained for his personal convenience sauna baths "at an astronomical cost of $250,000, a private gym, and full-time masseur," as well as a private dining room "staffed by six full-time employees including a Swiss chef." The old allegation about the supposed Indonesian bribe was raised again, and there were other claims: Henry had used company planes to transport his sister's dogs "from location to location whenever she felt her pets were in need of a change of climate" and "to transport caviar, Dom Pérignon champagne, Château Lafite wine, and special lean bacon for his use." There was one wonderful sentence: "In fact, Mr. Ford deploys company aircraft to maintain his supply of caviar at his office and residences as if the company ran a New York to Detroit air shuttle."

Everybody concerned, including Cohn himself, knew these allegations were either without foundation or too trivial to be of consequence. The supposed $10 million house in London was an office building for which I was myself responsible and which is still in use today. We moved from an old and far from functional building into the new one and even made a profit on the deal. No capital payment was required, for the office was, and is, rented. The gymnasium and the private dining rooms in the Dearborn office were available to, and used by, all the company's senior executives and were a great deal less glamorous than many other executive suites I have seen. I had never suspected that Henry had any kind of taste for caviar; a proper meal was only a proper meal, in his opinion, if it began with soup. The bit about the bacon was true. He liked American bacon, and company planes crossing the Atlantic did occasionally bring him new supplies; but if room was available on company planes, it was not unusual for many of us to take advantage of their convenience. I once transported a music stand and a bust of the duke of Wellington in this manner, but when company planes were used for occasional private trips, they were invariably charged and paid for as personal expenses.

The allegations were as dishonest as the man who made them, but the "no smoke without fire" syndrome became only too evident when the media jumped upon them with expected glee. America's libel laws provide no protection for its public figures, and there is no refuge to be found in pleading sub judice, for it does not exist. Trial by public invariably precedes trial by judge or jury. Nobody seemed to want to examine the credibility or the character of the man who framed these charges. In an article in the December 1978 edition of *Esquire* magazine—it was titled "Don't Mess with Roy Cohn"—Ken Auletta said: "A legal executioner, he's the toughest, meanest, vilest, and one of the most brilliant lawyers in America." Auletta pointed out that Cohn was lawyer for New York's most feared Mafia families and "a string of hoods," and journalists were understandably wary of a man with such a fearful reputation for litigation, who had made his reputation as senior counsel for Senator Joseph McCarthy and his Communist witch-hunt.

It has to be said that Henry himself made a tactical mistake that gave Cohn's allegations credibility they might otherwise have lacked. Nothing is more calculated to add circumstance to the campaigns of unprincipled self-publicists than a response that appears to take them seriously. On the other hand, no charge leveled against Henry Ford II could have made him more angry than one of professional misconduct, and on May 2, 1978, one week after Cohn first filed suit, he called a press conference in Dearborn and gave a detailed rebuttal of the charges.

"I asked you here today," he said, "so that I could answer [the] charges, no matter how ridiculous they may appear to be. The matter is already in litigation, and lawyers are defending the case through normal channels. But I am not going to wait for court processes to clear my name. I have nothing to hide, and that's why I'm here to meet this personal affront head on." Details in the Cohn suit suggested that it could not have been compiled without inside knowledge. Some of the better-informed journalists thought it bore evidence of an internal conspiracy, and when Henry began to deal with questions at the end of his prepared statement, it was clear that he thought so, too.

"Who do you think would bring these charges against you?" he was asked.

Henry replied: "Why were they brought against me; is that the question?"

"Are they completely not based on fact and absurd as you implied?" the questioner persisted.

"I don't have any idea why they are brought against me," Henry said. "I have my own thoughts on the matter, but I don't have any idea what the facts are."

"Would you like to share your thoughts on it?" he was asked, to which he answered: "No, thank you very much."

The Detroit press corps is not noted for its shyness and was not to be deflected despite this unsatisfying skirmish. "Mr. Ford," said one reporter, getting nearer to the heart of the matter as he saw it, "do you have any reason to believe that your estranged wife may be involved in any of this?"

Henry pondered the question. "I don't know whether she is or whether she isn't."

"Have you asked her?"

"No, I haven't."

The Ford Motor Company holds its shareholders' meeting every May. In 1957, the year of the first meeting, 2,940 people attended, and in subsequent years there were often well over 2,000, for there are those who consider it good entertainment, better, indeed, than many of the other events that take place on the stage of the Ford Auditorium, which Henry's mother gave to the city of Detroit. Gadflies and sharpshooters alike enjoy the freedom to cross-examine the chairman, and it was Henry's experience, as target for the day at this annual rite, that had persuaded him to hold the press conference. The exchanges at stockholder meetings are, for the most part, good-humored and friendly, even effusive when the company is doing well, and Henry hoped to dispose of the Cohn issues at an open press meeting, so that he might prevent their becoming the principal topic on stockholders' day. I doubt if it was ever much more than wishful thinking because Roy Cohn, whose principal weapon was publicity and fear of publicity and who knew a good opportunity when he saw one, attended the meeting himself, as attorney for those whose names were on the suit, and shouted accusations at Henry. Cohn was booed by many shareholders and told repeatedly to sit down, but he knew he was on to a good thing and returned to New York well satisfied.

The Ford lawyers spent months investigating every charge in the suit, delving with mounting frustration into even irrelevant details, and produced a fifty-page, close-typed report effectively rebutting—or so it seemed to me—all the assertions. Henry read it and delivered himself of a one-word observation. Across page one he wrote: "Irresponsible." But irresponsible or not, he had to submit himself to hours of deposition, hoping that this might bring the affair to an end.

Cohn, however, was not to be deterred by reason, and on January 30, 1979, he deposited with the Supreme Court in New York a 104-page response which piled question on question, naming just about everybody on the board of directors and many in top management and demanding more information. The court promptly threw out the submission, insisting that it had no jurisdiction; the suit should be filed in Michigan, where the defendants were living. But Cohn seemed undismayed and soon had another unlikely ally.

At the end of March Henry's nephew Benson Ford, Jr., who was twenty-nine years of age and engaged in a battle to gain control of a $7.5 million inheritance from his late father, announced that he was extending his action to include several suits against company officials. Benson insisted that he had a right to succeed his father on the board of directors, and to pursue this family feud, he took his troubles to Roy Cohn. His suit was lodged formally against Ford Estates, an office that administered the private affairs of the Ford family, and insisted that he had not been treated "on an equal basis with other members of the Ford family." For Cohn it was a gift from his own perverted gods.

Benson, who had settled in California in 1969 and taken nine leisurely years to obtain a degree from Whittier College, was an inherently nice but distinctly mixed-up young man, and when the dust had settled, came to my office one day to regret his behavior. He wanted then to get back into Henry's good graces and apologize for the trouble he had caused. He had fallen, he told me, among some "bad gurus" and had been wrongly advised; but it was all grist for Cohn's remorseless mill, and it took some months before his ultimate admission that there was as little justification for Benson's suit as for the earlier one. Indeed, his admission was not obtained until the Ford Motor Company settled the initial suit with an out-of-court payment to Cohn of $100,000. He had harassed and chastised the mighty with evident advantage to his own reputation, and the settlement was no more than blackmail. It was cheaper for the company to pay than to waste time on endless depositions, and it was a great deal less than the legal fees that would have ensued had the case gone to trial. Out-of-court settlements are never satisfactory, for they invariably leave in their wake cynical opportunities for doubt. Why should anybody pay to have his innocence established? There was, however, a verdict in this case, written in *The American Lawyer* by Steven Brill, who tabulated succinctly the pattern of Cohn's behavior.

He wrote:

Event 1: A lawyer, using his partner's children as the aggrieved "share-holders," decides to bring a shareholders' derivative suit against a company, charging the chairman with stealing. The charges are so scandalous, and the company and its chairman so well known, that the suit makes big headlines.

Event 2: After he files the suit, he tells a reporter, as he waves various papers in the air, that he has "an open-and-shut" case on all charges.

Event 3: The suit has not been filed in the right jurisdiction. It is thrown out.

Event 4: The lawyer vows to file the suit in the right jurisdiction.

Event 5: Telling the other side that he plans to file again, and that this will mean a rehash of the charges in the press, the lawyer inquires if a "settlement" might be possible.

Event 6: The company, which has denied all the charges but is beset by bad publicity on other fronts . . . gives the lawyer $100,000 in "legal fees" on the condition that he not bring the suit in the right jurisdiction.

Event 7: The lawyer declares that "it now appears" that the company chairman was not guilty of any wrongdoing.

Brill went on to point out how neatly Cohn had manipulated the situation. "The lawyer's supposed clients—shareholders—get nothing," he wrote. "Nor do they give up anything: the shareholders can sue again on the same charges. It's just that the headline-making lawyer can't represent them. Contrary to what would be required in any other share-holders' suit, a judge does not have to approve this settlement. With the first suit thrown out and the second one only threatened, there is no suit pending and, therefore, no judge with jurisdiction. In many circles this would be called extortion. . . ."

In 1979 there were few brave enough to make these arguments and no headlines to popularize them. It was not until Cohn died—miserably, of AIDS—that the extent of his villainy gained any widespread under-standing, despite actions against him in his lifetime for professional misconduct, an attempted prosecution for murder, and his eventual disbarment. As the suit against Henry dragged on, I tried many times to understand a society so timid that it could conspire to allow its innocents to be so ruthlessly bullied. When Nicholas von Hoffman published his book *Citizen Cohn* in 1988, I began to comprehend, but by then I had other things on my mind.

In the early months of 1979 another monarchy was being transformed into a republic, and its consequences for the Ford Motor Company were to be of greater moment than its own domestic revolution. Ayatollah

Khomeini returned to Iran and dismantled the Peacock Throne. We were perhaps too preoccupied to understand what Iranian fundamentalism would come to mean, and the business climate in the United States was good enough to encourage optimism. The first three months produced the highest profits of any first quarter in the Ford Motor Company's history. Henry was slowly strengthening the U.S. management; Red Poling had returned from Ford of Europe and was given command of the staffs—a position that would give him a quick course in relearning America and identify him as a growing power within the company. Other "high fliers" were given bigger responsibilities.

Henry's desk, normally bare of anything save a few immediate papers, was piled with speeches, upon which he worked assiduously in and out of the office. His plan for his future was to be communicated to the management and to the board, to the stockholders and suppliers and dealers. Evolution would be explained, and for the first time Henry was also going to give the family a talking-to. The concerns aroused by Benson Ford, Jr., had created some new domestic tensions. Brother Bill had been infuriated, even to the extent of telling Leonard Apcar of the *Wall Street Journal*: "I don't think Benson's qualified to sit on the board any more than the man in the moon." Henry and Bill therefore summoned a family meeting at Bill's house. Nothing of the kind had ever happened before; when the family got together, it was invariably for social reasons. Henry talked to me on several occasions about the things he was going to say, and he repeatedly used the word *speech*. "I know it's a family affair," he said, "but I'm not going to write things down on my cuff and then find I've left things out. I'm going to give them a speech." When he had completed it to his satisfaction, it ran to fifteen pages.

There were thirty family members at the gathering: Bill Ford and his wife, Martha; Bill and Henry's sister, Dodie, and her husband; and all the children with their husbands and wives. Benson caused a small hubbub when it was discovered he had brought a pocket tape recorder. When this had been resolved, Henry got down to the problems with Cohn and the issues Benson had raised. He assured his family that he really was going to retire as chief executive of the company and that there would be a new man in charge whose surname was not Ford. "Some people on the outside," he said, "see the change in management as something like changing from a Monarchy to a Republic. Others who look at things a little more dramatically are seeing it all as some kind of struggle for a throne. I don't see it that way and I hope you don't."

He said that he had been doing the job since he was twenty-eight years of age and began to remind them of a little history:

When I became chief executive in 1945, you could count the number of major stockholders on the fingers of both hands and have a few fingers left over. In 1956 we became a public corporation and now we have 349,000 stockholders all over the world. We also have 500,000 employees whose lives and those of their families depend upon Ford. We have 14,000 dealers in fifty-six different countries and they employ another 350,000 people. We have 15,600 suppliers, and Ford of Europe, by itself, is bigger than the Chrysler Corporation. Obviously Ford remains a family company in the sense that there are men and women called Ford—and some of them are playing an active role in the business. And I think people like that. And that must be considered by all of you as good news because it implies that, although we are not a family company any more, the Ford family does have a continuing role to play in its affairs. However, there will be no place in Ford for anybody called Ford if the family fails to set the right public example and this applies particularly to the younger generation and the generations to come.

He went on to explain that he had begun to devote a lot of thought to the future of the family and the company "as long ago as 1976 when I got sick." He discussed the McKinsey study and the formation of the OCE. "The first three members were Philip Caldwell, Lee Iacocca, and me. Iacocca was against the idea from the beginning. He did not want to play on the team and eventually he went. Bill then came into the OCE." Henry was determined to be explicit, and he was:

What I have been doing all this time is to create the best senior management we could—because good management is what eventually sorts the men from the boys. There has never been a successful company with bad management and there has never been a company that went out of business with good management. Perhaps you have seen some of the newspaper stories that said Edsel would succeed me. Can you imagine what would have happened if we had tried such a thing? You can say that I took over at twenty-eight. Edsel is now thirty— why can't he take over? The answer is that the world in 1979 is a very different world from the one we knew in 1945. If we had taken such an obviously inappropriate step, public, press, and financial community reaction would have been devastating. The Ford Motor Company must not only make the management changes that are necessary—it must be seen to be making them impartially, intelligently, and taking into account its duty to these people who own the company: all those stockholders. And I mean all the stockholders out there— not only the ones in this room.

He ended by asking them—his family—to recognize that the stock-in-trade of any large corporation is public confidence. "If this family rocks the Ford boat," he said ominously, "that boat could sink. It almost did once. The quickest way to bring a country or a company to its knees is to sow the seeds of dissension from within."

As for jobs for the boys, he added:

If Edsel or Benson or Billy or Buhl or Alfred or any other members of the family want to get to the top of the company, they'll have to get there by merit. It's what you are and not who you are that's going to count. This may prove a pretty hard fact to swallow but there's no other way around it. And I have to say to Benson and the rest of you that fighting family or business quarrels in the press and on TV doesn't do anybody any good. In fact, quite the opposite. All it does is to make the press happy. In these times, everybody likes to read hot gossip. We have managed to provide our share of it lately. When it's Ford against Ford, that's news, and its a license for the press to print snide remarks, downright lies, and gross distortions. The press is happy but stockholders and major investors are very unhappy indeed. You would not want to sail in a ship that always seemed to have trouble on the bridge and neither do they. There will soon be a fifth generation on the way and a sixth. I have not devoted my life to this company without believing that I was helping to secure it for the hundreds of thousands who rely upon it—and for our own family.

I had wondered at the reaction these plain words would receive. Henry said it "went down all right"; some of the younger ones told me they found it very interesting, full of things they had not thought about. When, after Henry's death, there was another—certainly unnecessary—squabble over inheritance, I reflected wryly on the extent to which the family had absorbed the things that were said on this occasion. But despite the one other public drama, fortunately short-lived and soon ended, the family meeting has had one lasting effect. The family still meets to talk business twice a year.

———————

For the stockholders' meeting on May 10, Henry was more concerned to extol the merits of the new management than to deliver an encomium for his own career. He had decided to retire as chairman and chief executive on October 1, handing the responsibility over to Philip Caldwell, and the first notes he drafted for his speech contained news of another appointment. Bill Bourke was to be elected president. Jack McDougall, who had played such a key role in bringing Fiesta to the European market, was to replace Bourke and take over North American Automotive Operations. The speech that was taking shape noted: "William Bourke has had a long seasoning in the hard realities of automotive operations, both here and abroad. He is an ideal complement to Mr. Caldwell in his new role." Henry had also written: "It should be of more than passing interest to you to note that Mr. Caldwell, Mr. Bourke, and Mr. McDougall all have served as chairman of the board of Ford of Europe."

When it came to tackling his own achievements, he was determined neither to seek nor to imply the need for any personal credit. The figures he had given the family to show the growth of the company since 1945 were to be repeated, along with some other signs of maturity—the fact, for instance, that Ford sales now exceeded $1 billion for every ten days. Knowing that Edsel understood he could not quickly expect to succeed to the chairmanship, he felt it would be useful to dispel any further public conjecture in this regard, and he had written: "There are no crown princes in Ford Motor Company and no privileged route to the top"—a phrase that would be widely quoted when the press came to report upon the meeting.

But the speech, when it was delivered, differed in one important respect from the first draft: The names of Bill Bourke and Jack McDougall were missing. In discussion with Philip Caldwell, Henry bowed to a delayed transition. Philip argued that running North America—making cars and trucks for the U.S. and Canadian markets— at a time when those markets were turning sour needed Bourke's continuing presence, and a brief delay would provide some more thinking time to plan the precise composition of a new management. As I have said before, Henry never gave anybody a job and then insisted how it should be done, and he had sufficient respect for Philip Caldwell's talents to believe that one step at a time might be a more sensible approach. I thought it unnecessarily cautious, although I could not quarrel with the principle involved; like Philip Caldwell, I always safeguarded the right to make my own appointments.

So when the stockholders' speech was finally delivered, there was only one announcement: Henry would resign as chief executive, as planned, on October 1; Philip Caldwell would succeed him in the principal executive responsibility and continue as vice-chairman. It was understood between them that in a matter of months Philip would also succeed to the chairmanship and Henry would replace Ed Lundy as chairman of the Finance Committee. "Phil will know where he is in six months," Henry said. "Then my day will be over."

I was surprised to some extent—despite my awareness of Henry's sense of duty—that he would remain shackled to the chairmanship for so long a period of time, no matter how logical it began to seem, for he was as anxious as the most optimistic emigrant to embrace a new life. An exact explanation of his state of mind was contained in a quotation from Dr. Johnson that he used at the end of the stockholders' speech. "Ten years before this country was born," he said, "Samuel Johnson said: '. . . as we advance in the journey of life, we drop some of the things which have pleased us. No man is obliged to do as much as he can do. A man is to have part of his life to himself. If a soldier has fought a good many campaigns, he is not to be blamed if he retires to ease and tranquility. . . .' I have doubts about the 'ease and tranquility' but with the rest I find myself, ladies and gentlemen, in complete accord."

It was a graceful exit.

When Philip Caldwell inherited executive control of the Ford Motor Company, nobody drew parallels with the way it had been when Henry Ford II was charged with a similar assignment in 1945. It would have taken very little to shake the insecure foundations in 1945; thirty-three years later they were strong and resilient enough to withstand a shock of much greater proportions. But only just.

The big American automobile was never entirely the totemistic emblem of conspicuous consumption so many of its critics claimed it to be. America was a big country with wide, beckoning spaces and superhighways, and even women, who might be considered less adventurous than men, often thought little of packing the family into a big wagon and ferrying it from Chicago to Florida or from equally distant cities to other locations in the Sun Belt. The traveling salesman packed his suit bag and golf clubs along with his samples and cruised from motel to motel with the air conditioning high and the radio (soon to be called an in-car entertainment center) as loud as his eardrums could stand. The truckers swept by in their enormous rigs like the argosies of trade they had truly become, more so as the railroads lost their glamour and preeminence.

The enormous change in the ethnic composition of the United States, in which Hispanics began to multiply, overtaking blacks in many regions of the country to become the second-largest group, turning places like Miami into Spanish-speaking cities, had its own impact. These groups still had big families, and many within their family clans were without cars of their own, so the big cars made sense; small ones were not roomy enough for them and their impedimenta. Mostly they bought used cars; but used cars start by being new, and there were times in the earlier seventies—even after the OPEC oil embargo of

1973–74—when Ford, along with other U.S. manufacturers, found itself short of big cars while the small ones began to jam the dealerships.

Until the mid-seventies the United States was a country where the essentials of life were always cheap and the luxuries expensive, and even they often seemed a good bargain to visitors from other developed Western countries. Compared with Europe's, the American car has always been a bargain. Moreover, sitting as they did on enormous reserves of oil, Americans believed that cheap energy—in particular, gasoline—was part of their birthright, and this point of view was underscored by the unwillingness of U.S. administrations or Congress to tax the stuff as governments did so heavily in Europe and Japan. Big cars were therefore practical and affordable, and their ownership conveyed no sense of guilt. But then something happened to challenge this comfortable view of life: the OPEC embargo. By the end of 1978 gasoline prices were some 80 percent higher than they had been in 1970. The small, fuel-efficient, and technically sophisticated car began to nudge the bigger ones out of the parking lots. California—where every new fad took root, from Davy Crockett caps to Hula-Hoops, from motels to outdoor movie houses, drive-in restaurants, and banks—led the way. The shrinking U.S. family, the single-parent home, the flood of women into the work force as they embraced their new freedoms—all made small cars sensible, and suddenly big was bad.

On top of this was the growing national disaffection with "Detroit," which, under constant attack from politicians, government regulators, and consumer groups, was seen to be monolithically opposed to any change that would meet the demands of the powerful environmental lobby. Cars were also becoming more expensive to buy and maintain, and the national economy was prone to periodic gloom with recession never far from the door.

By 1978, when small cars accounted for substantially over one-quarter of the U.S. market, General Motors had begun to offer a bigger proportion of "downsized" cars, beginning with its 1975 model year. Ford laid much emphasis on the introduction of its own small front-wheel-drive car, the Escort, but it was not due for production until 1980. The timing might have been more appropriate had it not been for the events in Iran. Between 1978 and 1981 gasoline prices increased by one-fifth in Western Europe and one-tenth in Japan; in the United States they doubled, and although U.S. prices were still cheap by European standards, the American customer did not take that point of view. For the only pocketbook against which he could make inflationary comparisons was his own. By 1979 the small-car share of the market had shot up to 54 percent, and imported cars had a grip on as much as one-fifth of the entire market.

It was not only, as Lee Iacocca put it, that "the Shah left town" but that occasional gasoline shortages quickly demonstrated the importance of a full tank of gas. It is fine to travel hopefully, but it is more comforting to be sure of arriving at the desired destination. Then, as more and more Americans began to rediscover the pleasure of small driver's cars—and new standards of uncomplicated reliability—they began to spread the gospel of miniaturism. Small was beautiful, and since the growth of small cars was led by the better-educated and better-off families, which usually had two or three cars at their disposal, it gained additional credibility among users and onlookers alike. Even those owners of small cars who found them less resourceful and reliable than their previous U.S. vehicles kept quiet about it. Imports were the trend, the thing to own; it was eccentric to bad-mouth them.

People and their purchases rarely change for any one single reason; one thing creates and leads to another. Change nevertheless tends to cohere, and it was not necessary for the American automobile industry to summon its psychiatrists or indulge in rueful introspection to understand why the world had turned upside down. The writing was on the wall, and the evidence was in the streets. Detroit might—and should— have foreseen the changing nature of its business. The truth is, however, that its managers were ill-prepared for the change in public demand and possessed no wands with sufficient magic to remedy the situation overnight.

I think I must have been half asleep myself at this time where my own future was concerned. I suspect I had not taken Ted Mecke's determination to retire with Henry Ford II seriously enough, and then, when Henry had changed his own plans—retaining the chairmanship—I had lulled myself into believing that Ted would extend his own period of service. I had known that for some time Ted had proposed, even advanced the idea of my succeeding him as the company's vice-president for public affairs, but I had never taken the suggestion seriously. There were only two Ford Motor Company vice-presidents who were not American citizens, and both of us worked overseas. I did not believe that Ford, despite the growing international nature of its management, would want one of them in the Dearborn hierarchy. I knew that all Ford managers are required to nominate their successors and are to an extent judged upon the effectiveness with which they develop suitable candidates. The management review system is unyielding in this respect, and Henry used to spend days every year sitting in management development reviews. I was happy to figure on Ted's own list but thought it more of a courtesy than a reality. Circumstances in the United States also persuaded me—from my cozier chair in Europe—that there was a lot more winter and rough weather on the west side of the Atlantic, and Ted Mecke was occupying a hot seat that could only become a great deal hotter.

I should have guessed that my name would not be allowed to linger on Ted's little list unless Henry shared his point of view, and in June 1979 I woke up. During a trip to Dearborn I received a call from Henry suggesting dinner for "just the two of us." I booked a corner table in the restaurant at the Hyatt Regency Hotel. He discovered the existence of some Lafite-Rothschild that was not on the wine list, and we gossiped the first bottle away. He then sent for another—"the night's still young"— and when that was nearly consumed, he said that my replacing Mecke was no joke (which, in a different context, I never thought it to be); it made every kind of sense for me to take over from him. We were an international company, and hadn't I been everywhere within it? Ford in the United States was accelerating into small cars, and who knew more than I about them? I said it was a ridiculous idea. I knew every airport and airport hotel in Europe and had keys to the antechambers of most governments. I was not, in any sense, an organization man. I didn't like meetings. In America I couldn't find my way unaided from Chattanooga to Little Rock and indeed would have had trouble getting to dinner parties in Detroit had it not been for a phone in the car upon which I could call for directions. "Use a driver," Henry said, practically. I said "they" wouldn't let me do what I wanted to do. "What *do* you want to do?" he asked, and, while I was thinking, added: "Do what you like." I said that the problems facing the company in the United States were enormous and needed both competent and instinctive responses. In Europe my reactions were like that; in America I would even have to learn how to spell again.

When the second bottle was finished—and I never remembered relishing Lafite-Rothschild less in my life—Henry said: "I know it's going to be backs to the wall, but all my friends tell me the British are never happier than in that position." We stayed late at the table. The restaurant hostess, who was young and had long blonde hair, came and sat at the table by my side. Henry said to her: "You'll get to know Walter; he's going to work here." The lady expressed pleasure, but I told her that Henry was pulling her pretty leg.

The next day I went home and recounted the conversation to my wife. Elizabeth asked: "Are you sure you can hold out?"

"Absolutely," I said.

When Henry was frustrated, he never returned directly to the attack, preferring to resort to his usual tactics of taking things for granted, and at other meetings during the year he began to slip "when you come" into the conversation. In October there was a meeting in Cologne under the visiting influence of Philip Caldwell, with whom I had worked closely in Europe. The U.S. Escort had been developed in a common program with Ford in Europe, and this was the principal item on the agenda for everybody except Philip, who told me he "understood" I would replace Ted Mecke and wanted me to know how pleased he was to hear the news. How soon could I move? I went back to Elizabeth again and said the hounds were moving in. A week later—after some days of doubtful introspection—she said: "I know what's on your mind. What do you want to do?" I heard myself saying that I would like to give it a go. "Well, then," she said, "we will." We did.

With a clear and determined plan in mind for his own remaining years and knowing he would soon be freed from the imperatives of being Ford's first manager, Henry Ford II began systematically to put his own life into order. He had navigated the stormy waters Roy Cohn had whipped up and piloted himself through the stockholders' meeting, and in July 1979 he began to think of casting himself almost symbolically adrift and indulging his own private pleasure in sailing as captain of his own real ship.

Henry had always loved messing about in boats. It was a pleasure he had inherited from his father and the days of his childhood. He began his own adventures at sea in chartered oceangoing yachts, cruising the waters of the Caribbean and the Greek islands. On September 21, 1961, however, he placed an order with a Dutch shipyard for a fine white cruiser of his own, and this was delivered shipshape and spanking new on April 30, 1963. He called her *Santa Maria* after the flagship of Christopher Columbus, although some who knew that Cristina's first name was Maria imagined a different derivation. The little ship in which Columbus set sail had been ninety feet long; Henry's *Santa Maria* was bigger by eighteen feet. He paid $460,000 and was initially charmed with the boat and all its newfangled instruments on the bridge, but the love affair did not last long. He went cruising when he could and chartered her in between to people he knew, including C. Douglas Dillon, the secretary of the treasury, but although she cruised at a comfortable eighteen knots, the *Santa Maria* had more room for crew than passengers. There were only two guest cabins, which gave her an unlucky complement of thirteen: six passengers and seven crew. When Glenn Hargrave, the captain, had a heart attack, Henry decided he had an additional reason for bringing the brief relationship to an end, and the *Santa Maria* was sold on September 1, 1965, for the same sum of money he had used to buy her.

He then went back to chartering until June 1973, when he flew to Genoa in Italy and bought a much smaller boat—a forty-one-foot Tiger sports cruiser—for $130,000 and had it shipped as deck cargo across the Atlantic so that he could use it in Michigan on the Great Lakes and the Detroit River. The Tiger, promptly renamed *Santa Maria II*, was also a disappointment. From the beginning its generators were faulty, its electrical equipment would work only on a European voltage, and the twin-diesel engines demanded frequent oil changes. Henry had Tom Kish, a burly and dependable member of the Grosse Pointe police force, trained as captain, but he was never able to enjoy the boat as much as he wanted since he was spending more and more time in Europe and managed to use it only six weekends a year over his period of ownership. In August 1977 he gave *Santa Maria II* to Palm Beach Atlantic College in West Palm Beach, Florida, for use at its school of oceanography and for another six years went back to chartering.

One of the boats he chartered was the *Southern Breeze*. She had been built in Louisiana in 1964 and was nearly 169 feet long—more than half the length of an American football field—and had a gross weight of 538 tons. There was accommodation for ten people in five double cabins, each with a bathroom, and in addition, there was a large main saloon, an upper sky deck, and a crew of thirteen. She was painted blue and had immaculate teak decks. The *Southern Breeze* did not bear, or seek, comparison with the floating palaces owned by such other private sea-farers as Aristotle Onassis, but I never heard anybody complain, and in April 1983, when Henry knew what he really wanted, he discovered she was for sale and gladly paid $3.5 million for the privilege of ownership. An extensive refit and restyling by John Bannenberg cost him another $2.5 million in 1984, by which time she was as beautifully equipped as anything of her size afloat. *Southern Breeze* was a good sea boat and made fourteen transatlantic crossings, but for Henry she was his own passport to the aquamarine havens of the Mediterranean and the enchanted waters of the West Indies. To begin with, it had made no sense to do other than charter her for occasional cruises because he could manage no more than infrequent trips, and he never wasted money. Nor was this an opportune time to invest $6 million, for he had decided to proceed with a divorce and a divorce was going to be expensive.

The divorce action came to court in Detroit in February 1980, fifteen years to the day after he married Cristina, but some years after the marriage had really ended. He had left Cristina on March 30, 1976, moving out of the large house they had occupied together on Lakeshore Drive in Grosse Pointe and into the Edgar Allan Poe cottage at the Dearborn Inn. He had expected this move to convince Cristina of the incompatability of their marriage and incidentally of the seriousness of his relationship with Kathleen Duross, but the two suites that formed the Edgar Allan Poe house were to be his home for more than four years. The Dearborn Inn did its best to make him comfortable, although in a businesslike fashion. In December 1979 he received a pointed little letter from the manager, which said: "Dear Mr. Ford: It has become necessary to increase our room rates beginning January 1, 1978, and the monthly rate for Poe 1 and 2 will be $1400.00, instead of $1312.50. All of us are honored and pleased having you stay at our Inn. Cordially, A. A. deVogel." The rates went up to $1,500 in 1979 and the following year to $1,600, whereupon Henry wrote a little letter of his own: "Dear Dutch: I received your note about the increase in rent for Poe Cottage. Needless to say I don't like it, but I guess I will have to go along with it." By then he knew, however, that he would not have to go along with his solitary way of life much longer.

I went apprehensively to the Wayne County Circuit Court in the City County Building in Detroit at 9:00 A.M. on February 19, 1980, convinced that Henry would once again provide the newspapers with a sideshow—an opinion that was soon verified. There were only sixty seats in the courtroom, but some forty were occupied by journalists. Cristina arrived with a niece and a wan smile, wearing a brave purple Saint Laurent suit. She would almost certainly have extracted a larger settlement had she not gone to court but had apparently been persuaded otherwise. Cristina had many good qualities, and it was sad to contemplate somebody with whom I had enjoyed good times going through the washing of linen in public. It seemed a long way from that April day in 1974 when Henry had sent a telegram to Henry Kissinger congratulating him on his marriage, and Kissinger had replied: "Are all Henrys so lucky in love?"

I also had some reason for believing Cristina had not forgotten the good times. I had been subpoenaed by Henry's lawyer to attend the court and "give such evidence as may be required," which was more than I bargained for. "What on earth," Elizabeth had asked, "does anybody know about anybody else's marriage?" Then, two weeks before the action was due to come to court, I was waylaid by a process server in the foyer of the Hyatt Regency Hotel, where I was living and waiting for our American home to be ready, and handed another subpoena, demanding that I should appear as a witness for Cristina. I asked Henry's lawyer what you should do when you are summoned as a witness by both sides in a divorce case, and he answered simplistically: "Just answer any question they ask you."

The first day of the action was occupied with adjournments, requiring the principals and their lawyers to disappear into a back room in the hope, which I think both Henry and Cristina shared, that they could avoid ending their marriage on the front page. I told Elizabeth that I would do anything to avoid having my own marital past exposed in this fashion. "Once they get into print," she said, "even small sins seem so much larger." And it was this thought that eventually carried the day, for the court was adjourned overnight and in the intervening period a settlement was agreed out of court, as we had hoped.

Although the settlement was achieved offstage, it was—in Detroit at least—a public sideshow, and this hastened Henry's determination to speed his passage toward the day when he could regard himself, and be regarded by others, as a truly private citizen. Within a month he had formally announced his resignation as chairman of the Ford Motor Company, agreeing to continue as an ordinary member of the board of directors and chairman of its Finance Committee. It gave him a large finger in the pie—the Finance Committee has to approve all major financial transactions and investments before they go to the board—but Henry still felt he might reduce his participation to eight of the ten meetings a year. "I'll know the big things," he said. "I guess I can cope with that."

The settlement also exacted a personal penalty, which he brushed aside as "the price you sometimes have to pay" but which nevertheless caused intense regret. Henry had never had vast sums of money, tucked up in investments or hidden away in bank deposits. His income derived principally from dividends in the Ford B stock that he owned and would not sell. Money had to be raised, however, to honor the divorce settlement, and he therefore selected ten important paintings from his collection and asked Christie's to put them up for sale. Christie's was chosen over other auction houses for a sentimental reason: His first wife, Anne—now Mrs. Deane Johnson—was on Christie's West Coast staff in Beverly Hills, California, and he thought the commission on the sale might be of value to her.

The ten works were all masterpieces: by Boudin, Cézanne, Degas, Gauguin, van Gogh, Manet, Modigliani, Picasso, and Renoir. The finest was Cézanne's *Paysan en Blouse Bleu*, a blue-smocked peasant sitting reflectively with his heavy hands at ease on his lap. Modigliani's majestic nude *Nudo Seduto*, of which art critic John Russell wrote, "To be naked is no longer a condition of anguish"—one of the major landmarks of twentieth-century painting—was another. There were two other wonderful nudes—Degas's *Étude de Nu* and Picasso's *Tête de Femme*—and two garden paintings by van Gogh from his Arles period. The sale was due to take place at 8:00 P.M. on May 13 at Christie's large saleroom on Park Avenue in New York. More than thirty thousand people went to the views, and poster reproductions of the works on sale went fast at $5 a piece.

Henry said he hadn't the heart to go to the sale; Anne and Charlotte decided also that it was best to stay at home, and it was agreed that I would go by myself and join them later at Anne's apartment. I went with a sense of parting; the paintings had long graced the house from which Cristina had only recently moved, and they had become a familiar and integral part of Henry's life. The sky at Deauville in the Boudin picture seemed to change its mood and color with the seasons.

"Don't feel too bad about it," Henry said. "I haven't seen them for a very long time, and they represent times that are gone. And I guess I can say I made a profit"—a near-philistine remark that in no way reflected his feelings. There was standing room only in the saleroom. Bidding was brisk and soon over. One of the van Gogh's—*Le Jardin du Poète*—brought gasps when it fetched $5.2 million—at that time the highest price for any painting auctioned in America. The gasps were almost as loud for the Cézanne, which fetched $3.9 million. Six of the ten paintings established new record prices for a work by the artist concerned. I was glad to be out of the place and grateful for the drink Anne gave me when I reported back to the flat. "Eighteen million three hundred and ninety thousand dollars," I said. Henry looked astonished. It was almost exactly twice the reserve and substantially over Christie's own estimate. "I think I can afford to take you out to dinner," Henry said. "I can also pay for my divorce."

That evening he made his last reference to the sale—and never mentioned it again. In black and red ink he made a reckoning of the sale under three headings: "Cost," "Reserve," and "Price Achieved." It was a small scrap of paper for such a large parting.

	Cost	Reserve	Price Achieved
Boudin	225,000	380,000	480,000
Manet	102,000	650,000	650,000
Cézanne	406,322.05	2,000,000	3,900,000
Renoir	200,000	1,100,000	1,200,000
van Gogh *garde*	371,273.85	2,000,000	5,200,000
Gauguin	63,000	700,000	2,900,000
Van Gogh trees	750,000	1,100,000	1,900,000
Degas	202,147.46	380,000	900,000
Picasso	85,000	400,000	660,000
Modigliani	28,000	450,000	600,000

He had paid less than $2.5 million and received more than $18 million, but Charlotte said to me: "There wasn't any profit, was there? It was just one great loss."

I said I could have borne to part with any of them except the Cézanne.

Henry laughed and said: "That's because you're a sentimentalist. I'm looking forward because that's all you can think about when these things happen." He did, however, confess—a little wryly—that the sale had provided more than he needed for the divorce settlement. Perhaps he need not have sold them all. Still, now he could buy the *Southern Breeze*.

This chapter of his life came to an end five months later, when he married Kathleen Duross and proved himself to be the kind of sentimentalist he had accused me of being. The marriage was eventually a quiet affair in Carson City, Nevada, attended only by Kathy's two daughters, Debi and Kim, Debi's husband, and Henry's longtime man Friday, Tom Kish. But he had planned it differently. In July he had called Victor Matthews, the managing director of Trafalgar House, the company that owned the last of Britain's great ocean liners, *Queen Elizabeth II*. He bought the wedding ring at Asprey's in London and thought it a splendid idea to be married on the ship in mid-Atlantic. Matthews was sympathetic and anxious to help but unable to do so. "It can only be done now," he said, "for British citizens and even then under special circumstances." Henry and Kathy came back together on the *Queen Elizabeth*, nevertheless, but settled for something less romantic. "It didn't matter," Henry told me later at a party given in Detroit to celebrate. "It was getting married that was the important thing. Kathy has waited a long time, and so have I."

Dr. Johnson, who had firm opinions on most things and had provided a sort of epigraph for Henry's departure, once told Boswell that the most pleasant prospect in any Scotsman's life was the road leading to England. In my new and elevated position in the United States I began to think that he had a point. I had either gone too far or in the wrong direction. The U.S. car market slumped to 10.5 million in 1979, as low as most people could remember, and showed no signs of optimism or recovery. In 1980 it fell farther, to 8.9 million. Even that was not the end of the slippery slope, for it went steadily downward to 8 million in 1982. Chrysler, which had been under the command of Lee Iacocca since 1978, was the hardest hit and was saved only by a massive and controversial government loan guarantee and by government insistence that in return for this lifeline, its employees should immediately agree to wage reductions. Ford was never threatened, as Chrysler was, by extinction since it was in a comparatively stronger position. General Motors felt itself, as ever, to be in the strongest position because it had brought more small cars to the market, but it, too, was in mounting trouble. The only people who could summon up any kind of cheerful countenance were those manufacturing or selling foreign products; imported cars soon began to account for nearly one-third of the market, and in some parts of California, Japanese penetration was 80 percent or more. In greater Los Angeles, where annual car sales exceed those of several major European markets, it began to seem as if American cars were an endangered species.

There was only one intelligent response to this phenomenon: better domestic cars, new models that could win back the American owner and driver by virtue of their own integrity. Patriotism was certainly not enough. The American newspaper columnists and television pundits, reinforced monotonously by the editorial writers, seemed to take a masochistic pleasure in using their own birches on the backsides of Detroit's dumb damn managers. Those who dared venture into Washington—to confront or seek to persuade consumer groups and government regulators or even members of the administration that the issue was not merely an industry problem but a national emergency—returned baffled and further chastised. It appeared to be no use to argue that the change in public mood and the circumstances of the market had come about too quickly for any industry to respond, certainly one with a three-year product life cycle. Those who chose the political highroad, arguing that the billions of dollars being spent to import foreign cars were producing a trade deficit of staggering proportions, found themselves listening to unfeeling homilies. When Philip Caldwell was summoned one day to a meeting in the White House, he had to pinch himself when he heard President Carter say that Detroit should learn from the Europeans. "Mr. President," Philip said, "we *are* the Europeans."

The Europeans, in any event, would have responded differently. In the first place, European governments knew very well that their national automobile industries were cornerstones of their economies, and most European producers were heavily protected, subsidized, or owned by their governments. Europe had suffered heavily in the wake of the 1973–74 OPEC oil embargo and had not escaped the consequences of the Iranian Revolution, but its producers were not regulated or abused as American manufacturers were. Moreover, the European motoring and editorial writers still retained some patriotic fervor where their national carmakers were concerned. The German press trod lightly on Volkswagen, if at all, and the French never forgot the influence of Monsieur Chauvin. In Japan it was clear that the newspapers and journalists believed themselves to be a part of Japanese industrial and economic success and dutifully worshiped at the shrines erected by Toyota and Nissan.

There was little point in sophisticated argument or discussion. Nobody could whitewash Detroit, although Detroit, to be fair, was asking not for forgiveness but only for understanding, only for an acceptance that the crisis in the auto industry had not been of its own making, at least not entirely. Recession and inflation, revolution and rationing, regulation and a government that seemed willing to let its own whales die in a harsh economic climate—all these were constituents of a complex situation and did not permit explanation in the two or three sentences permitted by inquisitors on the network news. There is no doubt that Detroit should have been less insular and quicker to respond to the American taste for smaller and better cars, but European manufacturers have sometimes shown as little prescience without being so roundly abused for their incompetence. National pride is not of necessity preconditioned by victory, as Britain had proved—in a different kind of war—with the defeat at Dunkirk.

This may seem too grand a comparison, but it did not appear unreasonably self-important at the time. The great automobile revolution began to remind some in Detroit of the beginning of the thirties. Since nobody knew how far was down or how remote recovery, the manufacturers had no alternative but to retrench. Well over three hundred thousand men and women lost their jobs in the factories that put the cars together and those of suppliers that provided the components. Forty factories were closed. More than two thousand dealers went out of business, and there were soup kitchens in Detroit again.

On New Year's Day 1980, when I landed in New York—en route to Detroit to discuss the launch of the new Ford Escort, the small car that was so badly needed in the unforgiving market—the worst of the crisis was still in the future. I had found a house in Ann Arbor, thirty miles away from the office. Henry had found one in Grosse Pointe, not very far from the place where he had suffered the first painful premonitions of angina. He had no intention of returning to the old house on Lakeshore Drive; that was bundled up with the rest of the past. We had chosen homes forty-five miles apart, but Henry also thought that a good idea. "McNamara lived in Ann Arbor," he said. "And Arjay Miller. All the intellectuals live there. It's a good place for you"—and it was. Ann Arbor is a university town, the home of the University of Michigan, and it has a flourishing life with good music, good conversation, and—as we found to our growing pleasure—good neighbors. Dingdong Manor, as my children called the house, was located in what I thought of as a cul-de-sac, although the road sign said—unprophetically, we hoped—DEAD END.

When I arrived in New York, Elizabeth was still in England, womanfully dealing single-handedly (apart from encouraging murmurs from me over the long-distance telephone) with the sale of our house there and the disposal of thirty years of clutter, including a roomful of children's toys and books that suddenly became precious artifacts when they were threatened and declared surplus to grown-up requirements. As it was March before the Ann Arbor house was ready, we lived, as I've said, for two months at the Hyatt Regency Hotel, only five minutes from the office. I had no excuses for being late and grew accustomed to starting work before eight o'clock in the morning.

Nevertheless, I was rarely at work before Philip Caldwell, who had refurbished an office next door to that of the chairman, furnishing it with an antique desk and chairs, a dignified grandfather clock, and a tapestry. It suggested elegance and calm, but the furnishings belied its true character, for Philip had a gargantuan appetite for work, an explorer's zest for figures, and a passion for order and discipline. He was neat, tidy, immaculate, and insatiable. I never saw him yawn and only once saw him pretend to tiredness. With his wife, Betsey, he shared a private passion for early American furniture but had no other interests or anything that might be called a hobby. Weekends were no different from weekdays, and there were few Saturdays or Sundays when we did not talk on the telephone. We once made a ten-day business trip with him, traveling to Johannesburg, Durban, Port Elizabeth, Mauritius, Hong Kong, Melbourne, and Hawaii. When we got to Hawaii and had one whole afternoon without official duties, I told him I was going to see Pearl Harbor, and he said he would come along. He had served there during the war and proved a good guide. On the way back to the hotel, he fell asleep in the car. He apologized when he woke, but I said I was delighted. I had some evidence at least that he was human. He could be beguiling company and seemed amused always by Elizabeth's occasionally risqué jokes, but he was, above everything else, a workman.

In the first months after his appointment as vice-chairman and chief executive, he had devised an operational strategy for the company. "We must get back to the basics of our business," he said. It might have been considered a simplistic viewpoint, but it was more easily said than done, for it implied coming to terms with reality: accepting without excuses the sins of the past, redesigning every car and truck, and rebuilding or reequipping every single plant. It was a strategy that also required a puritanical abhorrence of waste or luxury and—as salaries were pegged, bonuses withdrawn, and dividends passed—some considerable financial sacrifices.

It also required some other hard men to execute the grand design. Philip spent a long time putting a new executive team together, arguing the merits of the human cards he had to play. As the extent of the crisis facing the entire American automobile industry became more and more apparent, I began to wonder if Henry would delay his planned retirement as chairman to steer the company through what was beginning to look like the biggest challenge in its history, but he was too wise for that. "I feel good about Phil," he said one night at dinner. "It's going to be tough, but he'll get the job done." Tough it was assuredly going to be. Dealers were growing increasingly restless as they looked out of their lonely showrooms into the more confident faces of their competitors who were selling imported cars. The newspapers chronicled their despair, and the editorial writers composed threnodies that encompassed a much wider segment of American industry. The "smokestack" industries, they insisted, were doomed, and they were not without allies on Wall Street, who noted that there were now more people working for McDonald's— selling hamburgers—than for U.S. Steel.

As spring approached in 1980 and Elizabeth began to hunt for nurserymen who might provide the plants for the English garden she was determined to have, and the hickory trees began to stand upright when the gales gave way to calmer weather, Philip and Henry came to an agreement. On March 13 Philip gave me a sheet of paper on which he had written their conclusions. Henry would that day resign as chairman of the board of directors of the company and Philip would take over, becoming the first chairman and chief executive with a surname other than Ford. Henry would become chairman of the Finance Committee. Donald E. Petersen would become president. Red Poling would replace Bill Bourke as executive vice-president in charge of North American Operations. Bourke would replace Don Petersen, who had been in charge of all Ford operations overseas.

But Bill Bourke was not amused. He had justifiably felt himself heir apparent for a bigger job. Henry himself had used the magic word *chairman*, and a return to that international world where he had won his spurs seemed to smack of demotion. He retired from the company, bought a beautiful house in Virginia cradled in the Blue Ridge Mountains, and went on to become chief executive of Reynolds Aluminum and play a key role in the automobile war from a different front. We spent a few days with him in Virginia later, flew a kite in the garden, and raided his chicken coop for fine brown breakfast eggs. Having farmed cattle on his ranch in Australia, he had gathered a new American herd, which roamed the paddock nearby. He bore few grudges.

Despite my regret about the loss of Bill Bourke, I had no doubt that Henry and Philip had picked their lieutenants well. The business of Ford in North America—which meant the United States and Canada, with Mexico soon to be included—was designing and making cars and trucks and selling them to Ford and Lincoln-Mercury dealers. The future was contained within the disorder then apparent in the design center and the factories. Red Poling knew the shop floor and understood the mechanism of production. Don Petersen knew product. Philip knew what he wanted.

Don Petersen was considered by many people something of a dark horse. He had one attribute that would have won him easy acceptance into the circle around old Henry Ford: Like Knudsen and Sorensen and other "great Danes" who built the company in its early days, he was of Danish descent. He was tall, ascetic, thoughtful, and surprisingly tough, at least to those who judged by appearances. He had joined Ford in 1949 from the U. S. Marine Corps. In the sixties he had spent a year as executive assistant to Lee Iacocca and had long years of experience in product planning—he had invented the name—before taking over Truck Operations and then Ford International. He had been married for thirty-one years, and outside his family, he had few diversions.

No days were ever so long for me as those I counted during this period of my life. The house in Ann Arbor had big rooms. We installed a grand piano for my daughter, but it languished for the many months of the year she was in England at university. I had shipped three thousand books from England, together with the entire contents of the house, but found too little time for reading. Elizabeth had got herself an unpaid job at the Clements Library of the university—one of the most splendid antiquarian and colonial treasure-houses in the country—and was enchanted to find among its possessions nineteen love letters from Lord Nelson to Lady Hamilton. We bought a snow blower and came to terms with the snow and ice and learned respect for the wind-chill factor, but the winds, moaning at night and whipping the hickories, were no colder than those that blew across the economic map of the country.

Wall Street decided that Ford was no longer a good credit risk and valued the Ford Motor Company at only $2 billion, less than one-third of its book value. The company's debt rose to $4.9 billion. More than sixty thousand people lost their jobs. But the new cars were coming along, and miles of new machines were being installed. The United Automobile Workers—never previously the most considerate of bedfellows—showed a remarkably pragmatic face to this tottering world, and shop stewards became evangelists for quality circles, employee involvement programs, and intensive training. I thought often of Henry's remark about Britons and their resilience when their backs were to the wall; none of my countrymen could have set a better example.

Among them, Philip Caldwell, Don Petersen, and Red Poling reduced the company's annual operating costs by $4.5 billion, or $12 million a day, and between 1980 and 1984 spent more than $13 billion on new products, processes, and machinery as well as $9 billion on research and development, which meant new technology. The company's financial losses in 1980, 1981, and 1982 combined were substantially over $3 billion, and true to itself, Ford spent a substantial proportion of its investment overseas to reinforce that other world, which—for all sorts of pertinent reasons—had missed the eye of the American hurricane. Henry's Ford of Europe remained so significantly strong and profitable that it was able to lend its parent company millions of dollars to bolster its own shrinking resources.

The re-creation of Ford during these frugal years and the parallel endeavors of its equally troubled compatriots in General Motors, Chrysler, and American Motors were, by any standard of judgment, the biggest industrial revolution in history. It was undertaken and achieved entirely without government assistance. Indeed, the almost willful unwillingness of Washington to comprehend the basics of its own business never ceased to astonish me. In January 1981, when Jimmy Carter had limped back to Georgia and Ronald Reagan was learning his way around the White House, I went to Washington for the inauguration and felt I was dancing on the grave of industrial America. I wore a white tie and tails to the annual Gridiron Club dinner of the Washington press corps at which its guests—out of the corridors of power and away from their word processors—looked lightly on their blinkered world and banished the thought of budget deficits or trade gaps.

In 1982 I spent three weeks in Tokyo, Hiroshima, Seoul, Hong Kong, and Taipei, watching the big Japan and the little Japans, and then went to Perth, Wellington, and Auckland before coming home—as I now thought of it—to Los Angeles, where I lost count of the Japanese cars on the freeways and in the broad parking lots.

On the first anniversary of Henry's marriage to Kathy, I joined the two of them at Turville Grange, and we planted a tree in the garden to celebrate. The cook made a birthday cake, and we stayed up late. It was a rare relaxation, and we spent more time talking business. Henry's chairmanship of the Finance Committee was never the formal pastime he had expected it to be, and as the dividends dried up, he was again aware of pressures on his own personal expenditures. The pleasures of private life were often held at bay by the continuing concern about whether or not Ford would have enough money to pay for all the feathers on its emerging phoenix. There were occasions that otherwise would have rated grandly on his scale of contentment. Her Majesty the Queen had conferred upon him a distinguished honor, making him a knight of the British Empire. Had he been of British nationality, he would thenceforth have been known as Sir Henry Ford. Two years earlier I had been appointed a commander of the same order, and when the British ambassador in Washington called Henry to give him the news, he observed that honor had been properly done, for he outranked me once again. We went to the British Embassy in Washington together—Henry and Kathy, Elizabeth and I—for the ceremony at which Sir Nicholas Henderson, the British ambassador, presented the medallion of knighthood. But as we came back to Detroit, the mood of celebration quickly passed, and the party for his sixty-fifth birthday on September 4 was small and brief and confined.

He did not go to Turville Grange for Christmas—he said there was too much to think about—and we spent Boxing Day with him in Grosse Pointe. After dinner he did something I had never before experienced—certainly on such an occasion—and excused himself for half an hour to go over some papers. It would have seemed natural to me had Philip Caldwell been doing it, but Henry never took work home.

He called me at home on New Year's Eve. "I know you are both missing England," he said, "but we haven't won the war yet. Hang in there, though. We will."

In the end we did. Unshackled from the ways of the past and shaken out of our insularity, we had gone back to the basics of the business, as Philip intended, and, more important, no longer looked over our shoulder at General Motors. The new Ford and Lincoln-Mercury cars that were coming onto the American roads looked new and were new from bumper to bumper. They owed nothing to yesterday and had even begun to make a bridgehead in California. Red Poling's people were lean and hungry, and a new confidence was emerging.

"It is all," Henry said, "a matter of getting the right management." I thought I detected a sigh and might well have done so. It had taken him a long time to be able to make that statement.

CHAPTER NINE

Matters of Life and Death

In my diary for June 15, 1983—
the day Henry came to my house and asked me to plan his funeral—
there are only two words: "Morte d'Arthur." One of the problems with
enigmatic notes of this kind is that they become difficult to decipher with
the passage of time. Still, the note must have seemed appropriate on the
day it was written. With Henry's death, the sword would go back into the
stone and there would be a large vacant chair at the round table.

Having seen how methodically he proceeded with the ordering of his
business affairs as he surrendered his corporate titles, I could easily
believe he would be as practical with those that were personal. He had
started to put his private affairs in order the previous autumn. For many
years Max Fisher had owned a substantial summer house in Palm
Beach, Florida, and sometime later the Taubmans bought one, too.
Alfred Taubman was a friend as well as a business associate; one of their
ventures together with Henry was the purchase of Sotheby's, the international art auctioneers. Henry did not like Palm Beach. He thought it too
humid and nothing ever happened there, but he nevertheless purchased
a house on the same street as the Taubmans and the Fishers and not far
away from another owned by Douglas Fairbanks, Jr. The marble halls of
the rich in Palm Beach range in style from Spanish rococo to pink
palatial, but Henry's was comparatively modest. A large, cool drawing
room with almost a wall of sliding windows opened to a patio and a
swimming pool. The Inland Waterway was only ten or fifteen yards
beyond. On October 7, 1983, Henry became officially a Florida resi-
dent. The formality was important because it conveyed some consider-

able tax advantages; his real purpose, however, was to provide Kathy with a place of her own with winter sunshine in which she could live among friends after his death.

The house, which Henry and Kathy called The Cottage, was decorated under the supervision of Tom Parr, the English interior decorator who did all his homes, and was typical of Henry with bright floral chairs and sofas, an abundance of flowers, and an immaculate kitchen. It lacked a formal dining room; as its name suggested, the Florida residence was intended to be casual, and undress the order of the day.

There is an air of unreality about Palm Beach. It is too neat, too tidy, too hygienic, too soporific. When he was there, Henry lazed by the pool reading whodunits, venturing into town now and then to shop in the elegant stores and boutiques on Worth Avenue. He had a white Mustang convertible, which he liked to drive himself, insisting he was a good driver. One night he came home from a dinner party with Kathy and his English secretary, Wendy Alexander, and stopped at a distance from the garage that Kathy insisted was too close. He was equally sure it was not, but when he pressed the device that automatically opened the garage door, it rose under the front bumper and lifted the car into the air. "Damn silly door!" Henry said, but he was amused by the incident. It was the most interesting thing that had happened all day.

The following May he bought *Southern Breeze*—after Kathy and Turville Grange, the other true love of his retiring years—and, step by step, began to plan the pleasures of his new life and the disposal of his estate when it came to an end. His quest for tidiness rather than apprehension about death itself provided the motivation. In June 1983 he was three months away from the sixty-sixth anniversary of his birth but still vigorous in mind and body, and there was no reason to doubt he would have many more years to enjoy the pleasures he could now more readily afford.

Any suggestion that Henry might ever have had to stop and think about money, from the day he first held a coin in his hand, seems silly on the face of it. But he never wasted it. He knew what things cost and would pay the proper price; but he was never extravagant, and there was a period when, by his standards, he was hard up. Between 1980 and 1982 Ford lost more than $3 billion and for the latter two years paid no dividends to any of its stockholders. Since Henry owned 1,961,632 Class B shares and had to maintain three homes and two wives and a staff, he was only too aware of the personal consequences. Wendy Alexander framed and kept in her office a letter from him at the time—it was dated January 23,

1981—that said: "Dear Wendy, Please don't spend any money." But a remarkable recovery began in 1983, and the Ford Motor Company ended the year with a profit substantial enough to wipe out the losses of the previous two and to restore Henry's income to the expected level.

Dividends or not, his estate was obviously going to be large. In addition to the Ford stock and the new house in Palm Beach, he owned Turville Grange and the residence in Grosse Pointe. Despite the sale of his ten paintings, he retained many other notable pictures. Unlike his mother and his first wife, he had never been particularly interested in furniture, but he had collected some splendid pieces of Fabergé and fine porcelain.

When it came to thinking about the funeral, however, I was more preoccupied with the value of the man himself rather than his possessions, although it was obviously necessary to reach some immediate specific conclusions, including the nature of his own religious preferences, where the service was concerned. Henry had become converted to Roman Catholicism upon his first marriage. It had not been an easy thing for him to do, and indeed, the very idea of his marrying a Roman Catholic proved something of a shock to his grandparents, although it has to be said that when Henry wrote them a letter to break the news of his engagement and Anne's religion, they responded with more consideration than might have been expected. Henry retained among his personal papers only two letters, which he evidently treasured above all others. He kept them securely hidden in a small green metal box— rather like a cashbox—which was itself lodged in his safe and contained nothing else save a rosary. One of them said:

Dear Henry—Your letter came this morning and am writing at once to let you know how we feel about the news. We have loved you devotedly since the day you were born, and the girl you take for your life companion will share in our love. We are all protestants and it will be strange to have a catholic in the family, but we will take it as we should. I have many friends who are catholics. Father Coughlin, who is so disliked by so many, we count among our friends. Years ago, when your father was younger than you are, I thought of this same thing and I decided that it would be right, be she catholic or protestant. All we wished was that he would love her and that he would be happy.

The letter was signed "With all our love, dear Henry—Callie and Granddad." Callie was always easier for the children to say than Clara, and Grandmother was too formal, so she had become Callie over the years. That says something about the relationship, as does the letter, about the remarkable woman who wrote it.

Henry's adherence to Roman Catholicism did not endure, for he was excommunicated after his divorce from Anne and his marriage to Cristina, and by 1983 there was no doubt about the denomination of faith in which he wished to be buried. It was to be a Church of England service and as traditional as possible. It was also to be small and private. His ashes were to be scattered to the winds and waters, and there was to be no grave, no headstone, no memorial of any kind. While we were sitting in the house discussing, a little awkwardly, these affairs, I said that the death of Henry Ford II would not be a private affair. Many thousands of people would want to share in it, as they had in his life, and any man's death should take account of the living. It was a brief discussion. Henry said: "This is one decision that isn't going to require a board meeting. I guess I'm entitled to have my own way."

Elizabeth was about to make a trip to England, and while she was there, she went to see some friends in Guildford Cathedral. She brought back with her a handful of service sheets from other funeral and memorial services that provided some points of reference in composing one for Henry. She comes from a long line of choristers and musicians and is sure and convinced about such matters, and I had myself been a Sunday-clean and pure-voiced choirboy in my own youth. I sent Tom Kish to inspect all the appropriate churches and chapels in Detroit and its suburbs. A little later, when we had something to suggest, Henry came out to Ann Arbor again and made Elizabeth sing the hymns she had chosen. He liked "For All the Saints Who from Their Labours Rest" but hesitated over the anthem "Let Us Now Praise Famous Men." It was the "famous" he didn't like; it sounded a bit self-important. He did not think of himself in that way. I had the *Oxford Dictionary* on my bookshelves— all thirteen volumes—and I laid volume four on the carpet and said that *famous* merely meant "well-known." "Don't argue about it," I said, "and we'll get on famously." This diverted us for a full ten minutes, but it stayed in. Stanford's setting of Nunc Dimittis—"Lord, now lettest thou thy servant depart in peace"—was approved, and Henry then added one last flourish, writing on the typescript in red ink after the concluding organ voluntary: "few bars of *Saints Come Marching In.*"

I said, "Absolutely no—over my dead body," but he was not to be shaken. "Nobody," I persisted, "finishes a funeral service like that."

Henry said: "Nelson Rockefeller did." I did not believe it. "Look it up for yourself," Henry said. So I did, and I discovered that the twenty-two hundred people who had attended the Rockefeller memorial service at Riverside Church in New York, including the president and vice-president of the United States, had been sent away to what the Reverend William Sloan Coffin, Jr., had called a "little unusual" recessional and *The New York Times* described as "the zesty melody" of "Sweet Georgia Brown," played by Lionel Hampton and his jazz group. I told Henry he had got the tune wrong, but he said it made no difference. The principle was the thing, and that had been clearly established.

There remained the matter of the memorial service, which seemed unlikely to prove controversial except that to begin with, Henry could not see the need for one at all. So I went over it all again. He was the head of a larger Ford family, not merely of those who had been born with the name. Human beings have a right to mourn in private, in public, or not at all; but he could not disappoint people after his death by refusing to grant them a last act of companionship, particularly if they had played a part—no matter how small—in his life. Henry was still grudging about it. "I suppose so," he said. I suggested he should accept the idea and leave the details to the family, Ted Mecke, and me. The funeral service could provide the basis for the larger and more public one. The Cathedral Church of St. Paul was the obvious place for it to be held. Within a day or two all this had been committed to paper, together with a letter of instruction to Kathy and Edsel, and everything transmitted to Frank Chopin, his lawyer in Palm Beach, to be typed in proper legal format and become the first amendment to his trust deed.

When Henry retired from the chairmanship of the Ford Motor Company, he had taken a small suite of offices in Parklane Towers, twin buildings the company had erected in Dearborn as part of its own property development in the area. He always regarded them disrespectfully as the "washer" and "dryer" (although he had been dutifully consulted upon their design and appearance), and they had, from inside and outside, much of the impersonal character of a laundry. With the plans for his funeral out of the way, Henry began to apply himself in this office to the continuing business of ensuring that all remained shipshape and Ford fashion "should anything happen."

This self-imposed task included tearing up the past. I found him in his office one day, in his shirtsleeves, ferreting through a cupboard and standing almost ankle-deep in torn paper. He had forty or fifty filing cabinets in an anteroom, and he was carefully going through them drawer by drawer shredding a large proportion of their contents. I said it was sacrilege to rip up history in this fashion, but he insisted that it was his history and of no damned consequence to any other person.

There was something contradictory about this destructive impulse, for there could be no doubt about his dedication to the family heritage and its traditions as well as his single-minded determination to secure its survival. Nor was he without interest in the history of the Ford Motor Company from its earliest days. I never did reach a satisfactory conclusion about this dichotomy. The nearest I ever came to an explanation was a remark of his sometime later, during a late-night conversation in Palm Beach, to the effect that "I am me, and when I have gone, I've gone; the company and the family are two different things." But even that was not true, and I don't think he believed it any more than I did; if the rest of his life proved anything, it was that they were indivisibly one. The explanation that still seems most likely is that he was a private and secret man, made more private—even into unnecessary concealment—by the long passage of his life and its skirmishes and ambushes. He knew his own worth and could calculate his own weight, but the value and the reckoning were really his own damn business.

One other motivation, I suspected, was his lifelong insistence upon tidiness and order. All his possessions in all his homes were carefully cataloged, often with detailed provenances. His estate was as neatly ordered as the books enumerating its content, and they were as immaculately symmetrical as the shirts in his chests of drawers or the cashmere socks in his cupboards. He was getting everything ready for his departing, and what could be more sensible than ridding himself, in the process, of every inconsequential thing so that he could carry on living with a desk as tidy as his conscience—a conscience, moreover, that was now clear enough to indulge in personal pleasures without any lingering feeling of guilt?

This was certainly my opinion, and Henry gave every indication of being in agreement, so far as it was possible for him to do so, for there was always a sense in which pleasure came harder to him than business. It seemed to require more working at, almost as though business were the familiar joy and pastimes no more than the word implies: ways of passing time not otherwise devoted to things that really mattered. Although he was no longer chairman of the Ford Motor Company, he was pleased to become chairman of its European Advisory Council. We had started it together with John Loudon, and I continued to run it through all the years I was in the United States and after I returned to Europe when I made two or three trips a year to wherever Henry was, to discuss such things as locations and agendas. In Madrid in July 1983, on a reconnaissance for a forthcoming meeting, he was still involved to the extent of sitting down with the banqueting manager of the Ritz Hotel and discussing such details as receiving lines for the coming occasions and place cards for the guests. (He always chose the food and wine.) It seemed to me that he had never been so relaxed. He decided that since we were unaccompanied, we would be wasting company money by having two suites in the hotel and suggested we should share: separate bedrooms and bathrooms but one drawing room, where we could stay up late and talk. We stayed up very late until it was very early and the night was very short, and the next morning I was standing naked before a mirror, unsteadily shaving, when I was aware of another naked form looming somewhere behind my back. "My God, Walter!" Henry said. "Your belly's almost as big as mine. You must get a bicycle, too." It was not a reasonable remark because Henry had many bicycles and they were obviously better for his health than his waistline, and I was usually in much better shape. It was, however, an indication of the sense of mischief that could always be found—when it was willing—not far beneath the surface of his character.

I expected to see little of him for the rest of the year. Working with Philip Caldwell was a full-time occupation, and I had many other things to do. We would be separated at Christmas. We had asked our children to come to Ann Arbor, and Henry had gathered his traditional November shooting party and was planning to spend the rest of the year at Turville. Where Henry's shooting was concerned, the places varied little: Biddick Hall in County Durham—Lord Lambton's estate—and the Black Swan at Helmsley in the Yorkshire Dales; occasionally there were invitations to Blenheim or Lumley Castle. The guns were usually the mixture as before. His guests included Edsel, brother Bill, sister Dodie, Lord Hambleden, Lord Wilton, John Bugas, David Metcalfe, and Evelyn de Rothschild—all with wives and husbands. His favorite shoots both were well over two hundred miles from London, and getting there became part of the fun. One year, when there were sixteen in a Black Swan party, Henry chartered a motor coach, but mostly they went by train. Henry religiously kept a game book, dutifully noting each day's bag, convinced he had done less than well for his guests if the numbers ever sank too low.

Kathy's children were with them at Turville for Christmas, and we talked as we always had on Boxing Day whether we were together or not. It had become something of a tradition ever since Elizabeth had explained how its name had been derived, through the opening of poor boxes in English churches on the day after Christmas and from the days when apprentices would knock on the doors of their masters' customers to have their boxes filled with small gifts or money. Henry was a delighted connoisseur of such anglophile trifles. (He was, for example, interested in the derivation of English pub signs and was quite surprised to find one near Turville called The Black Boy. It would not have been considered enticing in Detroit. So he was pleased to know that all the Black Boys in Britain are named for King Charles II, who was born with such a dark and swarthy complexion that his mother even thought she had given birth to a black child.)

Turville Grange was always beautifully decorated at Christmas, with a big tree in the hall. In Ann Arbor the snow was knee-high and our footsteps lay deep beneath it, and when we told Henry and Kathy we were sorry not to be with them, we meant it. Henry liked Christmas. He liked the formality of it, the having friends to luncheon and dinner, and the conversation. He liked giving and opening presents. It was often remarked that nobody ever found it easy to decide upon a Christmas (or any other kind of) gift for Henry—what, after all, could you give a man who had everything?—but we never found it difficult to find a book, a record, a special photograph, or a gadget to entertain him. One year we gave him long johns to keep him warm while shooting; for another, we found an old solitaire board with Victorian glass marbles that baffled him, as it does most people, until Elizabeth, who knows how to solve the puzzle, sent him written instructions to explain the mystery. A week later she received a letter in his large familiar hand. "Dear Elizabeth," he wrote, "You were most kind to send me the solitaire solution. I will memorize it and win lots of money from my friends. We so enjoyed having you and Walter and the children the other evening. It was really great fun and we all had just enough claret."

It was an unnecessary letter, for his pleasure was evident, but I never met anybody who said thank you so scrupulously; the merest trifle would be promptly and considerately recognized no matter where it came from, and for the most part, the notes would be written by hand. He was equally thoughtful where his own Christmas gifts were concerned. They were never lavish, but they were always appreciated because it was clear that he had taken trouble to match the character of the gift to its recipient. For his children he often selected a picture or a personal possession from one of his homes. Sometimes, when he himself had a passing fancy for a new gadget or electronic puzzle, he bought a score of them. The families of his staff mostly received Christmas hampers.

Our telephone conversation at Christmas 1983 was not confined, however, to the usual seasonal exchanges, for his affairs were not yet in the order he intended. In January I was due to go to South Africa and Henry intended to return to Florida to work with Frank Chopin on a new will and eventually settlement of his estate. He was also concerned with the changing of the guard in Dearborn and said he would like to spend some time with me when I got back from my journey.

Philip Caldwell reached the age of sixty-four on January 27, 1984. Under his chairmanship, Ford had made a remarkable recovery—to all intents and purposes a rejuvenation—but Henry knew that its new and reinforced foundations were not yet secure enough to withstand the impact of another economic or market crisis without the prospect of some damage. The next management would have to be chosen with as much deliberation as the one presided over by Philip. He was especially concerned to achieve an orderly, unremarkable, and judicious transition, free from controversy or drama, and now that the company had the wind in its sails again, the time seemed ripe for decision.

The disposition of Henry's estate did not appear to be a matter of controversy, and I anticipated no reason for my own involvement. Henry devoted many months of thought before he finally made up his mind what to do, and went to great lengths to avoid anything that could lead to conflict. There need never have been any misunderstanding, and even now the subject would be worth no more than a passing mention were it not for the fact that Martin Citrin, one of the three trustees, committed suicide within a few months of Henry's death, and what appeared to be a simple matter of definition turned into something much more complex and confused.

Henry decided that his three children had been adequately enriched during his lifetime and that all that was necessary was to provide homes and income for his widow and ensure, after her death, that the entire estate should pass to his six grandchildren. He therefore wrote a will that would provide Kathy with a comparatively modest sum upon his death and give her a number of purely personal possessions. At the same time, he created a revocable inter vivos trust into which he immediately placed everything else, appointing himself sole trustee during his lifetime and naming Edsel, Kathy, and Martin Citrin as three equal trustees at his death. Martin Citrin had a business of his own, making and selling medical equipment, and both he and his wife, Myra, had been friends of Kathy's for many years. Martin had been severely stricken by poliomyelitis as a young man; he was burly and walked with difficulty on crutches, but he was a gregarious and cultured person and made light of his affliction, which his friends soon learned to take for granted. Henry spent long hours with him in Dearborn and Palm Beach, as well as on the *Southern Breeze*, talking about his estate and his intentions, and he felt that Marty would faithfully discharge the responsibility. If there were any queries, Frank Chopin, who was appointed lawyer to the trust, would be there to advise.

The trust was specific but unremarkable. Turville Grange was to be sold, as was the *Southern Breeze*, and the proceeds put into the trust. The houses in Grosse Pointe and Palm Beach (and subsequently, by amendment to the trust deed, an apartment in London) were to be kept during Kathy's lifetime for her use, and the trust was enjoined to "maintain the standard of living she enjoyed" and to which "she has become accustomed." Kathy was to have the income of the trust during her lifetime— it was to be conducted to provide the maximum possible through judicious management—and after her death the entire estate would be divided into shares of which every grandchild, save Edsel's eldest son, would be given one. He was to have two, naturally and properly enough, for he was the eldest son of the eldest son and had been christened Henry Ford III.

The will and the trust deed, each page initialed "HFII," were sworn in Palm Beach on May 17, 1984, before Mabel Joyce Huey, a public notary. Between this date and February 4, 1987, Henry signed six amendments to the trust. The first, eight days later, gave instructions about the funeral, and others covered such things as compensation for trustees (no family member was to be paid) and other bequests. The third amendment, signed May 1, 1986, showed that Henry—at the very end of his life—was at last recognizing the growing dangers facing public figures and also provided remarkable testimony to his faith in Arjay Miller. It specified that "in the event that the Grantor should be kidnapped or otherwise held against his will," Arjay should assume Henry's role as guardian of the trust and that "the said Arjay Miller shall have full authority to do whatever is required to secure the Grantor's release." In this he was given "exclusive power." Arjay was both taken aback and honored when Henry sat down with him and asked that he should accept this responsibility. He was never, fortunately, called upon to perform it.

On the occasions when Henry talked about "getting on with the will," I made the most superficial responses—partly, I think, out of a desire not to think about it but also because I had an avuncular relationship with Anne, Charlotte, and Edsel, and one of long standing with Kathy, and felt it improper to risk exerting any kind of influence no matter how light or casual upon such private concerns. There was, notwithstanding, one issue over which I could not avoid involvement and argument. Henry came into my office one day and gave me what he said was a six-page summary of his considered intentions where the estate was concerned and asked me to have a look at it. "It's not right," he said, "not yet anyway. Tell me what you think." He then explained that what I was holding in the plain brown envelope was essentially a summary of his will and trust, a sort of statement of intent, which he intended to deliver before a television camera. The completed videocassette would remain with his lawyer until his death, when it would be shown to Kathy and his children. They would then be able to see and hear him speaking his will, and this, he felt, would remove any remaining doubts about his desires. I had never heard of any such thing before—although it is now common practice in the United States—and without even opening the envelope, I said it was an unnecessary and even gruesome thing to do. "They will be badly enough upset anyway," I said. "Why inflict this upon them?" But Henry was adamant. The widow of his good friend and ally John Bugas had cried on Henry's shoulder when John's will was disputed, and Henry was determined to avoid such an outcome. He knew what he was doing. He was "all there." He was sure his family would understand. It was obviously something he was resolved to do, and I therefore agreed to have a look at the text and provide any editing that seemed necessary. Apart from Frank Chopin, there was obviously nobody else with whom he felt able to discuss the document.

I took it home and read it aloud, making changes here and there, and soon sent it back with a note: "I haven't altered this very much. I have been pleased to do it for you, but I didn't enjoy it." I said I thought it was a little clearer and perhaps a little gentler, and it certainly was to me. He was happy with the revised text and recorded it in Palm Beach on May 24, 1984, calling me afterward to say the deed had been done, although it wouldn't win any Oscars. The cassette shows him sitting, unnaturally stiff, in a gray suit, a plain shirt, and a striped tie, holding the text in his hands; reading deliberately through his half-frame glasses. On October 30 he sat at his desk in Turville Grange, and with a thick black fiber pen—in a large hand with not more than fifty or so words to a page—he wrote a letter of explanation and then sent that off to be included with all the other paraphernalia of willing and trusting that had engaged him for well over a year.

He wrote:

Dear Kate—A note from me at this time I am sure you will not understand but let me try to explain. You know how much thought and effort I have put into the planning of my estate. I therefore wanted to explain it to you and my children by means of a videotape which will be given to you with this letter by the manager of the Ford Estates Office. This tape explains specifically what my estate plan is in some but not complete detail. For more detail, my lawyer, Frank Chopin, can fill you in. Will you please show this tape to my children as soon as you receive it or as soon as you can. Please show this letter to them as well. The tape and the letter are to be kept in your possession in the future. This whole scheme may seem rather strange, but to me it makes sense. I am sorry to have to do it this way. You have been a wonderful wife and made my life so happy. Thank you, my darling. All my love, Henry.

I met Henry two weeks later in Florida. He said all the "will stuff" was put to bed, and we did not dwell upon it again. And I did see some wisdom in the tape much later, when I also came to believe there was another reason for my own involvement; although the message itself should have been plain enough, I think he wanted somebody else to be able to say: "This is what Henry wanted."

On the tape, Henry said: "I have thought through the planning of my estate very carefully, and I want to be sure that my wishes are fulfilled. I hope you will all agree that I have been fair and equal about everybody and everything. I want to tell you my children, Charlotte, Anne, and Edsel, that I have not left you any of my property. This is not because I don't love you or care for your financial well-being. I think that you have always known that I do care. I love you all very much. Indeed, before making my will and trust, I reviewed your own property holdings— much of which you acquired from me—to be certain of what each of you has. As a result of that careful review, I know you won't be hampered or harmed in any way by excluding you from my estate." The text continued: "There are really one or two things I want to do. First, I want to provide for Kate, and second, I want to provide for the family over the long term—for my grandchildren and even for generations beyond them." The explanation was detailed and concise and, although— despite the immense care with which Henry made his wishes known— there were some differences of interpretation by various members of the family and lawyers after his death and that of Martin Citrin which necessitated hearings in a Florida court, the cassette exists as a permanent and clear reminder to future generations of Henry's intentions.

For all its cold, repetitive language, the trust deed not merely detailed Henry's long-considered desires but also provided a remarkable insight into one other aspect of his character: his respect and affection for the small band of personal servants who lived his life with him—or at least a great deal of it—and helped smooth the bumps. The old platitude that no man is a hero to his valet has been attributed to Byron, Carlyle, Goethe, and several other less eminent thinkers, but it was never true where Henry Ford II was concerned. He was a hero to them all.

Jim Cumming, who emigrated to the United States with his family from Scotland when he was four years old, became Henry's secretary in June 1945 and remained in the job for thirty-nine years until retirement. Bernie Bohn joined Jim Cumming as assistant secretary in 1954 and—apart from two years after Henry's retirement, when he worked for me—also stayed the whole course, replacing Jim upon his departure from the company. Tommy Romano (whose christian name was really Domenico but who happily settled for Tommy) was hired as a butler in 1965, when he was working on the cruise ship SS *Shemara* and Henry was on board enjoying an excursion. Tomasz Szarek was inherited by Henry from the Radziwills when he bought Turville Grange from them, and both these Tommys continued to work for Mrs. Ford after Henry's death.

Mike Merrick was Henry's driver and watchdog from 1945 until he retired in 1978. Another Tommy—Tommy Shields—joined Mike as late-night driver in 1963, took over the job completely when Mike gave it up, and stayed with Henry to the end. Ted Schutza and Ed Waryas went to work as day and night watchmen at Henry's homes in 1964 and 1965, respectively, and served without break until their sixty-fifth birthdays in 1988.

These eight good and loyal servants and friends gave Henry 214 years of combined service, and there was never any doubt about his regard for them or theirs for him. When Mike Merrick retired, Henry hired the General Dearborn Room in the Dearborn Inn and gave a dinner for him and his wife and twenty-two members of his family. Jim Cumming, Bernie Bohn, and Tommy Shields were also invited with their wives; the only other people present were Henry and Kathy and Kathy's sister, Sharon, and her husband. It was an occasion when that other Ford family of dedicated servants and allies—keepers of the faith and of many secrets—stopped to take pleasure in each other. Many of them were working at this time for Cristina, and their loyalty was often tested. It says a great deal for all of them that they never wavered.

At the end of the dinner Henry presented Mike Merrick with a model tractor and several toy-size implements, including a plow and a disk.

There was not enough room in the inn for the full-size versions. They were delivered, spanking new, to Mike's farm in Pinckney, Michigan. Henry also sent him a letter the next day: "In the event they are not all the things you need, please let me know so this can be corrected."

When Mike Merrick's retirement party took place, Henry was living in the Dearborn Inn and lacked a suitable place of his own in which to entertain. By the time Jim Cumming retired in 1984, however, Henry and Kathy were happily established in the new Grosse Pointe house, and Jim's retirement dinner took place there, with the Cummings, twelve of their friends, plus Henry and Kathy. Henry presented Jim with the larger part of a silver dinner service from Tessier and went on to complete the set, adding other pieces on the three following Christmases.

Nor was this an end to Henry's gratitude. The only named benefactors in his trust—outside Kathy and the family—were Jim and Bernie, all the Tommys, and the handful of other domestic companions. Among them they shared something like $750,000.

───────────

There is no entry in my diary for May 17, 1984, but the date remains in my memory for reasons beyond the fact that it was the day Henry notarized his will and trust. My stint in the United States had come to an end, and we shortly returned to England. The contents of the house were packed into two enormous containers, and Elizabeth said a tearful good-bye to our neighbors and wished she could have shipped them, too. Going home was a more leisurely affair than the journey into our American years. We had flown from London in 1979, looked at six houses in Ann Arbor, picked one, and gone home the next day. All our possessions were later flown over in a Boeing 747, and we were established and organized in three months. Five years later there was no need for such speed. We found a house in England in a matter of weeks, but it took a year to get it ready for occupation, and our worldly goods made a more leisurely return by sea and into storage.

We camped in a flat in Shepherd Market, and I was glad to be spared the immediate necessity to make a home again. Philip Caldwell had decided there were matters of business in Europe to which I ought to turn my attention, although I still had some things to do in the United States. We therefore agreed that I would commute between London and Detroit for the remaining months of his chairmanship and attend to specific tasks in America as well as those to which I was newly committed on the other side of the Atlantic. I saw Henry only occasionally that summer. In June he boarded the *Southern Breeze* at Nice with Kathy, her two daughters, and Paula Sarvis, her closest friend. He went back to Dearborn for the July board meeting but returned immediately to Athens, where he boarded the *Southern Breeze* again and continued his holiday.

Before the summer had ended, however, he was clearly itching to get back into the business and, in particular, into the management of the company after Philip Caldwell's impending retirement. It was not a subject that concerned Philip; he worked to the last minute of the last day of his sixty-fifth year. He would have happily soldiered on, but Henry had thought it right to engineer his own retirement before his sixty-fifth birthday and wanted sixty-five to remain the end of the line.

Changes at the top in large corporations always carry with them an atmosphere of papal expectation and conjecture—one expects to see holy smoke, signaling that a choice has been made—but on this occasion there seemed little likelihood of debate. Donald Petersen had been president through Philip's years as chairman and had proved himself a good product man with a perceptive concern for the human side of business and a proper respect for manufacturing quality. Tall, lean, and thoughtful, he spent his private time—such as it was—in thinking pursuits as a member of Mensa. He was eager for change but never in a hurry, and something in his character suggested the reflective man within. His only hobby was collecting rock samples, and he adorned his office with prize specimens.

Don Petersen was persuaded that the turnaround in the fortunes of the Ford Motor Company would not have been possible without what became known—in the inevitable jargon of business—as "employee involvement," which required the recognition that the human instinct was still supreme, even in an age when technology had begun to take over the entire process of mass production. Petersen knew that people who brought their brains and enthusiasm to work would find more fulfillment there and do a better job, and he set to work to commit to paper a corporate philosophy that he called "Mission, Values and Guiding Principles" and begin systematically to change the culture of the corporation. At the same time he brought Dr. W. Edwards Deming into the company to teach the human and statistical principles that had made him the guru of the Japanese industrial empire so that he might spread the gospel of quality within the Ford Motor Company as a way of life. Henry Ford II, who had enunciated his own concern for what he called human engineering many decades earlier, observed, listened, and approved. Nobody in the company took it for granted, but Henry had no doubt in his own mind that the next chairman of the Ford Motor Company had selected himself.

He was equally content to contemplate Red Poling as president in Don Petersen's place, for the North American operations Red had commanded were almost jaunty in the self-esteem they had rediscovered under his leadership. Invention and daring had been given their head in the design centers, and in the factories, foremen and even operatives on the production lines were now entitled to stop the production process if they thought they were not delivering high quality. The accumulating profits were duly noted on Wall Street, and the company, which had only recently been considered a doubtful risk, was seen to have survived and to be heading for more enduring achievement.

Henry was, in fact, more concerned at this time about Ford in Europe than in the United States. At the end of his holiday he called me to say he was out of touch with the European product program, and I arranged to have all the latest cars available at the test track in Belgium together with prototypes of those not yet in production. We spent a long, hot August day on the track driving the circuit, banking at speeds well over one hundred miles per hour, bumping over the rougher sections in cars with turbocharged engines, four-wheel-drive, and a revolutionary automatic transmission.

Where cars were concerned, it is probably most accurate to say of Henry that he knew what he liked. He had great respect for engineers, and in the forties and fifties scarcely a product committee went by (and he attended them all) without his insisting on the need to hire more of them; the younger, the better. He was stimulated by adventure and new ideas, but he retained a certain orthodoxy. This was not a contradiction in terms, certainly not in his dictionary of design; his taste was for advanced engineering but traditional looks. Soft, feminine shapes were less pleasing to him than defined contours. After he bought Turville Grange and had somewhere in England where he could garage cars, I provided him on every trip with a new "special" of some kind, and he worked out a test route around the Henley lanes, trying them occasionally on his friends. His preferences were always crisply declared. Nevertheless, he was very willing to be overruled. He would pace the design studios and say firmly that he did not like the model on display. Some looked fat, some ugly, but "if that's what you fellas want . . ." All that he required was that the "fellas" should justify their own taste with argument and conviction, for he showed remarkable respect toward people who knew their own minds and markets and would fight for their points of view.

For all his vigor where new cars were concerned, he was curiously diffident about Philip Caldwell's retirement. He half expected Philip to initiate a discussion on the subject, for they worked in harmony and Philip regularly consulted him on the major strategical concerns. Eventually, it seemed, the subject hung in the air between them at their meetings, and members of the board of directors began to quiz Henry about the future. In the end it was resolved as I had anticipated. Don Petersen was proposed as chairman, and Red Poling as president, and the board gave the selection its unanimous approval. In mid-November the company's senior managers from all over the world came together for a meeting that had been planned as a farewell to Philip, and a reflection of his enormous achievements, and, incidentally, as a public baptism for Don Petersen and Red Poling. It was also intended to be Henry's last hurrah.

I had dinner with Kathy and Henry in Detroit on October 11 at the house one month before the meeting. It had pleased him to rechristen her Kate. He had never liked "Kathy," and there was perhaps a Shakespearean reminiscence in her new name. I had never seen him quite so relaxed. In five days he was off to England for some shooting. Then there would be the management meeting. His private affairs were in order. A new chairman and president would soon be in command for a period of some five or six years, which would take them well past his seventieth birthday. "I shall have to find something else to do," he said. "Will you give me a job?"

He was more serious than I thought, and the New Year provided some clues to the direction toward which his thoughts were turning. He professed no desire, so far as the company was concerned, to do more than "keep an eye on things." There would be more family meetings to continue the education of the younger generation. He readily undertook special missions when asked, making contact with heads of other automobile companies and using his welcome in the corridors of power to provide an impetus for new ventures or the resolution of old ones. But this did not seem to be enough, and he began to wonder if there might be some role he could play in public affairs. He always recalled with pleasure his days at the United Nations and on the various Washington committees and organizations, and as the economic managers of the Western world seemed badly in need of some assistance with their own affairs, he thought there just might be at least a walk-on part for him in the unfolding drama. It was by no means an intrusive desire. What made Henry's contribution to the Ford Motor Company of unique importance and relevance was that he carried his nationality lightly, he was entirely without insular preconceptions, and he brought to all his considerations the experience of a worldly man who could consider things from afar and provide perspectives out of sight of most people in American business and industry. Somebody once called it lateral thinking. He was particularly concerned about the growing tensions in world trade and felt, as did many others, that the developing money industry was no substitute for making things.

He had models of his own who provided justification for his thoughts. Many of Henry's European friends—John Loudon, Lord Richardson, Lord Plowden among them—had retired from distinguished careers in international business, banking, or industry and applied themselves, often without payment, to public institutions or the antechambers of government. Henry was by no means sure about the field of activity in which he might most usefully be engaged. He talked things over with Arjay Miller and had similar conversations, often over dinner, with others whose judgment he valued, such as Harold Shapiro, the president of the University of Michigan (now in a similar position at Princeton), and former Ford colleagues who had worked with him in his previous government associations, including Ted Mecke and Rod Markley, Ford's wise and experienced former vice-president of government affairs in Washington. I produced a long memorandum on the subject and was surprised by the intensity of his interest. I was also pleased at the possibility of a new avocation. There is no knowing what might have come about—whether or not he could have found a niche as an elder statesman—because he was again reminded of his mortality.

Henry had one other business interest that occupied some of his time. He was vice-chairman of Sotheby's. He enjoyed this strange new world and provided sound advice for Al Taubman, who was bent on transforming a somewhat sedate auction house.

He invited Al Taubman to join him on the *Southern Breeze* for a summer cruise off Majorca, and on August 20, 1985, he flew from Luton in England to Palma with Kathy, her two daughters and her son-in-law, Jerry Guibord. Al and Judy Taubman arrived in Palma the same day in their own private aircraft. Four days later Henry called me at home from the yacht and asked me to fix an appointment for him with his doctor, Peter Odgers, at London's Cromwell Hospital. "There's nothing wrong, is there?" I asked. Henry said it was nothing. He had had a fall and wanted a checkup.

Henry had fallen heavily, late at night, on the upper deck and appeared to have stunned himself. He lapsed into unconsciousness, and Jerry was sufficiently alarmed to give him the kiss of life; but he soon recovered awareness, and the admittedly inexpert opinion was that he had banged his head sharply and might perhaps have a slight concussion. As a precaution, the *Southern Breeze* changed course and Henry was taken to a hospital in Ibiza for a more professional inspection which was reassuring. He nevertheless thought it wise to interrupt his holiday long enough to see Dr. Odgers, and on August 26 he came back to London with Al Taubman, leaving the rest of the party on the yacht. Nobody thought his knock on the head sufficiently serious to involve the others, and it was arranged that they would stay moored in Palma until Henry's return.

As it turned out, he didn't go back. Peter Odgers ruled out a return to Majorca and made an appointment for further consultations with Dr. George Hart at the Radcliffe Infirmary in Oxford. Meanwhile, he was told to stay at Turville and rest, which was the last thing he wanted to do, and he insisted on living normally. On August 27 Wendy Alexander called me; she was convinced that it was far from being a casual incident. Henry was finding it difficult to talk coherently and he had a far from lucid luncheon with Al Taubman at the London office. I went to see him and thought I could detect a slight spasm on the right side of his face— the consequence, I suspected, of a minor stroke. His speech was still slurred and his conversation much less precise than usual. I sat with Wendy in her office and we wondered whether or not his condition was a consequence of the fall or the other way around.

Tomasz, who was at Turville, had been instructed to keep an eye on him and moved into the bachelor bedroom adjoining the one where Henry slept. Henry was out of sorts for another two days and was visited by the doctor at Turville. Kathy came back to London on the evening of August 30, and Bruce Steinhauer, Henry's personal doctor from Grosse Pointe, who was also the head of the Henry Ford Hospital in Detroit, flew in the same day. As Henry's speech returned to normal, he looked again to be in good form and was certainly in high spirits. He remembered nothing of the accident, describing it in one of his favorite phrases: It was just one of those things.

It was not, however, just one of those things, although it made no difference to the rest of his life. The fact was that he had suffered a stroke, which was confirmed after his death, when an autopsy was performed. Eight days after the fall he went back to Detroit for the board meeting, and he flew the Atlantic three more times in October and November, spending Christmas again at Turville Grange. I asked him if he had suffered any continuing consequences from the fall. "Never felt better in my life," he said.

CHAPTER TEN

Unfinished Business

In the spring of 1987 Henry and Kathy flew to London in their own Boeing 727: two bedrooms; one bathroom; all other relevant conveniences. The Ford Motor Company had owned a similar aircraft—a commercial 727 converted for private use—many years earlier. As Europe and the company's operations there grew in importance, sometimes as many as fifty people from Detroit— or more distant locations—were involved in the management meetings that took place each March, June, and October. The Ford Gulfstreams began to know their way from Detroit to Gander and Shannon before landing in London or Cologne, Bordeaux, or Valencia. Henry gave no evidence of being a nervous flier and traveled enormous distances—in everything from Hawker Siddeley 125s to the Concorde and regularly used helicopters—but he made no secret of the fact that he preferred to cross the Atlantic in planes with more than two engines. This, plus the growing executive traffic from west to east, led to the acquisition of Ford's first Boeing.

It did not, however, remain long in the fleet. I flew in it once, and it was certainly comfortable; but the energy crisis made it an evident luxury. No arguments could justify the use of so much aviation fuel for the transportation of so few passengers, and Henry ordered its sale. It was purchased, ironically enough, by the shah of Iran, who had his own oil wells.

By the time Henry came to buy a Boeing of his own, the oil crises had passed into history, big cars were reasserting themselves on American roads, and the old feelings of guilt had vanished. He inspected seven different aircraft, selected one, and was surprised to discover how many other people were buying 727s for private use. The other six on offer were all snapped up before he signed his check. There were sensible and practical considerations that led to his apparent extravagance. The "kidnapping codicil" to his trust agreement was proof of Henry's growing awareness of terrorism. As a director of the company he was entitled to use company aircraft on business, but he frequently found his own travel plans in conflict with Don Petersen or Red Poling or other executive directors, and he genuinely felt they outranked him where such things were concerned. He could charter company aircraft for personal use when they were available, but the costs were substantial. His brother Bill often did so, but he was rarely outside the United States, and Henry was everywhere and could scarcely keep a company aircraft at his command in Europe no matter the cost. After its maiden flight to London, Henry's Boeing was soon working hard. It returned to Detroit before taking off again for Dallas, then for Florida, back to Detroit, and coming over once more to London. "It's like a flying carpet," Henry said when I chided him for his indulgence, "and I don't have to ask any favors of anybody." He reminded me that his children were well provided for, as was Kathy, "so I might as well spend the money while I'm alive and enjoying it."

The 727 could also gobble up great masses of cargo, which promised to be useful since Henry had recently purchased a London apartment and would therefore have a convenient method of transporting furniture and pictures. I felt there was something more to it, although I did not know what. Perhaps he really was going to settle in England and wanted his own plane based there, too; he had, after all, tried to arrange its English registration until this proved too difficult. Maybe it was a sign of new resolution or a new direction in his life, a desire possibly to be free and independent and no longer obliged to seek any favors.

That April Henry and Kathy both were as happy together and as amusing as I had ever known them. Kathy disappeared to Paris for a couple of days for dress fittings. She looked longingly at a Stradivarius being auctioned at Christie's—"a little bit better than my violin," she said, but she was only joking. It fetched more than £400,000 and was sold to a professional Italian violinist. On the Saturday of the Easter weekend, when the weather was particularly lovely, Elizabeth and I went to Turville for the day. I had a box at Covent Garden the following week for three one-act ballets and asked Henry if they would like to come with us. Kathy quickly said yes and Henry was pleased with the idea. He was some distance from being a balletomane; but *Checkmate* is invariably captivating, and the company was at the peak of its talent. Four days later I went back to Turville, again for luncheon; we had shepherd's pie, and Henry confessed ruefully that he had given up wine and smoking and— look what it had done. He had taken six pairs of trousers to his tailors in Savile Row and the good Messrs. Anderson and Shephard had let them all out four inches.

This was a period of great contentment in his life. There was a shine to his eyes and a briskness in everything he did. His curiosity—always one of the most beguiling aspects of his character—was much in evidence. It had been partially satisfied that morning. In his retiring years Henry kept up with Ford's new cars and trucks by periodic descents upon the design and engineering centers and test tracks—through the presentations that were regularly made to the board of directors—and by reading the motoring magazines. He had read several articles, including a couple of cover stories, about a car that Ford of Britain had unveiled at the last British motor show. It was called the AC Ace and was a descendant of the AC Cobras Carroll Shelby had godfathered for Ford in the spectacular sixties. I was similarly placed in regard to the Ace.

In the late seventies my wife came home from the hairdresser one day and explained that a friend had told her of a young woman she knew whose clever husband was rebuilding Ford GT40s and Cobras; they both thought it would be a good idea for me to see what he was doing. Since peace is good for marriage, I had gone to see the car and the young man, Brian Angliss, and was unusually impressed with his Cobra restoration. I stayed in touch with him, and a few years later, when I was working in Dearborn and Brian was building new Cobras on the original tools at a small Brooklands factory—on the site of England's greatest racing track—I helped him gain respectability in the United States so that his Cobras (all one hundred a year of them) could be sold in an orderly and convincing fashion. The Ace had taken him a large step farther. The Cobra success enabled him to buy the remaining assets of AC Cars, and with the help of our design studios in Cologne, he built—largely from Ford production components—a masculine and good-looking two-seat sports car. I had liked it enough to campaign for its exhibition at the Birmingham show.

The automobile business is serious and dull and demanding and consists of numbers and machines and cost analyses, and a lot of the people who run it are like that. It is as well they are. But it has been the inestimable good fortune of everybody who works in the car business that the product of their labors can give rise to extraordinary passions, enduring love, and occasionally total obsession. The entrepreneurs who undertake to satisfy this longing are often lucky in love, and automobile shows are the places where trysting begins.

The AC Ace found her lovers at first sight. We were careful to say there were no plans for production because at that stage it was true. Henry might have seemed an unlikely suitor, but he liked cars, he lamented the absence of a modern sports car in the Ford range, and, reading one evening about the Ace, he asked me if he could see one, whereupon we arranged for Brian Angliss to take the prototype to Turville Grange and be prepared to explain.

Henry was dressed for the occasion in jeans and a blue Ford motor sport rally jacket. He said he would talk about the Ace later, but first he was going to drive it, and with Brian at the wheel, they were soon through the lanes and on their way to Oxford. After five or six miles they swapped places, and Henry took over the driving, heading for the nearest motorway. It was a good, tight prototype with a nice wide stance and long wheelbase, and even with its then standard development engine, it was quick, quicker than either of them was able to prove on public roads. After about an hour they came back, and we sat in the drawing room to talk about the car. Bill Coles—originally Henry's shooting instructor but then, with his wife, Annette, majordomo of Turville Grange—served coffee from a silver pot, and Brian had time to explain what AC Cars was about and his hopes for the Ace in particular.

Henry, in his new bright-eyed mood of adventure, was much taken with the prospect. After Brian had departed with the car, we talked about it over luncheon, and in the afternoon Henry sat down with the telephone. He called Alex Trotman, then president of Ford of Europe, and his son, Edsel, in Detroit, and began to discover certain logical apprehensions about engaging in such a venture. Even limited production automobiles are required to pass the same stringent tests for safety and emissions as those that come off the production lines in their hundreds of thousands. The same standards of engineering, development, and manufacturing quality must be maintained. Some brave souls who have ventured into the specialist car business with different ideas and faith in shortcuts have lost their self-respect as well as their shirts. Boutique sports cars have a habit of losing money for their manufacturers, as even Commendatore Ferrari found out.

Henry, however, was not to be deterred by the recitation of such considerations or by muttering about caution because he had heard the story a hundred times before, and to ensure that his suggestion to "look into it" was being taken seriously, he told Edsel (then Lincoln-Mercury's general marketing manager in the United States) that maybe he would go it alone. Instead of asking the Ford Motor Company to buy AC Cars and put the Ace into production, perhaps he would buy it himself; it probably would not cost much more than the Boeing 727 he had just acquired. "Wouldn't that be something?" he said between telephone calls as we sat in his study. The more he thought about it, the more he enjoyed the prospect. "Just think of it," he said, "we could call it Ford Motor Company if I owned it. God, that would make them sit up!"

In essence, this was no more than Henry being Henry. Throughout his working life he would sometimes deliberately throw unacceptable ideas on the table, partly to gain attention but more often to extend the range of thought that was being brought to the issue under consideration. In April 1987, however, there was more to it than that; his rekindled determination to stimulate strategic thinking in and about the Ford Motor Company gave me, at least, the impression that he woke each day looking for action of some kind. "Are there any other AC Cars about?" he asked.

As it happens, there were, and a trip to Italy reminded me of one in particular. We went to stay with two hospitable friends, Joyce and Gordon Wilkins, at their little palazzo near Bergamo for the Mille Miglia. To many people this remains the supreme motor race, and it was, indeed, of sufficient stature in its heyday to raise the pulses of both Hitler and Mussolini to the highest level of competitive tension. Even after the outbreak of the Second World War, Mussolini kept the race going, and some of my older German friends found no difficulty getting leave from the Luftwaffe and the Wehrmacht to participate. It has monumental significance in British motoring history because the last time it was run—over one thousand miles of Italian roads, hairpins, and mountain passes; before anxiety about road and spectator safety brought it to an end—it was won by Stirling Moss, who covered the route with his codriver, Denis Jenkinson, in ten hours. I have known both Stirling and Denis for many years and have often enjoyed a free drink from motoring enthusiasts merely because I could claim their acquaintance. In recent years the Mille Miglia has become a historic and rather less competitive drive over the same distance. It lasts two days and brings out beautiful cars and Italians by the thousands. The last time Stirling was there, he was pursued into the woodlands by a group of nuns who remembered him flashing by when they were no more than schoolgirls in black smocks and white stockings.

Elizabeth and I had flown from England to Bergamo with Prince

Michael of Kent, who is a connoisseur of motorcars and constructively engaged in motor sport and business. He is a confident fast driver, and he was entered for the event, sharing an Aston Martin DBR2 with Aston's executive chairman, Victor Gauntlett. They both were members of the same house party, and I had an opportunity to talk to Victor. I knew Aston Martin was for sale before I got to Bergamo—one of my colleagues in charge of European business development had it on his mind and desk—but I had no previous opportunity to think and talk about it to the man who was running it or appreciate its newer cars as much as I did when, at the end of the race, Prince Michael and Victor swept Elizabeth off to the airport in a new Volante and she disappeared with her hand on her hat and a wave and was out of sight in seconds.

I told Henry about the Mille Miglia and Aston Martin less than a week later in Detroit. He knew the Livanos family, one of whom owned the larger part of the Aston Martin Lagonda Company, and made some private calls to satisfy himself it was for sale. Victor Gauntlett and Peter Livanos were sensible enough to see that they could keep the famous marque alive and prosperous only under the aegis of a rich and benevolent uncle. "What shall we do?" Henry asked, and I said I would certainly buy it. Apart from the practical considerations, I have always believed that the giants of the automotive world have a duty to keep the traditions of their industry alive.

On September 1—twenty-eight days before Henry died—I had dinner with Peter Livanos and Victor Gauntlett and with my colleagues Ken Whipple, Alex Trotman, and Bruce Blythe, and we had by then agreed to buy both AC Cars and Aston Martin Lagonda. All that remained were the legal niceties. Henry had been pleased with the progress that had been made and was delighted that Don Petersen was committed and supportive from the beginning. "It won't change the universe," Henry said, "but it is the kind of thing we should be doing."

In the firmament of Ford it was true that the two new stars were modest additions to the galaxy, but they had a particular relevance at this time. For the whole of 1987—and, indeed, from the time that he really got back on his feet after the mild stroke he had endured on the *Southern Breeze*—Henry was increasingly concerned with two things: what sort of enterprise the Ford Motor Company should be and what role, as guardians or guides, the family itself should play.

The speed and completeness of the change in its fortunes were ever-present reasons for focusing attention upon the first issue. In the worst days of the early eighties, when Henry was most fearful for its future, he had even—for a brief and perhaps fanciful period of time—contemplated having the Ford family buy the company back into private ownership. He had talked it over with Arjay Miller but soon found reasons for dismissing the fantasy as no more than that. It was not, however, as fantastic an idea as it might seem—particularly in these days (no more than a decade later) of frenetic multibillion-dollar take-overs. The market value of Ford stock fell from a high point of $51.87 per share in 1978 to a low of $15.75 in 1981. Henry could then have bought sufficient shares to give the family 51 percent ownership for less than $500 million. For $2.5 billion he could have bought 100 percent.

Yet, in less than ten years, its cash reserves alone had grown from $7 billion to $8 billion to $9 billion, and this provided a resource substantially larger than that needed to sustain and develop the purely automotive side of the business. There was more than enough for the Ford *Motor* Company, but the company was more than that. Its finance and insurance operations were more substantial than those of many international banks. The value of Ford stock rose in one year—January 30, 1986, to January 30, 1987—by 78 percent. The Ford Motor Credit Company completed its twelfth consecutive year of record profits in 1986—the U.S. car crisis of the early eighties notwithstanding—with net income of $611 million. The good news was everywhere. In 1986 more than 2 million Ford vehicles were sold outside the United States, three-quarters of them (1.5 million) in Europe. Two-thirds of all America's overseas communications and virtually all the world's intercontinental television programs were transmitted by Ford Aerospace satellites. A jury of European journalists named the Ford Scorpio Europe's "Car of the Year," and the Ford Taurus won a similar honor in the United States.

The tottering company, which had received young Lieutenant Henry Ford into its arms with a decidedly muted expression of confidence, was now—forty-three years later—the second-largest car and truck producer in the world; the second-largest finance company in the world; the third-largest tractor producer in the world; the second-largest glass company in the United States; the seventh-largest U.S. savings and loan company; and the eighth-largest U.S. steel company. In 1986, moreover, Ford's pretax earnings were larger than those of General Motors and Chrysler put together. The last time Ford profits had exceeded General Motors' was 1924.

By any standard of measurement and analysis, these results were a remarkable tribute to Philip Caldwell, Don Petersen, Red Poling, and many others on the board of directors and to that international management over which Henry had fretted and planned and plotted and maneuvered for the greater part of his life. They were, in a sense, the final tribute to, and justification for, his own life and the single-mindedness with which he had discharged that near-sacred duty thrust upon him in his raw and youthful years. But he was not investing in a goddamned newfangled hearing aid so that he could hear hallelujahs, and Don Petersen and Red Poling had given specific instructions within the company to prevent eruptions of euphoria. So far was so good, but the global, motorized, traffic-jammed, high-tech village that the world's motor industry had become was more competitive than ever. Ford was continuing to invest billions of dollars and weigh some bumper harvests, but the watchword from the Dearborn Glass House was still frugality.

Henry had become involved in a number of strategic discussions with other large automobile manufacturers. A merger of Ford's European operations with those of FIAT foundered, despite the common interest of Henry and his friend Gianni Agnelli to make it happen. An alliance of some kind with Austin-Rover in Britain was betrayed at birth by some gentlemen who could see no farther than the butter on their own bread and, more substantively, by rampant xenophobic chauvinism, for which Britain has become disturbingly famous. There were sensible talks with Volkswagen's Kurt Hahn that resulted in the combination of Ford and VW operations in Brazil into a joint company called Autolatina—now big enough to be counted among the leaders of world vehicle manufacturing. The association with Mazda—once Toyo Kogyo—resulting from Ford's 25 percent ownership was developed and reinforced. Henry made time for briefings and discussions on these and other potential alliances and brought his unique stature and experience to many confidential exchanges of view. Nobody could open doors more quickly, including those at the back, and nobody was more trusted.

But Henry's specific concerns were of wider scope. The growing financial resources of the company had permitted the purchase of First Nationwide, the U.S. financial services company, for $483 million in 1985, and another $330 million had been spent to create Ford New Holland, which reinforced Ford's tractor and implements operations. Other smaller acquisitions were made to reinforce existing activities by the various components within Ford's automobile, aerospace, and financial services world. The question in Henry's mind was not the validity of acquisitions of this kind but whether or not the time had come to see Ford not merely as a motor company but as a corporation in which the word *motor* might mean no more, say, than it did at FIAT, where the parent organization was involved in everything from machine tools to newspaper, magazine, and book publishing. It even had a football team. (So, in a sense, did Ford. Henry's brother Bill owns the Detroit Lions, but that is a private preoccupation and pleasure—not a company affair.)

Henry approached these concerns by several typical, if roundabout, methods. Toward the end of 1986 he asked Sidney Kelly, the company secretary, to set down on paper the precise rights and powers of the Class B stock of the Ford Motor Company. He had asked for a memorandum on the subject previously, but that had been written in January 1975, and he wanted to be accurate and up-to-date in his understanding. It was an interesting paper. Kelly pointed out that the members of the Ford family, among them, owned some twenty million shares of Class B stock. Although this was less than 8 percent of the total capital stock of the company, it represented 40 percent of the voting power. There was no discrimination where dividends were concerned; common stock and B stock received, unit per unit, precisely the same dividend. The issue was one of power. Practical control of a publicly held corporation rests with its operating management, which is itself elected and removable by the board of directors. Power to select a majority of the board therefore represents effective control, and all the other facts and figures in the seven-page memorandum emphasized that 40 percent of the vote was power enough.

Kelly pointed out that the company's certificate of incorporation made the balance of power easy to understand. The aggregate Class B stockholder vote would equal 40 percent so long as the number of outstanding shares did not fall below 15,187,470. If it did, the voting strength would drop to 30 percent. Below 8,437,483, each B share would fall in line with the common stock, which meant it would have only one vote.* Henry checked the 1986 memorandum with the one from 1975, satisfied himself that the numbers were right, and agreed with Sid Kelly that if the past rate of sale of B stock by family members was taken as a yardstick, the 40 percent power was probably good for a minimum of fifteen years. Some diminution in B stock was to be expected and of no consequence; indeed, Henry himself had thought

* These figures were correct for 1986. A subsequent split in the stock has altered the numbers. It now requires roughly double the number of units of B stock to secure the 40 percent and 30 percent vote. The family, however, owns thirty-eight million shares, well above the required level.

about Kathy's holdings after his death and had suggested that she should sell some to diversify her income. The reality was that the family could continue as a bastion of the company's security comfortably into the twenty-first century and the Ford Motor Company's one hundredth birthday, provided, of course, that the family retained Henry's own sense of tradition and continuity and—most important—common purpose.

Henry worked out his ideas that summer mostly in the library at Turville Grange and in his remote little office in Mayfair. He looked up his old papers on McKinsey and talked to some of the outside members of the Ford board of directors. He invited his nephew Bill—his brother Bill's son—to Turville and asked him how he saw the company developing. Young Bill was working in Ford of Europe's truck operations in Britain, taking a back seat and learning as fast as he could, and he was not prepared for this examination; but he impressed Henry by speaking of the company as he saw it from his own experience and as he thought it could be. Back in Detroit, Henry talked to Edsel. He was keen that both young men should play a bigger role in the company. I was amused by his new preoccupation with elevating his son to something more nearly approximating a crown prince. I chided him about his past fixation about nepotism, but he did not mind the reminder. "It will be a different thing when Bill and I have gone," he said.

I tried to put my finger on the pulse of this quite evident change of mood that infected everything Henry did that spring and summer. It was to an extent like having a younger Henry back again. He was once more surrounded by papers in his office. I would call in for meetings at his request and find myself still there two or three hours later. It was an enjoyable time but difficult, too.

I had developed over the years an instinctive technique when Henry was about to embark on a new venture or initiate change whether in public or private life. The best phrase for it is the term *slow-walking*. It consisted of being deliberately slow in both understanding and response, almost to the extent of appearing ignorant—asking questions rather than suggesting answers. It was not altogether like playing devil's advocate because in Henry's often complex approach to new ideas or tactics, the ideas themselves and their execution were not sufficiently shaped to be defied or contradicted. More than anything it called for a certain vagueness, lack of interest, or hesitation about becoming involved. I am sure Henry knew it was a game because he played it very well. It was called making up his mind.

The process, so far as I was concerned, came to a hiatus while Henry went off in pursuit of something that was pure nostalgia. He was determined to go to Pamplona in Spain for the running of the bulls. He had a list of sorts in his mind of things he had never done and wanted to do and places he had never visited, and Pamplona was high on the list. Thousands of Americans over the years, and many from other countries, have been lured there each July for *Sanfermines* after reading Ernest Hemingway's *The Sun Also Rises*. In the twenties Hemingway went to Pamplona year after year to join in its nine days and nights of tauromania with other aficionados of the bullring. *The Sun Also Rises* was one of Henry's best-remembered books, along with Kenneth Tynan's *Bull Fever*. He had known some of the people whose lives were impersonated in Hemingway's story, and one long night in the Ritz in Paris he had stayed up late with Hemingway himself, talking about St. Fermin's fair or festival, and Hemingway had urged him to go there and see for himself. Henry mentioned it to me several times when we were site hunting for the factory in Spain, for Pamplona was at one time on the list of possible locations, but he had never made it.

The Sun Also Rises was published in 1927, and Henry thought it proper that he should be going to Pamplona exactly sixty years later. It was a suitable omen. And he was sentimental about another coincidence. Hemingway's novel is published outside the United States with a different title—it is called *Fiesta*—and that was the name Henry had personally bestowed on Ford's first small car in Europe, which had proved the inspiration for the company's by now substantial operations in Spain. It was nice to be able to tie up the ends of one's life in this fashion. We all carry with us on every journey some kind of premonition, comfortable or otherwise; Henry's angels appeared to be smiling on him from a bright blue sky, and Kathy was looking forward to the holiday. If he had been eighteen, he would have been running with the bulls, but he was less than three months short of his seventieth birthday. Still, he had a hotel balcony that would provide a splendid view of the spectacle and tickets for several bullfights.

He had arranged to go to Pamplona with a small party: Mary Wells and Harding Lawrence, Sandy and Ed Acker. Mary Wells Lawrence, the first lady of Madison Avenue, is a stimulating companion. She had built and established one of America's most creative advertising agencies—the "I Love New York" campaign, which put a red heart on everything from cars to coffee mugs, was one of her successes—and her husband, Harding, was a former chairman of Braniff Airways. Ed Acker was the head of Pan American. The Lawrences have a beautiful villa at Cap Ferrat on the French Riviera, and Henry flew with Kathy to Nice in the 727 on July 2 to join them there. They all flew to Spain on Henry's magic carpet three days later.

Pamplona, which stands on a plateau in the foothills of the Pyrenees, is noisy with the pipes and fifes and drums of the marching bands and the sounds of flamenco while *Sanfermines* is taking place, and the Plaza del Castillo is jammed with dancing Spaniards in white shirts and trousers, red scarves and cummerbunds, and Basque berets. San Fermin is the patron saint of the city, and there is a religious procession of baroque opulence, fireworks galore, and every excuse not to go to bed. Bullfights are held on all but one of the nine days, and every morning at eight, six bulls, which are to be fought in the afternoon and evening corridas, and twelve steers are released from their corrals at one end of the town to run through the narrow streets to the bullring, challenging amateur bull-fighters on their way (and in their way) to try their skill and courage. To be sure of a good position from which to view and belong to the spectacle, it is wise to get up at six o'clock in the morning and listen to the rise in the common heartbeat, which reaches bull-fever pitch as the time for the running approaches.

Henry and his party were certainly dedicated tourists: They went to watch a game of jai alai and had a 7:00 A.M. breakfast in the Bullfight Museum. The bullfighter Morenito de Maracay joined them for lun-cheon, and they later watched the ritual ceremony as he was dressed for the ring. They toured the Sarría winery and attended several bullfights in the afternoon and evening, watching the brave bulls die. Henry was no expert, but other visits to Spain over the years had made him knowledge-able enough to explain some of the finer points to the others in the party. They were welcomed everywhere, but there was no fuss, which was remarkable in the circumstances.

Pamplona is in the Basque country, and Basque terrorists are not the most gentle people in the world. I had been concerned about security, but knowing of Henry's aversion to security men, I had decreed that there should be none. Tomás Cavanna, an intelligent young executive from Ford in Madrid, had joined the party with Henry's agreement to lend a hand, but that was as far as protection went. Henry's arrival had obvi-ously not passed without notice. The airport at Pamplona is not very large, and only one small aircraft—from Madrid—arrives each day. The Boeing 727 stood out like the *Queen Elizabeth* in a swimming pool. But the regard for Henry throughout Spain, from president to peasant, was general and sincere, and the newspaper editors decided they would not mention the presence of Senor Ford at *Sanfermines* until the day he left. They recognized, too, that being incognito was the bigger part of his pleasure. This brought a few white hairs to the head of Tomás Cavanna during the first night of the party's stay, for he was called to the office of the director in the Tres Reyes Hotel at 4:00 A.M. to be told the lobby was full of policemen; there was a bomb alarm. For two hours they searched and talked and made telephone calls, weighing the risk to the hotel (and Henry) from the ETA (the Basque terrorist organization) if the threat proved real, but Tomás—calm and logical—had his way, and when daylight came, the warning was seen for what it was: a hoax.

Hemingway has a sentence in his novel that describes "a feeling of things coming that you could not prevent happening," and it seemed especially apt to me when I read the book again recently. It was said that Henry picked up the virus that killed him on this holiday, but there was no premonition in Pamplona at that time, by any member of the party, except of future contentment and companionship. Nor was there any evidence; Henry was coughing at night, but he was also smoking cigars again.

They left Pamplona on July 9 and returned to Cap Ferrat to stay again with the Lawrences until the seventeenth, when they all went off for a cruise on the *Southern Breeze*. The Lawrences felt at home; they had chartered the yacht before Henry bought it. On July 27 Henry and Kathy came back to London, having disembarked at Corfu.

I have traced and retraced Henry's movements in the four weeks that followed—no easy thing to do, for he was rarely at rest. On August 4 I had a long meeting with him at which it was evident he had not devoted his break entirely to holidaying. He had more papers to read and discuss. On August 12 he went to Frankfurt for a Ford meeting concerned with the development of its European business and stayed there overnight. On August 13 he flew directly to New York and stayed at the Lowell Hotel for a meeting with John Weinberg of Goldman, Sachs, and that afternoon he left for Detroit. He had various meetings there, including a session with Don Petersen, and he got back to London on August 20. On August 24 we spent some time together in the London office, and he revealed his plan.

He had finally completed and polished to his satisfaction a paper he intended to present to a meeting of the company's Finance Committee two days before the September board. It ran to three pages, and he had completed and signed it six days earlier in Dearborn. It was not particularly remarkable or in any way revolutionary. He had come to the conclusion, the paper said, that it was time for some hard thinking about the future of the Ford Motor Company. He was going to seek out and appoint a management consultancy group—just as he had before with McKinsey—to make sure the company itself was not being too restrictive in its outlook or too conventional in its evaluations. "I do not have any unshakeable preconceptions or theories," Henry had written, in a typical burst of bluffness, "and I intend to ensure that the study will be open-minded in its concepts and global in its scope."

He had also prepared a family letter, postdated September 8, the day of the Finance Committee meeting at which he intended to present his paper. This said:

It is the opinion of the senior members of the family that it would be advisable to hold a family meeting to discuss various problems that are coming up from time-to-time at the present as well as what the family position would be for the future after Bill and I are no longer members in any way of the Ford organization. I am calling a meeting on Friday, December 18, at 2 P.M. in the Bugatti Royale Room at the Dearborn Hyatt Regency Hotel for this discussion. I do hope that you will make every effort to attend because it is most important that all of us be there in order to arrive at conclusions that will be the wishes of the majority.

The letter was not intended to be as enigmatic as it sounds. What he had in mind was some kind of voting trust that would ensure that the B stock was voted as a whole and that ownership of the stock would not be diluted below the level required to maintain a 40 percent share. I read the letter and the paper. I said: "I don't know why you are pushing yourself so hard. There is no urgency about what you are doing and you are beginning to look tired again."

"I'm fine," Henry said. "Don't worry about me. I'm going to have a nice quiet rest for my birthday."

CHAPTER ELEVEN

And the Saints Came Marching In

Nobody outside the family ever made a fuss of Henry's birthdays, and even the family response was no more than a matter of cards and calls and presents. Before their marriage Kathy had once arranged for a local Detroit jazz band to serenade him early outside his bedroom window; the gesture had not been appreciated. The approach of September 4, 1987, however, prompted more general interest. Don Petersen and others on the top floor in Dearborn began to receive letters from people in the company suggesting some kind of celebration, some form of recognition; this September, after all, Henry Ford II would be seventy years of age. It was not a birthdate Don was likely to forget, either, because it was also his own; he had been born on September 4, 1926.

Earlier in the year, when I was in Dearborn, I had been given some of the letters and asked what I thought would please Henry. The suggestions were various, ranging from endowment of university chairs to a management dinner. I said I thought he would be horrified by anything of this kind. In the first place, he did not see himself as an ancient gentleman, ripe or ready for memorialization; in the second, he was a private person and had never allowed business into his private life except when and where he chose. I nevertheless said I would ask him. As I expected, the news was not calmly received, and we had a pointed discussion, in which I said that he was reacting foolishly. The suggestions for celebration had arisen from the genuine affection of many people who rightly recognized his stature in the world and properly regarded seventy as a milestone worth a garland or two. Henry's little furies mostly subsided as quickly as they arose to the surface, and he was dutifully apologetic. It *was* very nice of people to think of him and his birthday, but he had had a better idea anyway and would not be in the United States on the anniversary.

The better idea was another "Pamplona"—one of the other locations on that list-in-his-head of places he had never visited: Baden Baden. Baden Baden in Bavaria is one of John Loudon's favorite places, and the Brenners Park Hotel there one of his most enjoyable watering holes. In a sense that is precisely what it is, for Baden Baden, as its name implies, grew out of a spa, and over many generations, the Germans have come there for rest and to indulge themselves in that special German fixation known as taking the cure. Nor were the visitors only German; the crowned heads of Europe and their retinues had descended on Brenners over the years along with many other more distant courtiers.

I thought it a good place for Henry. He had looked tired and was, without question, traveling too far and too often; even in the comfort of his own aircraft it was still a wearisome business. The visit was secretly planned. It was to be Henry and Kathy alone for a few days, celebrating themselves and taking it easy. Kathy's younger daughter, Kim, was invited later, and Edsel quietly bought himself a ticket when he discovered the plan so that he could make a quick dash from Detroit and surprise his father on the great day. Henry and Kathy flew from London to Strasbourg on September 1 in the 727 and then drove to the hotel.

Henry was delighted to see Edsel but clearly not well enough to enjoy any sort of celebration. He had some kind of bronchial upset, and Kathy was sufficiently concerned to call Detroit and ask Bruce Steinhauer, the family doctor, to make the trip to Germany. The photographs taken in Brenners on Henry's birthday were not of the usual kind: Kathy, Kim, and Edsel, Bruce Steinhauer, and Henry—in nightshirt and toweling robe—just about managing a smile. Henry spent most of the day in bed, and Dr. Steinhauer went around to the pharmacies in the town, buying antibiotics, but he soon decided it made more sense to fly Henry back to the United States despite the length of the journey. They all returned to Detroit on September 5, and Henry was doctored at home for a day or two.

On September 9 it was decided that he had pneumonia badly enough to be admitted to the Cottage Hospital in Grosse Pointe, a mile or two from his home—a branch of the Henry Ford Hospital in Detroit—but his condition did not improve, and three days later he was moved to the main hospital and put into intensive care. I was much occupied with business reviews at this time in London; October puts the budget to bed for the following year, and these autumn days are the working bridge between the old year and the new. I called Kathy once or twice. Wendy Alexander was in London, and I talked more frequently to her. We agreed that Henry's illness was perhaps not all that surprising. We both thought he had tired himself unnecessarily with all his business and private journeying, and people are most vulnerable to pneumonia in this condition. And he was in intensive care, and if there was one place in the world where they would certainly take care of him, it had to be the hospital his grandfather had built and his family had sustained.

I did not know what to do for the best. One pair of hands is all the comfort one person needs, but I had a long-standing instruction from Henry to "be there" at any time of crisis. All indecision was removed on September 15, when Kathy called to say I should catch a plane. The doctors had diagnosed a form of viral pneumonia, a strain that had come to be known in recent years as Legionnaires' disease. Henry was heavily sedated, but he could comprehend what was said to him, and he still had a good chance of pulling through. A tracheotomy had been performed to permit the administration of oxygen. There was no immediate panic.

I did not feel reassured. I spent the morning in London canceling business appointments and excusing myself from meetings, taking time and care not to suggest either the reason for my journey or any specific concerns. I then caught the evening British Airways Concorde to New York and another flight to Detroit, where I was met by Bert Pearl, one of the company's unfailingly considerate drivers. I arrived at the house just before midnight. A dozen or so people were sitting at the long table in the dining room finishing dinner. It was superficially a jolly party, and I was, for a moment, surprised, since the women were in evening dress and the men in black ties. I had forgotten that Henry had planned a dinner that evening in honor of his English friends Vivienne Duffield and Jocelyn Stevens. The invitation had gone out on August 28, and Henry, from the hospital in Grosse Pointe, had insisted—perhaps as an act of defiance—that the party should continue without him. He sent messages to all concerned to this effect.

Edsel's wife, Cynthia, was there, along with Walter Buhl Ford (despite the surname, not a direct relation; he had married Henry's sister, Josephine); Sam Sachs, director of the Detroit Institute of Arts, and his wife, Beth; Kathy's sister and brother-in-law, Sharon and Richard Amluxen; Kathy's daughter Debi and her husband, Jerry Guibord; and some good and close friends: Paula Sarvis; Mort and Mary Jean Lieberman;

Anne and Peter Spivak. Jocelyn Stevens, whom I had known for many years through his career in English publishing and journalism, is rector of London's Royal College of Art, and he wanted to see the treasures in the Detroit Institute of Arts. He believed, I think as I did, that the party was a sign of optimism. I got back to the hotel and woke Elizabeth in England with a phone call. It was seven o'clock in the morning there.

I went to the hospital with Kathy and Debi to see Henry that afternoon. The Henry Ford Hospital is a large brick establishment—forbidding to me, as all hospitals are—and Henry was in Unit WC547 on the fifth floor, a glass cubicle with one window to the outside world and the other facing inward. Five similar enclosures in the unit were all occupied by other patients, and in the hub of the room, green-suited nurses sat at a control unit. It was the kind of place where people speak in whispers. I stood for a while in the cubicle by Henry's side and held his shoulder and then his left hand. There was no response and nothing to do save pray. He had been given cortisone, Valium, and morphine. Kathy had changed into a track suit immediately after the party was over and had spent much of the night with him, sleeping in a room that had been found for her and returning to Grosse Pointe in midmorning. She was already familiar with the tubes and the machines and the hum and digital click of this modern robot medicine. She knew what the displays meant and had quickly learned the names of the doctors and nurses. At such times, lacking all knowledge and any kind of experience likely to be of practical help, one sinks into the banalities that can bring comfort only to those close enough to share the same feelings of impotence. One finds oneself saying: "He has a good color"; "He's in the best possible hands"; "I'm sure he understood what I said"; "Of course, they know what they are doing." You never say "die."

The doctors were expert in this kind of conversation. God knows how many times they had been through it before. But saying something was what mattered. It didn't have to mean anything. I talked to John Popovich, director of the intensive care unit; Sol Pickard, the senior staff cardiologist; Dr. Louis Saravolatz; and a kidney specialist whose name I never knew. Bruce Steinhauer, who in his more formal attire was chairman of the board of the hospital, spent hours in attendance in his white coat and comfortable shoes.

They talked openly and wisely about their patient, and when Charlotte called me at the hotel that evening from New York, I was at least able to say more than "As well as can be expected," which was what the hospital was telling everybody else who inquired. Charlotte was anxious to be there, as were Anne and their husbands and children. Edsel and Cynthia were in the hospital day and night, although it began to seem as if not being there was the more positive response; we all could continue to believe Henry would pull through. On September 18 I went to Edsel's office to discuss the things that would happen should this not prove so, and at Kathy's request, I then packed my bag and moved into the house. It had become apparent that it was the best place to be, and indeed, a bizarre happening quickly convinced me a barricade or two would not be out of place.

A security man had been posted near the door of the intensive care unit, but the vigilance provided was not up to Secret Service standards, nor did anybody feel it necessary to go to such lengths. There were also other people to consider. Relatives visiting patients in the other five cubicles would not have welcomed any hindrance to their own freedom of movement. They sometimes cast a glance in Henry's direction or asked how he was getting on, but for the most part they were enclosed in their own concerns. People came and went, and all of them evidently had some reason for being there. So when a Roman Catholic priest walked into the unit, nobody thought it odd or asked him his business. Priests are the people to whom we entrust our souls, and why should security guards show less respect?

The Reverend John Mericantante III, an associate pastor at the Immaculate Conception Church in Hialeah, Florida, strode into Henry's cubicle and, soon after 11 A.M. on September 18, administered the last rites. When I first heard the story, I did not believe it. I told Debi and her husband and insisted that nobody should tell Kathy; it would dangerously shred the thin strands of hope from which her confidence was suspended. But it was not possible to keep the intrusion secret. Father Mericantante, it appeared, was a friend of the Iacocca family and had come to Detroit to participate in the wedding of Lee's daughter Lia. The wedding naturally had journalists in attendance, and Father Mericantante had volunteered the news of what he had done at the hospital and his outrageous behavior there, although he obviously did not see it in that way. He said he had been driven by chauffeur to the hospital in a Chrysler limousine and had merely taken the elevator to the fifth floor and to Henry's bedside. He had lots of different explanations for his actions: His father had worked for Ford as a regional manager in New England; he had been asked to perform the sacrament by a member of the Ford family, although he was not willing to say which one. Lee Iacocca was quick to deny any involvement. When Kathy came down to the small library in the evening, wrapped in a dressing gown after a fitful afternoon's nap, all of Detroit's television channels were reporting the news, which turned out to have some value after all since it made her so angry that her fury eclipsed for the whole evening the other thoughts that had weighed upon her so heavily. There are times when getting mad has a therapeutic value, and this was certainly one. Kathy later complained to the archbishop of Detroit, who was preoccupied at the time with the impending visit of the Pope, who was due to arrive any minute on his first visit to the city. I did not discover if anybody ever apologized.

The following evening I went with Debi and Jerry to dinner with Edsel and Cynthia at their Grosse Pointe home. They had thoughtfully suggested a break in the vigil. We had separated Kathy from all but emergency telephone calls and sent her early to bed. Edsel's three boys were rumbustious company. Sonny—Henry Ford III—tall for his seven years and slim, was already looking, I thought, something like his great-great-grandfather. Life is demanding of the firstborn, and he was quieter than his brothers because, after all, being older brings very early a self-imposed sense of responsibility. Calvin displayed the most astounding energy and was a bundle of bounding mischief. Stewart, only just toddling, looked as if he would be as big a handful before too long. When I went to the hospital the next day, alone with Kathy, something had been added to Henry's room. On the wall, affixed with sticky tape, there hung a painting of a wavy blue sea, a few blue clouds, and an enormous beaming yellow sun. Underneath the picture was written: "To Granddaddy. Get well soon. Love, Sonny."

The doctors had given Henry massive doses of steroids but said he had come slightly out of his drugged sleep during the night. The night nurse had asked him to move his limbs, and he had nodded and obeyed. A specimen from a biopsy had been sent to Atlanta for further expert diagnosis. I leaned down a little over Henry's cot and said: "Think of all the work you have done and the plans you have and all the unfinished business. And bloody well concentrate on getting well. . . ."

Kathy said: "They say he can understand even though he cannot reply."

I said if anything would get through to him, that would.

Kathy decided to have Edsel and Cynthia around that evening for hamburgers and hot dogs barbecued on the terrace and to show a film afterward in the downstairs cinema. The invitation stemmed, I thought, from an unacknowledged belief that behaving normally might somehow make everything that way. Martin and Myra Citrin and Paula Sarvis were also invited. It was still warm enough to sit outside and enjoy the meal and the company. Mort Lieberman had produced for after-dinner entertainment a copy of *The Rosary Murders*, a whodunit derived from a book by a well-known Detroit writer. There was an astounded gasp when the film began. The opening shot showed a dead priest lying on a bed in an intensive care unit.

It was Henry Fielding who once said that death is not so terrible as dying, although the two are frequently confused, and those long days and nights I came to know how true it is. Medical staff members sweep by in their white or green anonymity and nod kindly as they pass, but they are self-contained in their own duty. You are offered coffee in Styrofoam containers and sticky buns, and you are asked all the time if there is anything they can do for you. Of course, there isn't. And they can't. You stand awkwardly, trying not to get into anybody's way, counting the numbers in the little glass windows of the machines, watching the blip that tells you he is still alive although there is no other evidence to convince you. The man himself ceases, under your very eyes, to be the one you knew. He would never have let his side whiskers grow that long. And he looks different. Perhaps he is. And how can he ever regain his own functions from the gadgets that have taken over? What sort of man will he be if he comes out of it? You stand outside the cubicle for four or five minutes while something is changed and smile at a young woman leaving the one next door. You cannot think of anything to say to each other. How long has he been unconscious like this, lying unknowingly while other people and things fight the war inside his body? Nine days. The doctors say he is putting up an astonishing fight, but is it now one he would want to win? You know you are being silly, but you find it all an affront to his dignity. How much he would have hated lying like this on a public cart . . .

On September 22 the doctors reported the first signs of improvement. Kathy had spent the night in the hospital and was outwardly quite different. She came back to the house and changed and went off to the Caucus Club for luncheon with two women friends. I answered the telephone a couple of times, once to Gianni Agnelli, to whom I gave as much news as there was. I then packed my bag and moved back to the Hyatt. I was constrained in the house and probably constraining to other people. The women could, I decided, sit around *déshabillé* more easily if I were not there, and they could also stop worrying about whether I was eating enough. Moreover, Wendy Alexander was on her way from London to join the other ladies in waiting, so I went back to the Hyatt and opened a bottle of red wine from California and thought about the Napa Valley where it had come from. At midnight Kathy called me in the hotel to say Henry had had another tracheotomy to clean the lung that was principally infected. I must have fallen asleep over a B movie on television, for it was the noise of the early newscast which woke me the next day.

I had extra telephones installed in the hotel suite. The doctors told Kathy that if Henry survived, he would be a semi-invalid all his life. We had a plane standing by to bring Charlotte and Anne and their families from New York. I talked to Charlotte once or twice a day, and this day I said I did not believe her father would survive the night. She said she could not bear to see him, nor could she bear the idea of his continuing to live his life attached to a kidney machine. Kathy had become extraordinarily calm and spoke always optimistically. I knew she was thinking differently, for she asked me when Elizabeth was coming out. I said Elizabeth thought we had enough helpers and did not want to be in the way. I told Elizabeth I did not want to see Henry again. The previous evening I had come out of the hospital on a clear, cold night with an anemic moon in the sky, too weak even to make shadows, and the clouds had come quickly, and then it was all dark and I was full of foreboding.

On September 29 Kathy woke as she usually did at 3:00 A.M. She drifted back into sleep, and Dr. Popovich woke her at 4:20 A.M. Bruce Steinhauer called at the house a few minutes later to drive her to the hospital. Debi woke early and discovered her mother was not in the house, so she called Wendy, and together they went to the hospital. They stood in Henry's room and watched the digital counter on one of the life-support machines as it fell to register zero. The time was 7:21 A.M. At 7:30 A.M. Kathy called me at the hotel and said: "The poor guy . . . He had so much to live for."

Death really is better than dying, for you can bury your own thoughts beneath the mound of things that have to be done. I had visited and surveyed Christ Episcopal Church in Grosse Pointe Farms some days earlier, and Kathy and Bernie Bohn—Henry's U.S. secretary—and Wendy Alexander and I had sat in Henry's office one day and compiled a list of names of those who would be invited to the funeral. I had gone privately to St. Paul's Cathedral in Detroit to make sure it would be available for the memorial service. Henry's letter, giving instructions for the disposition of his body and the funeral, was delivered to Kathy and Edsel at the house. The last paragraph said: ". . . while I cannot direct the feelings or the behavior of other people, it is my most earnest wish that I shall be remembered in an atmosphere which enables those who participate to recall the good things of my life and not to linger on the regrets that death inevitably brings in its wake. If a man is remembered properly, it can be a matter for rejoicing rather than sorrow, and it is my most sincere desire that the last chapter of my life, rather than my death, shall be celebrated in this spirit."

A small family dinner was arranged at the Little Club in Grosse Pointe the night before the funeral. Kathy arrived in the bright scarlet dress Henry liked best of all, but this gesture could not overwhelm the feelings or obscure the trickles of sadness in the eyes of the grandchildren who were there. Elena and Allegra and Alessandro were visibly upset, and Kathy comforted Edsel when he made a brief speech and found one sentence hard to finish. The funeral itself was small—family, family servants, and close friends—and Elizabeth was pleased that the service she had planned so carefully and with so much thought did sound very much like those that were held in the little churches on the corners of the country lanes near Turville. For those who attended, the words, even the unfamiliar ones, meant what they said.

We let Henry down with the epilogue—the intended rousing rendering of "When the Saints Go Marching In." Church authority had thought the idea "not quite right." As a compromise, the tune was more or less played on the carillon as the mourners left Christ Church, but you had to be a remarkable musician to know that. We did much better, though, at the memorial service when this took place on October 8. We had prevailed upon the Preservation Hall Jazz Band to come to Detroit from New Orleans, and it was a noble gesture, for they were old men; some of them very old indeed. They could not be placed in a gallery in the cathedral because one or two found it hard to climb stairs of any kind. And so they sat either side of the main door. I was asked how I wanted "The Saints" to be played. I did not know there were different ways. "Oh, yes," they said, "we can play it fast, kind of normal, or real slow." Real slow, they added, brings tears to your eyes.

And so it was that when the memorial service came to an end in Detroit's St. Paul's Cathedral on October 8, 1987, and the dean had pronounced the dismissal, Kathy sat unmoving in the front pew with the entire Ford family within touching distance, and the Preservation Hall Jazz Band played "When the Saints Go Marching In" as I think Henry would have wanted it, although not as he enjoyed it in his lifetime: real slow.

There had to be one other memorial service, of course, in London.

Carol Price, the wife of Charles Price, the United States ambassador in London—the most thoughtful and resourceful lady ambassadress I have ever known—offered to help with the planning, and with her assistance, we settled finally on St. George's Hanover Square as the place and November 18 as the date. I was not there. I felt emptied of everything—even thought—and because some weeks earlier, long before any intimation of Henry's illness, I had booked a holiday in Jamaica, I resolved to leave London as I had planned. Since the children grew up, we have always taken summer holidays in November, for summer is when England is at its best and the country is emptier than usual. I told Kathy with great reluctance that I would plan it all and the form of service would be the one Henry had chosen—indeed, it would be even more appropriate in a church in the heart of Mayfair where George Frederick Handel once worshiped and conducted the choir—but I was going to take Elizabeth and bury our heads in a Caribbean sandhill until I could see straight again.

Envoi

When all is said and done, all is never said. I come diffidently toward the end of this memoir, knowing it to be the end rather than the conclusion. The consequences of the life of Henry Ford II are not yet apparent. Nor do they stand like corn in the silo waiting to be weighed. There are many more harvests to come from the seeds he sowed.

Virginia Woolf said that the purpose of biography is to give a man some kind of shape after his death, and I feel comfortable with that definition, though she might have added "or woman." Shape is something you can come to terms with, even measure; a good pair of eyes sees more than a mirror. But there is more to it than meets the eye.

Michael Holroyd spent fifteen years researching and writing the life of Bernard Shaw and then, in one sentence, defined the task and the dilemma when he said: "It's absolutely essential in a biography to recapture the truth—whatever that truth is—insofar as it can be recaptured." He went on to say: "While we are alive, we all need protection, we all need to tell lies, not to have things revealed about us; and that is extremely understandable and proper. But after we are dead, it seems to me that the dead can be kept in employment by giving something that they could not give in their lifetime: they can give some more truth."

My response to that, when I read it, was "yes . . . but," and Holroyd also recognized the need for some qualification:

. . . it is very difficult to change people's perceived ideas on somebody because we all change our opinions with great reluctance. We've got our categories for people, our typecasting, our stereotypes. When somebody comes along with a new biography and says, "hey, this person was not like that," our first reaction is to say, "no, I don't want to change my idea, I know where I am." I don't think any biography changes people's opinions of the subject immediately. It takes about a decade, I think, for anything to work through.

For my part, I do not believe the living are necessarily the best witnesses for the dead. All too often they bring to the remembrance of things past an entirely modern set of values or judgments. Moreover, within each human shape there is an inner mystery, and the evidence upon which the writer bases his judgment is at best circumstantial— even in a life as well documented as that of Henry Ford II. And the evidence itself is suspect. It is the fate of many public figures to become transformed into essentially fictional characters during their lifetime, and Henry never ceased to wonder at the process when it applied to him.

On two, perhaps three occasions he felt sufficiently sullied by a piece of writing or something said on television to consult a lawyer, but each time he was given the same answer: American courts grant no private life to public figures. Anybody of public consequence has to expect his privacy to be made public, too. One famous counselor said: "Don't let it worry you, Mr. Ford. People don't really believe what they read anyway." It was not much consolation although it was true that many of the more fanciful inventions were too silly to be taken seriously. I often thought it a pity that writers who had every opportunity to discover the truth rarely got under his skin except in the sense of bringing him unhappiness— since, it seemed to me, the truth was more interesting than the fictions they eventually produced—but he eventually developed an outer layer impervious to almost everything of the kind.

No writer can avoid bringing his or her own preconceptions to his or her own task. One spent several years determined to prove that Henry was the reincarnation of his grandfather. Another seemed convinced he was an alcoholic although, during his research, his own wife had to be treated for incipient alcoholism and he thought it prudent to forswear all intoxicating liquids. She was not an alcoholic, as it turned out. She had drunk too much at times, as had Henry. With the scattered press clippings from Henry's three marriages, one sought to paint him as a Don Juan, which was equally ludicrous. Nor was he devious. His marriages ran into unnecessary problems—one was prolonged long after all affection had been spent—because he funked the unpleasantness of domestic confrontation, and this sometimes magnified the differences and added to the hurt later on.

The books, the superficial eye of television—with its obsession for instant judgment and one-liners—and the gossip columns were themselves damaging to a man who was quite secretive enough, even with his family, for they increased his secretiveness. Writers sent him their books with warm, even generous dedications on their title pages and seemed unaware how wounding they had been. As a guest in the country I was saddened to see how often America diminished or trivialized the very men who should have been the sources of its pride and were, in fact, the architects of its success. Henry said it didn't matter. He alone—perhaps even more alone—knew what had to be done, and he was going to do it.

It is a pity that this is not his book, as it might have been and could have been. At dinner in London one night in January 1986, he was sufficiently tempted by the idea to promise Lord Weidenfeld, chairman of the London publishing house Weidenfeld & Nicolson, he would undertake the telling of his own life story. I joined them both on a couple of occasions in the London office to discuss the project, and six months later, we had luncheon together in the Plaza d'Athénée in New York. Henry liked and trusted George Weidenfeld, and they were on good terms with each other. By the time coffee arrived, Henry had more or less agreed he would sit down with me and his diaries and we would write the book together, but within a week he wrote to George retreating from the project. "How do you make sense of your own life?" he asked. "How does anybody? How do I explain what I did or why? Sometimes I didn't know; I just did what was necessary." A more pressing reason, I came to believe, was that Henry had begun to appreciate how much time and effort would be required and he had more important items on his agenda: the continuing future, for example, of the Ford Motor Company. And nothing could ever be allowed to come before that.

I suspect, however, that the ultimate deterrent to his own reminiscences was that lifelong guardian, the man within himself. Leon Edel, one of the greatest biographers of our day, has challenged his fellows and followers to come to terms with, and not to fear, the techniques of modern psychoanalysis in the writing of lives, and it is tempting to pop Henry on the couch and try to materialize that hidden ego. Indeed, despite my own belief that no man is better understood than by his deeds, that what he did, essentially, was what he was, it has obviously been impossible to live another's history vicariously and to share another life so intimately without occasionally listening to one's own inner voice asking why.

It is always a difficult question to answer although comparison with the history of the other great automobile dynasty produces at least a clue.

The history of the Fords and the Agnellis has as many differences as similarities, for the two cultures are as far apart as popcorn and pasta. But there are some telling parallels.

Giovanni Agnelli, a former cavalry officer, was one of a group of young men who founded a company that became FIAT on July 1, 1899. This was a little less than four years before the creation of the Ford Motor Company. Giovanni's grandson, who was also named Giovanni, was born on March 12, 1921. Henry's grandson, who was similarly named after his grandfather, was born on September 4, 1917. The difference in their ages was three years and six months, very nearly the same as the difference in the age of the family companies. The young Giovanni and the young Henry both lost their fathers early. Henry's father, Edsel, died on May 26, 1943, when he was twenty-five, and Giovanni's father, Eduardo, was killed in an air crash on July 14, 1935, when he was fourteen. Young Giovanni was a lieutenant in the Italian Army in the Second World War; young Henry held similar rank in the U.S. Navy. The founding grandfathers of the two great companies died within two years of each other: Henry Ford in 1947 and Giovanni Agnelli in 1945.

That is where the similarities end. In 1946, one year after Henry Ford II had assumed control of the Ford Motor Company, young Giovanni was asked by Professor Vittorio Valletta, his grandfather's principal and most trusted aide, whether or not he wanted to take control and run Fiat. "Gianni" said no and spent the next twenty years living a rich and leisured life with a villa at Beaulieu, a private yacht, a personal aircraft, and a number of what they used to call bright young things. Professor Valletta, who was facing in Italy many of the same postwar problems afflicting Ford in the United States, then used Marshall Aid funds to rebuild Fiat, and it was not until Valletta's death in 1966 at the age of eighty-two that young Gianni Agnelli became chairman, taking over a healthy and going concern. He was forty-five years of age and had prepared for his demanding role working three years under Professor Valletta as managing director. By then Henry Ford II had saved the Ford Motor Company.

Gianni Agnelli and Henry Ford II were more than names to each other; they were abiding and close friends, both of them remarkable men. They were, I think, in the Pacific—on a boat together—when Professor Valletta died and the U.S. Navy was sent to pass on the news to the new ruler of Turin and, in a real sense, of industrial Italy. There is very little doubt in my mind that Henry, married so early to Anne and the Ford Motor Company, envied Gianni's early freedom and his chance to sow his wild oats early, when they are most fertile. But in 1943, when arrangements were made over his head for him to leave the navy, Henry never doubted his duty, nor did he question it. His efforts to make some kind of amends for his late pursuit of pleasure provided welcome grist for the gossip columns in his forties and led to his second marriage.

The comparison is interesting, and it may be so. But there was always a certain boisterousness about Henry's high spirits, and he could never make his pleasures last for more than a few days at a time—even in retirement, when there were other ears to listen for the tocsin. Retirement came easily to him. Men who sit in the corner offices of tall buildings are sometimes bereft when the papers stop coming and the telephone sits silent and cope badly with the problem of having nothing to do. But it has been my experience that people with the aptitude for leadership are no less resourceful in their private lives. There is a certain loss of convenience for the man of power when he forfeits the services of the attendants who waft him through immigration and customs formalities along the red carpet of the VIP suite to the executive jet. For some, it is a salutory experience to discover how to buy an airline ticket, send a parcel, and stand patiently in line. Where Henry was concerned, however, none of these considerations applied because there never was a loss of power.

It is true that a lot of the paperwork landed on other desks and there were fewer telephone calls, and when I called to ask for half an hour of his time, he would often say: "Half a day, if you like." But he remained chairman of the Finance Committee and a member of the board of directors until his death, and although he had once vowed to retire altogether at seventy years of age, he showed no signs of reminding anybody of this declared intention. He was, moreover, the prime motivating figure in reminding the Ford family of its heritage and power and company management of its global responsibilities. I believe the reason Henry was able to exhaust his private pleasures after a comparatively short period of time was that business was his only pleasure. He would good-humoredly cancel things that I knew he was looking forward to— even one of his precious shoots—if something came along that seemed important to the Ford Motor Company in some fashion. Nor did it have to be anything of major significance to challenge his personal pastimes. "I don't want to let them down," he would say, or, "They expect me to do it." If I suggested that "they" expected too much (as they often did) or "it" wasn't important, he would still shrug my objection away. If it was Ford business, it did not have to be all that important to take precedence over genuinely valued private joys.

There was no shortage of dedicated and loyal men at the top of the

Ford Motor Company in all the years I knew it, but I never encountered anybody else who would instinctively make such choices. It was easy to equate a part of Henry's dedication—perhaps even most of it—to the well-known fact that his name was on the building, but other industrial or commercial princes, whether or not they had oil in their blood, often lacked similar dedication. The fact of birth or heritage is not a guarantee of devotion to the family business, and devotion has never been sufficient in itself to ensure effective or successful leadership.

I think I came nearest to an understanding of the man within Henry in January 1986. I flew to Palm Beach, and Don Braun, Henry's trusty handyman, picked me up at the airport. I could not find him at first in the crowd and walked outside the terminal. People were standing in groups, looking up at a jagged smear of black in the sky, and when I got to the house, Henry and Kathy were sitting in front of the television. The space shuttle *Challenger* had blown up soon after lift-off from Cape Canaveral, and the jagged cross we had seen floating as a smear, high over the ocean was all that apparently remained. We stayed at the television set for some time.

The evening promised to be relaxed despite the shock of the space disaster. I was prevailed upon to dispense with my tie, borrow one of Henry's sweaters, and behave like a normal human being. Henry had booked a table at a small bistro. We had a couple of bottles of wine among the three of us, and when we got back to the house, Kathy went to bed while Henry and I sat in the library and talked. He had come to Palm Beach to execute a minor amendment to his trust, and while he was there, he had agreed—largely at Kathy's insistence—that he should spend an hour or two with a writer who was researching a book on the Ford family. He would not be long in Palm Beach. He had promised to attend a reception in New Orleans for Ford dealers. There was a Sotheby's meeting in New York and luncheon there with Lord Weidenfeld.

Henry proved to be in a reminiscent mood, influenced perhaps by his agreement—no matter how reluctant—to talk about himself to the writer and by the need to give George Weidenfeld an answer about a book of his own. He had excavated from somewhere a book of early photographs of himself and his immediate family and showed it to me so that I could leaf through its pages. But then he said he thought he would have it back. "Perhaps I'll give it to you one day." I was not at all sure he would do any such thing because Henry in this mood could be deliberately provocative and innocently tantalizing. He could enfold things of no importance in wrappings of secrecy or vagueness and then cross his hands on his stomach and confess to startling intimacies. But I knew enough not to show interest in the album. I said something like "It's good to have an album like that. They must have been happy days." And this unleashed the longest consecutive reminiscence, almost an interior monologue, on family and Ford that I had ever heard him give. By this time it was early in the morning and Henry had caused a small blaze in the kitchen during a break when he had expressed a desire for toast and insisted he knew how to use the toaster. When we resumed our seats in the library, the thread had worn thin, and we both were ready for bed. At three o'clock in the morning he showed me how to control the television set in my bedroom; one network was still covering the *Challenger* disaster. "They didn't have a choice," Henry said. "They were like me. They had to do what they had to do." When he had gone, I made a note of these few words on a pad by the bed, and I did not go to sleep until I could see daylight through a chink in the curtains.

I believe in retrospect, and after much greater familiarity with all the albums and papers and diaries he did not destroy, that it is both simpler and more complicated than that. I also think one must beware in taking his remarks at face value as a straightforward epitaph for a complex man. Duty is what gets done because of what you are. It's a consequence, not a cause, and Henry's attitude, deeds, and behavior indicate—certainly to me—an almost puritanical view of life. It is an idea that would sit badly with people who remember the wine he drank, the bottoms he pinched, the small deceits that were nevertheless deceits even though their motivation was considerate. But I think more precisely of the essence of puritanism, which is the recognition of individual responsibility, as the linch pin of life—what R. H. Tawney called "the qualities which arm the spiritual athlete for his solitary contest with a hostile world."

If this seems too fanciful, it can gain credibility by being brought down to earth. Even where the closest members of his own family were concerned, Henry would not interfere in their lives or try to change their direction beyond a statement of his own point of view. All things considered, it was not his business. In business itself I was often surprised how easily he would allow himself to be overruled or outvoted if he felt an opposing point of view was "their business." He was certainly stubborn, but many among his peers were no less so. Ed Lundy certainly was, and he was granted victory in many difficult engagements with Henry.

Acceptance of individual responsibility in the puritan tradition goes farther than a sign on the desk saying, "The buck stops here." It implies, in addition, certain moral standards. Henry could not tell a lie and despised those who did. The most contempt I ever heard him express was toward some engineers who had distorted a process to pass a regulatory test. This viewpoint does not, however, create an overoptimistic expectation of other people's virtue; it is, and was, a hostile world, and Henry knew it. So he was pleased with loyalty when he found it and valued it highly, and he could tell it as plainly as a jeweler can recognize a hallmark; but he did not expect it or take it for granted.

I think perhaps that I have inadequately conveyed his enormous sense of fun and the pleasure of his company. He had an appetite for enjoyment, and those who took the trouble to pierce the defenses found themselves surprisingly at ease in his company.

Perhaps the conclusion must be that it is possible to define the shape without finding the whole man within. The Egyptians once believed that Osiris weighed the souls of the dead to discover if they had led just lives and spoken the truth; but it is a method that is not open to us, and it is not necessary to sit or stand in judgment.

The Japanese learned their business from Henry's Ford Motor Company. The Chinese and the Russians knew where they would find a welcome, no matter how turbulent the times or prejudiced the politicians. It made cars for the people, and the top people sometimes looked down, as top people do; but the common people were having more fun, and the cars they were having fun in were mostly those with the little blue oval on the front.

Ford made trucks for people who built and moved things and tractors so that people were not hungry, and when the company turned to outer space, it played a controlling role in putting a man on the moon. Henry enjoyed the congratulations but could not see the point because he thought we had enough to be worrying about down here on earth.

And down here on earth the Ford Foundation gave more—all in young Henry's time—to more good causes and optimistic causes and daft causes than any other. And everywhere that you could find the best-known trademark in the world (one Henry always refused to "modernize") you would find dealers and suppliers and hundreds of thousands of men and women who knew something from their own experience that was not always obvious. The thing about Ford, they would tell you, was that it was a family. That's what made it different from other companies. It was the glue in the tube, the core in the apple, the spice in the pudding.

I once thought to challenge Captain Nemo and sent a Ford Cortina with two drivers around the world in what I hoped would be forty days. It actually took forty-one. Eric Jackson from Barnsley in England, who was driving the car across the Afghanistan border and was cast down a little by the seemingly endless panorama of sand and rock, suddenly spied a man waving a flag with the Ford oval emblazoned on it and carrying two cans of cold Coca-Cola. "We stopped and talked for a bit," Jackson told me when he got back. He was very proud to have met Mr. Ford.

HENRY FORD
(1863–1947)

mar.1888
Clara Jane Bryant
(1866–1950)

EDSEL BRYANT FORD
(1893–1943)

mar.1916
Eleanor Lowthian Clay
(1896–1976)

William ("Bill") Clay Ford
(1925–   )

mar.1947
Martha Parke Firestone
(1925–   )

Josephine ("Dodie") Clay Ford
(1923–   )

mar.1943
Walter Buhl Ford II
(1920–   )

Benson Ford
(1919–1978)

mar.1941
Edith McNaughton
(1920–1980)

Henry Ford II
(1917–1987)

mar.1940; div.1964
Anne McDonnell
(1919–   )

mar.1965; div.1980
Maria Cristina Vettore Austin
(1926–   )

mar.1980
Kathleen King Duross
(1940–   )

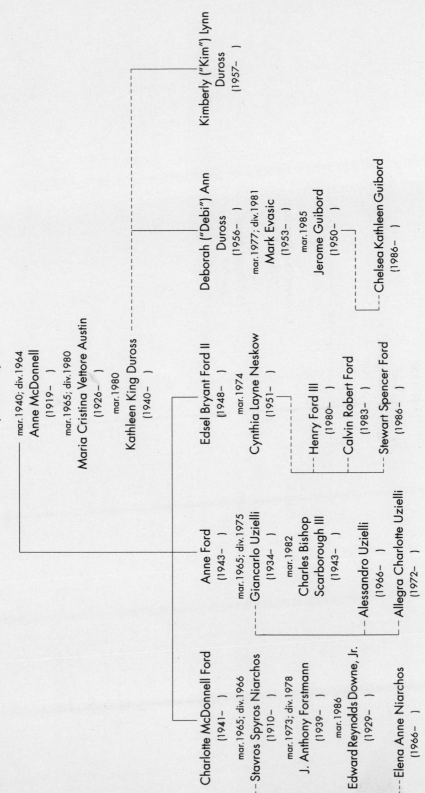

HENRY FORD II
(1917–1987)

mar.1940; div.1964
Anne McDonnell
(1919–)

mar.1965; div.1980
Maria Cristina Vettore Austin
(1926–)

mar.1980
Kathleen King Duross
(1940–)

Kimberly ("Kim") Lynn
Duross
(1957–)

Deborah ("Debi") Ann
Duross
(1956–)

mar.1977; div.1981
Mark Evasic
(1953–)

mar.1985
Jerome Guibord
(1950–)

Chelsea Kathleen Guibord
(1986–)

Edsel Bryant Ford II
(1948–)

mar.1974
Cynthia Layne Neskow
(1951–)

Henry Ford III
(1980–)

Calvin Robert Ford
(1983–)

Stewart Spencer Ford
(1986–)

Anne Ford
(1943–)

mar.1965; div.1975
Giancarlo Uzielli
(1934–)

mar.1982
Charles Bishop
Scarborough III
(1943–)

Alessandro Uzielli
(1966–)

Allegra Charlotte Uzielli
(1972–)

Charlotte McDonnell Ford
(1941–)

mar.1965; div.1966
Stavros Spyros Niarchos
(1910–)

mar.1973; div.1978
J. Anthony Forstmann
(1939–)

mar.1986
Edward Reynolds Downe, Jr.
(1929–)

Elena Anne Niarchos
(1966–)

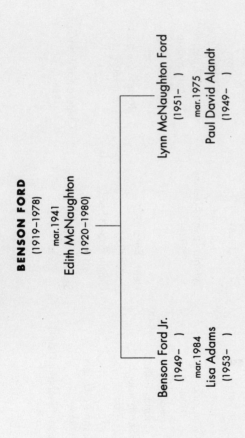

BENSON FORD
(1919–1978)

mar.1941
Edith McNaughton
(1920–1980)

Lynn McNaughton Ford
(1951–)

mar.1975
Paul David Alandt
(1949–)

Benson Ford Jr.
(1949–)

mar.1984
Lisa Adams
(1953–)

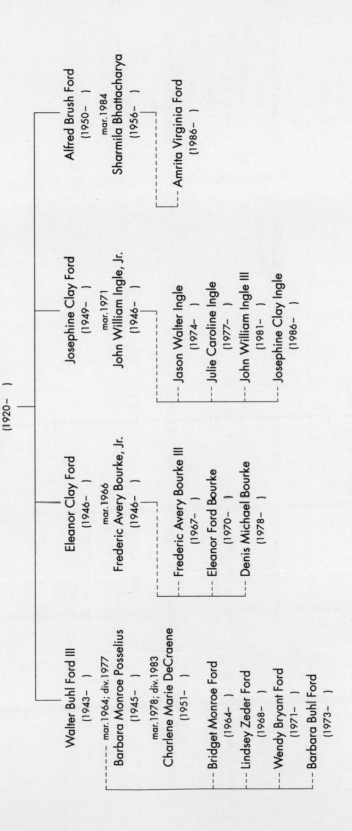

JOSEPHINE ("DODIE") CLAY FORD
(1923–)

mar. 1943
Walter Buhl Ford II
(1920–)

Walter Buhl Ford III
(1943–)

mar. 1964; div. 1977
Barbara Monroe Posselius
(1945–)

mar. 1978; div. 1983
Charlene Marie DeCraene
(1951–)

-- Bridget Monroe Ford
(1964–)

-- Lindsey Zeder Ford
(1968–)

-- Wendy Bryant Ford
(1971–)

-- Barbara Buhl Ford
(1973–)

Eleanor Clay Ford
(1946–)

mar. 1966
Frederic Avery Bourke, Jr.
(1946–)

-- Frederic Avery Bourke III
(1967–)

-- Eleanor Ford Bourke
(1970–)

-- Denis Michael Bourke
(1978–)

Josephine Clay Ford
(1949–)

mar. 1971
John William Ingle, Jr.
(1946–)

-- Jason Walter Ingle
(1974–)

-- Julie Caroline Ingle
(1977–)

-- John William Ingle III
(1981–)

-- Josephine Clay Ingle
(1986–)

Alfred Brush Ford
(1950–)

mar. 1984
Sharmila Bhattacharya
(1956–)

-- Amrita Virginia Ford
(1986–)

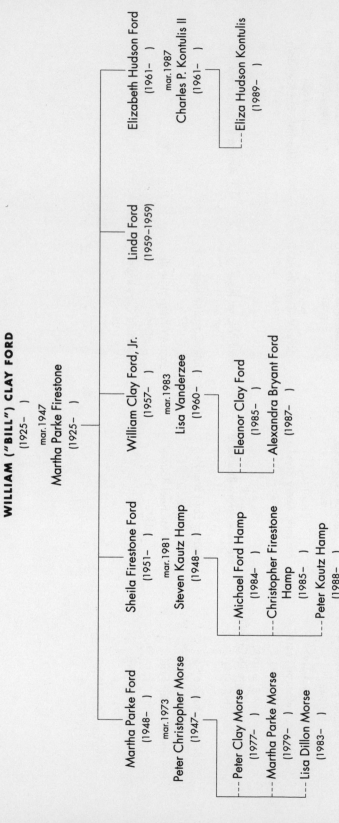

WILLIAM ("BILL") CLAY FORD
(1925–)

mar. 1947

Martha Parke Firestone
(1925–)

Martha Parke Ford
(1948–)

Peter Christopher Morse
(1947–)

mar. 1973

--- Peter Clay Morse
(1977–)

--- Martha Parke Morse
(1979–)

--- Lisa Dillon Morse
(1983–)

Sheila Firestone Ford
(1951–)

mar. 1981

Steven Kautz Hamp
(1948–)

--- Michael Ford Hamp
(1984–)

--- Christopher Firestone
Hamp
(1985–)

--- Peter Kautz Hamp
(1988–)

William Clay Ford, Jr.
(1957–)

mar. 1983

Lisa Vanderzee
(1960–)

--- Eleanor Clay Ford
(1985–)

--- Alexandra Bryant Ford
(1987–)

Linda Ford
(1959–1959)

Elizabeth Hudson Ford
(1961–)

mar. 1987

Charles P. Kontulis II
(1961–)

--- Eliza Hudson Kontulis
(1989–)

Index